Playing with America's Doll

Emilie Zaslow

Playing with America's Doll

A Cultural Analysis of the American Girl Collection

palgrave
macmillan

Emilie Zaslow
Communication Studies
Pace University, New York
New York, USA

ISBN 978-1-137-56648-5 (hardcover)   ISBN 978-1-137-56649-2   (eBook)
ISBN 978-1-349-93655-7 (softcover)
DOI 10.1057/978-1-137-56649-2

Library of Congress Control Number: 2017944764

Cover design by Henry Petrides

Printed on acid-free paper

This Palgrave Macmillan imprint is published by Springer Nature
The registered company is Nature America Inc.
The registered company address is: 1 New York Plaza, New York, NY 10004, U.S.A.

For Eric, Sam, & Zoe

Acknowledgments

In 1995, Pleasant Company sent a package announcing a new doll to the State University of New York at Buffalo where I was a student in the MA program in Women's Studies. This package made its way into the hands of Liz Kennedy who, walking through the hall one day, casually mentioned to me that I ought to take a look at it. This began a decades long project that has been developed with encouragement and support from many.

I have been lucky to find a home in the department of Communication Studies at Pace University where I am grateful for my inspiring students and my supportive colleagues—Barry Morris, Satish Kolluri, Mary Ann Murphy, Adam Klein, Marcella Szablewicz, Seong Jae Min, and Aditi Paul. I am deeply grateful to Abbey Berg for her friendship, mentorship, and support. A special note of appreciation is due to Jillian Halderman and my students in the spring 2016 Media & Gender course for their research assistance. I was fortunate to have some fabulous mentors and teachers along the way at SUNY at Buffalo and in Media, Culture, and Communication at NYU. I also wish to thank Alexis Nelson, Kyra Saniewski, and Mireille Yanow at Palgrave Macmillan for their editorial support.

My sincerest gratitude to Pleasant Rowland, who I have not yet had the pleasure of meeting, for her open invitation to universities, those many moons ago, to critically engage with her dolls, as well as to Susan Jevens and Julia Prohaska at American Girl for answering my many questions. Three authors who have written for American Girl—Valerie Tripp, Denise Lewis Patrick, Connie Porter—have so generously shared their time and creative visions with me. I cannot thank them enough for their insights. And, although I cannot acknowledge them by name, I owe a great deal to the mothers and daughters who spent time with me discussing American Girl, some with great enthusiasm. Thank you also to Nancy Deihl and Jo Paoletti for taking the time to share their knowledge about American children's fashions.

My family and friends have made this book possible. Lucy and Richard Zaslow have supported its writing with meals, childcare, critical engagement, and love. I thank my mother for teaching me the art of writing and my father for always challenging, debating, and questioning concepts and their articulations. Gail Braverman has generously shared her mastery of the English language as she meticulously read every word of this book. I am indebted to my sister, Carrie Zaslow, who had a big influence on my understanding of imagination and play. Thank you to my extended family and friends who have shared links and laughter. Laurie Diamond, thank you for the meaningful songs and the never-ending confidence you have in me. Special thanks to Liz Zenobi for her American Girl knowledge and enthusiasm and for the wonderful photos and to Judy Schoenberg who has offered sustaining friendship for over forty years and has been by my side in girlhood studies for half of that. SOMA friends, thank you for banana bread, lunch breaks, glasses of wine, fire pits, and noticing the muscles in my face relax when I submitted this manuscript. My Brooklyn women, always—even when we are all far apart. Jaleesah Edouard, thank you for being someone we could rely on.

Sam and Zoe have not only required me to take off time to play, grab cookies at the bakery, help with homework, and have dance parties in the kitchen, they have also been understanding of my project and asked questions that have enhanced my thinking about children's literature and toys as political texts. You two are awesome people! It is difficult to express my boundless appreciation for Eric Braverman, who not only made the writing of this book possible but who reads all of my work, talks to me about dolls, pushes me to think critically, encourages me to laugh and relax when I need it most, and co-parents with playfulness, patience, proficiency, and plenty of pizza.

Contents

LIST OF FIGURES

CHAPTER 1

Introduction: Unpacking America's Doll

Addy and Samantha sit on my desk encouraging me to write. These two enthusiasts are not my daughters, not my friends, and not my pets; they are two American Girl dolls. Since 1986 when the American Girl Collection of dolls and books was launched, the company has produced eighteen-inch dolls with stories to accompany many of them. If Barbie is our nation's most popular doll, American Girl comes in second; as of February 1, 2017, its corporate website claimed that over twenty-nine million dolls have been sold in the last thirty years and their accompanying stories are on the shelves of nearly every school and community library. American Girl dolls—unlike Bratz and Barbies, who are young adults and promote a sexy version of femininity that highlights big breasts, miniscule waists, and curvy hips—are young girls with soft undeveloped bodies, buck teeth, and child-like facial features. Unlike Disney princesses and Barbie dolls, American Girls are not passively waiting for a prince to rescue them, nor for a Ken to ride with them up to their dream house.[1] Unlike princess fairy tales, American Girl stories do not encourage girls to tether themselves to a mirror; their narratives do not insist on what Rebecca C. Haines has called the "princess pretty mandate."[2] Instead, American Girls are courageous, resilient girls who take risks and often use their voices to engage in everyday democracy. At $115 per doll, American Girl is a toy for the elite, but the dolls' stories, which situate each of them in a particular historical time period, make the brand popular and accessible. Created by educator and entrepreneur

© The Author(s) 2017
E. Zaslow, *Playing with America's Doll*,
DOI 10.1057/978-1-137-56649-2_1

Pleasant Rowland, the brand had a feminist inspiration: to create stories about girls who took themselves and their participation in American life seriously.[3]

Like many media scholars, I approach this study with two lenses; I am both a fan and a scholarly critic.[4] As Henry Jenkins has argued, utilizing these dual lenses allows for the researcher to shift fluidly between two epistemologies: the knowing attained through theoretical analysis and the knowing attained through communities of fandom and user-engagement.[5] While I am not a member of the American Girl fan community, I cannot deny that I have loved reading the American Girl stories that line the bookshelf in my office, not only because they offer rich material for analysis, but also because they are often simple pleasure. Even when I doubt the complete veracity of their history, I enjoy their historical settings, with hairstyles and clothing to match. I find it difficult to resist cheering on these girls who fight against normative femininity and sexist views about girls' capabilities and value to society. These girls defy expectations and use their voices for change. Depending on the character, the change can range from personal independence to gender equality, workers' rights, or social and racial equality. Take Caroline Abbott, a white girl growing up on the shores of Lake Ontario during the War of 1812, who confides in her family that her fervent wish is to be a sailor. I feel Caroline's disappointment when her cousin, Lydia, remarks, "You can't be captain of a ship!" and shares her own dream of following the conventions of femininity: getting married, living in a big home, and raising six daughters. Alongside Caroline, I experience the disconnect she feels when Lydia cares more about protecting her skin than enjoying the warm sun on her face. I feel wounded when her father, a shipbuilder, also questions Caroline's nautical dreams, not only because she is young, but also because she is a girl. I cringe when a nosy neighbor suggests that Caroline ought to be at home learning how to cook and do needlework.

It is difficult for me, then, not to take pleasure in the fact that Caroline doesn't let these negative reactions stop her; she puts in the effort to learn about knot-tying, sailing, and ship building. I delight in Caroline's mother, who runs the family's finances and business and also leans on her daughter as an ally when Caroline's father is taken prisoner by the British with whom the United States is at war. I celebrate when Caroline is able to give her imprisoned father an embroidered map marking British loyalist strongholds so he can be safe should he find a way to escape. How brazen she is when, in the presence of the British soldier who guards her father,

Caroline performs a daring act: "Moving only her finger, she pointed straight at Papa. Then she touched the X and shook her head slightly. *Not—safe!* She mouthed the words silently."[6] Does it feel silly to read about a nine-year-old taking a dangerous voyage to an enemy fort and secretly giving her father an escape route? Absolutely! Yet Caroline's story, along with those of her fellow BeForever historical characters is not about a passive, weak girl, or a girl whose focus is on boys and cosmetics, nor is her story about a young woman following her dreams or owning her sexuality.[7] Instead, these tales are about young girls whose minds and bodies are robust, active, creative, and ripe with agency. They may be dreaming about a future but they are living in the moment of girlhood.

Consider the newest BeForever story about Melody Ellison, an African American girl growing up in Detroit at the height of the Civil Rights movement. Unlike Caroline, whose story takes place 150 years earlier, Melody's whole family supports her desire to question social norms and expectations. This support helps Melody not only use her voice in the service of her family's well-being but also in the service of social change. Author Denise Lewis Patrick weaves the experience of racism and being the object of others' fear and hate into a story about love, music, family, community, protest, and social justice. After I finished reading Melody's story, I sat with my nine-year-old daughter and read it again because I wanted to share it with her, and then I passed the book along to my eleven-year-old son. I wanted them to feel as angry and sad as I did when Melody's sister is denied a job at a bank because she is black and to witness Melody and her brother being followed around a department store and then accused of stealing. I wanted them to feel the frustration, along with Melody's cousin, as her family continues to be rejected by one racist landlord after another in the neighborhoods in which they seek to live. The shameful histories of segregation and racism are not news, but there is something magical about Melody, who does not just give readers an age appropriate and intimate narrative about the need for fair housing laws, racism, and inequality, but who also feels real fear and fights for real change. Melody feels immense pain and terror when she learns about the four young girls who were killed when a bomb exploded in their Birmingham church. She has to overcome her fear of going back to her own church, which has always been a place of safety and communion. With the support of her family and community, she does conquer her fear and turns it into action. With her neighbors, she creates a protest against the local department store that mistreats black customers; with her friends, she organizes a playground revitalization committee because the city is not maintaining the public space in her moderate-income community of color; and with her voice, she sings songs of racial equality. Along the way she learns lessons about political struggle, community organizing, and leadership. One of the thrills of Melody's story is that it is not just about a heroic girl who saves the day; it is about the process of learning how to be a leader. Melody learns from her elderly neighbor that, "You are never too young or too old to stand for justice."[8] And, when Melody questions her leadership of the Junior Block Club she has formed, she learns from her father that, "A good leader helps everyone see that they're part of a special team. Leading takes patience, just like gardening...You're a wonderful gardener. You know how to make things take root and grow. As your club works together, it will become stronger."[9] Like many of the American Girl stories, Melody's creates a picture of American identity that involves thinking critically about the status quo and participating to make change.

Most of the mothers I spoke with in my research share my pleasure in giving their children stories of girls who, as one mother describes them, "are willing to take a little bit of a risk for what is right," and "fight for causes that they believe in." With the aim of protecting their children, mostly daughters, against a culture that sexualizes them early, and in which tween television on Disney and Nickelodeon depicts characters who are filled with "attitude" and are "disrespectful to adults," the mothers I spoke with turn to American Girl for a media source that is not "over-sexed" and as one mother, Violet, explains, will communicate to their daughters that "You just have to be the best person that you can be...You tell the truth ... and you just always do what's right." Girls, too, recognize that the dolls are not just beautiful but that they also, as fourteen-year-old Ruby explains, tell stories about "the struggles that the girls went through in history, and the different aspects of people's cultures, and how they affect your gender." Many girls expressed an appreciation for the age representation of the dolls as girls, rather than young women, because they remind them of themselves and their friends and because their imaginative play can revolve around more child-like activities like horseback riding, playing in the woods, and going clothes shopping. A few of the older girls also shared that the collection fed their interest in history, bolstered their grades in social studies classes, and left them feeling "really cool [when they began to study these time periods in school] because I knew all this stuff that no one else knew."

Although I have encountered these narratives with the curiosity of a fan and the concern of a parent, I first began to explore the whole American Girl brand, and continue to do so, through the lens of feminist media analysis. From this perspective, my critical analysis extends beyond the books to the entire American Girl mediascape of dolls, accessories, and retail experiences. So, too, does my analysis extend to the brand's conflicting and contradictory textual and material narratives about femininity, race, ethnicity, immigration, and what it means to be an American.

Nearly every time I tell people about the research I am doing on American Girl, they ask for a quick binary appraisal; "Should I buy these dolls for my daughter or not? Should I keep her away from the stories as long as possible?" But, of course, there is no simple answer. This is a massive brand, with over five doll product lines, as well as a magazine, and a library of advice books, started by Pleasant Rowland, but now owned by the Mattel corporation. Even within the brand's core collection of historical dolls, which is the focus of this book, there are fourteen characters, in thirteen time periods, that span over 200 years, and with books that are written by nine different authors. In addition, the ideological constructions of gender, race, ethnicity, and nation within these collections are multidimensional. The textual narratives frequently present girls as countering the prescriptive femininity of the times in which they live and ascribe a high value to the political work in which many of the girl protagonists engage. However, the accessories product lines emphasize hair care, fashion, bedroom furniture, and food play, all of which echo traditionally normative feminine playthings. Further, representations of race and ethnicity are multifaceted and inconsistent; with dolls of color and stories about Native American, Latina, African American, and Jewish American protagonists, girl consumers are asked to value the cultural diversity of American society and celebrate differences, but only sometimes asked to consider the institutionalized discrimination with which they live.

Throughout this book I explore the inherently paradoxical position of the American Girl brand as a form of commodity activism. Like other manifestations of girl power media culture, American Girl is a collection of material goods produced and purchased within a capitalist system but also a material form of resistance to historical power dynamics. Sarah Banet-Weiser and Roopali Mukherjee argue that scholars must historically situate commodity activism and seek to understand the muddiness of production and consumption practices in an era of activist consumption. They suggest that scholars steer clear of an either/or analysis in which

commodity activism can be understood either as "corporate appropria-
tions, elaborate exercises in hypocrisy and artifice intended to fool the
consumer, [and] sophisticated strategies aimed at securing even larger
profits" or, on the other hand, as examples of the "nettled promise of
innovative creative forms, cultural interventions that bear critically ... on
modes of dominance and resistance within changing social and political
landscapes."[10] Through this dualistic lens, American Girl would either
serve as an example of the market cooptation of feminism, watered down
enough to appeal to the masses and leave little trace of oppositional or
emancipatory promise, or contrarily, as a site through which feminist professionals bring to bear their resistive feminist messages to challenge the
dominant paradigms of femininity in the toy industry. This book, however, seeks to recognize American Girl as a product both of a massive corporation whose messaging is organized around a capitalist imperative and
also of critical feminist writers and product designers whose intentions are
politically inspired. So, too, I understand American Girl consumption not
only as jumping on the bandwagon of a trend to conspicuously consume
a luxury doll, but also as a political act, through the consumption of an
available, adorable, and palatable feminism. This consumption is driven in
part by the parental goal of shaping a generation of resilient, self-directed
girls who recognize the power of their voices (and not just their sexuality)
as a critical part of their (American) identity. The act of consuming these
contradictory texts is neither autonomously agentic nor representative of
the full capitalist incorporation of individual subjects.

These stories and dolls are a part of our cultural discourse about girlhood;
they create meaning for girl readers about what it means to be a girl and what
it means to be American. I started studying the American Girl collection in
1995 as I was writing my Master's thesis. The company was less than ten
years old and I was less than twenty-five years old. Since then, the company
has been sold to one of the big toy conglomerates and has expanded in
numerous directions. However, many of the same people who were there
from the company's start, or at least its early days, are still on staff or writing
its books. To unpack these definitions of American and girlhood created by
the brand, this book uses three methods: (1) interviews with American Girl
authors and industry executives; (2) textual analysis of the American
Girl BeForever books, dolls, and accessories; and (3) interviews with girls
and mothers about their experiences selecting, buying, reading, watching
and playing with American Girl dolls, books, and movies. This multi-method
analysis allows for a multifaceted understanding of the collection through

exploration of its production, textual meaning, and audience experience. I explore the ideologies encoded in the collection's narrative and material objects, the intentions of those who are involved in the production of the collection, and the experiences of mothers and girls who buy, play with, and love their dolls.[11]

My interviews with the cultural producers of American Girl include those with three authors who have collectively written for eight of the brand's historical book series as well as two online conversations, conducted twenty years apart, in 1997 and again in 2017, with public relations representatives for the company.[12] Focus groups and individual interviews with ten mothers and thirteen girls between the ages of five and fourteen were conducted in a primarily upper-middle-class suburban community during the winter of 2016. This community is located in a mid-Atlantic state and in a county in which over seventy-five percent of all voters cast their ballots for the Democratic Party presidential candidate. Seven of the mothers identified as white, one identified as Afro-Latina, one as African American, and one as Asian American. Of the girls, eight identified as white, one as African American, one as Asian, one as African American/ Afro-Latina, and two as African American/Asian/Irish. In total, these thirteen girls owned forty-five American Girl dolls. The discussions with these girls and mothers emerged through open-ended questions about doll play and the meaning of dolls and their stories. Girls move seamlessly between commenting on books and on movies and while my analysis focuses on the series books, it applies equally to the movies which share their themes. These interviews are supplemented with posts by mothers in online forums and blog posts about American Girl. This small and generally politically liberal sample is not representative of the entire country and I certainly do not aim to make generalized conclusions about the entire population of American Girl doll owners. However, the inclusion of audiences in this research has allowed for a richer understanding of the ways in which girls and their mothers interact with the brand narrative.

OVERVIEW

Chapter 2, "Branding the American Girl: The Making of Cultural Icons," introduces readers to the world of American Girl from its inception to its present-day endeavors. Since their introduction in 1986, American Girl dolls and books have been a major part of the play landscape for millions of girls in the United States. This chapter lays a solid foundation needed to properly analyze the brand's representation of gender, race, ethnicity, and American identity. The text delves into the early life and career of the company's founder, Pleasant Rowland, and the serendipitous circumstances that led her on the path to creating the dolls that would change the toy industry on a grand scale. It explores how a boutique doll company independently launched by a forty-five-year-old woman in 1986, and advertised through 500,000 catalogs, became a division of the multinational Mattel toy corporation. This chapter traces American Girl's development including the importance of gender empowerment narratives to its mission, the introduction of its line of historic dolls, the development of multiracial and ethnic dolls, and its turn toward contemporary girlhood.

Chapter 3, "Situating American Girl: Tools of Socialization in a Changing Culture," provides historical frameworks both to understand the study of girls' books and dolls as well as the emergence and growth of American Girl in the last three decades. Because narrative is central to the American Girl brand, this chapter begins by briefly reviewing scholarly studies on children's literature as a tool of socialization and a tool of political dissent for authors, publishers, and parents concerned with countering racist and sexist messages in popular culture. It then traces the literature on dolls as cultural texts that not only serve as loving playthings but as tools of intersectional cultural learning that embody and shape meaning about what it means to be an American girl and woman. I shift to explore the changing social and cultural environment in which the American Girl books and dolls could be positioned as teaching a particular kind of innocent, educated, empowered girlhood. This chapter historically situates the popularity of American Girl within a neoliberal girl power media culture, backlash against feminism, and burgeoning conservativism. As fears about girls' psycho-social development in an oppressive patriarchal culture moved from the halls of academia to mainstream media, American Girl marketed itself as a girl power text that could counteract what Mary Pipher called a "girl poisoning culture."[13] As concern about girls' culture morphed into a moral panic about the ways in which sexual power was becoming a synecdoche for female power, the pre-sexual American Girl dolls, representing kind and fair nine-year-old girls, became sought after by parents who wanted to protect their daughters.

As I explore in Chapter 4, "'Baby Doll, You Made the World a Little Bit Better by Speaking Out for What You Believe In': Narratives of Femininity and Political Action in the BeForever Collection," girls in the BeForever series books, whose narratives are situated within American history, are not in the shadows, but are agentic participants in their own lives, the lives of their families, the lives of their communities, and sometimes even the life of their country. Employing a neo-historical fiction genre, discussed in Chapter 3, the collection is able to offer representations of girlhood in which girls often resist the domestic location of their mothers and do not see homemaking as their destiny nor as fulfilling. In this way, the books are very much attending to the liberal feminist needs of the present day but framing them in historical tensions and conflicts. This chapter explores how readers can both celebrate feminist progress and also imagine their own role in the next battle over gender roles and social injustices. The chapter further documents how under the Mattel corporate umbrella there has been a surprising increase in the depiction of protagonists who see themselves as change agents and offer readers models of activism as well as strategies that they can use to become involved in their communities.

If the books have provided a growing emphasis on social action since American Girl was acquired by Mattel, the collection of accessories and clothing has become more deeply invested in the shimmery pastel femininity often associated with traditional dolls. Whereas the accessories and furniture in the collection had previously revolved around the passions and interests of the specific character and were accurate to her time period, since Mattel acquired the brand, accessories highlight traditional feminine cultures such as beauty culture, food culture, and bedroom culture. Thus, stories of social action are fundamental to the brand but exist beside a discourse of domestic and aesthetic femininity.

The next two chapters analyze the tensions, conflicts, and challenges of representing racially and ethnically diverse American experiences. I ask: Which American stories are told, by whom, and with what intention? How are racial and ethnic identities represented by American Girl in narrative and material form? And, when do the market interests of American Girl impact the brand mission of historical accuracy and diversity? In Chapter 5, "From 'This Where Freedom Supposed to Be At' to 'She Knew She Would Never Stop Speaking Out for What Was Right': Racial Logics and African American Identity in American Girl," I explore the variations in face molds, some of which intend to signify racial or ethnic features and the specific narrative representation of African American experiences in American history. From Addy (the company's first historical doll and series about an African American girl, released in 1986) who escaped slavery and experienced racism, freedom, and the reunification of her family in the 1860s to Melody (released in 2016) who works with her family and community to fight for social change during the Civil Rights movement of the 1960s, this chapter focuses on the narrative and material representation of African American experiences in American Girl's historical collection.

Chapter 6, "'This Is My Home': Representing Race, Ethnicity, and the American Experience in American Girl," shifts to explore the representations of Native American, Latino, Jewish, and immigrant protagonists in the historical collection. I explore the narrative positioning of readers in the simultaneous performance of noticing and not-noticing racial and ethnic difference. Unlike the stories of African American girls, that revolve around issues of power and institutionalized racism, in the books about Native American, Latino, Jewish, and immigrant girls, readers are encouraged to notice ethnicity and to celebrate cultural diversity, but remain blind to the constraining structures that maintain hierarchies around which social relations are organized. The final chapter, "Constructing American Girlhood" brings together the arguments presented throughout the book, reflecting upon the central question of how this brand imagines, represents, and ultimately constructs femininity, race, ethnicity, and national identity through its material and narrative representations.

IN THE BUSINESS OF LITTLE GIRLS

Pleasant Rowland often said—and her successors at American Girl have echoed this—that she was not in the doll business but in the "business of little girls."[14] American Girl, these executives believe, is not only involved in the production of dolls but the production of girls. Indeed, the books children read and the toys with which they play normalize particular ideologies and encourage particular ways of interacting with the social world.

While I was writing this book, Dr. Lisa Damour, director of Laurel School's Center for Research on Girls, wrote an article for the *New York Times* claiming that contemporary American culture, in which both traditional and social media consistently objectifies the female body, is detrimental to girls' mental and educational health.[15] Authors Peggy Orenstein and Nancy Jo Sales respectively wrote *Girls & Sex: Navigating the Complicated New Landscape* and *American Girls: Social Media and the Secret Lives of Teenagers*, both documenting a hypersexualized culture in which pornography and sexism have become a part of everyday teen girl culture. Young women, Orenstein argues, are growing up "in a porn-saturated, image-centered, commercialized culture in which 'empowerment' is just a feeling, consumption trumps connection, 'hot' is an imperative, fame is the ultimate achievement, and the quickest way for a woman to get ahead is to serve up her body before someone else does."[16] Even if, as some feminist media scholars argue, these kinds of concerns are alarmist and based in a moral panic that fails to recognize the empowered sexual agency of young women, there is a general scholarly consensus that an empowering sexuality cannot fully exist prior to puberty and that the representations of sex and sexuality created for and by older teens and young women have an impact on younger girls. Psychology professors Sharon Lamb and Zoë Peterson, who sometimes have differing opinions on the impact of hypersexual culture on teens and young women, reconcile their debate when younger girls are entered into the discussion; they write, "There are good reasons for us as adults, who have more knowledge and life experience than [a young teen] does, to not want her to feel desire so potently at this young an age, to not want her to make autonomous and absolute decisions that may place her at emotional or physical risk."[17] Rowland understood herself to be that knowledgeable adult—a self-directed, women's college graduate—who was creating a product not simply to turn a profit, but to protect girls from a sexualizing culture. This book explores the complex and contradictory constructions of girlhood as American Girl continues to produce both a profitable good and a tool of cultural resistance.

NOTES

1. Rebecca C. Hains, *The Princess Problem: Guiding our Girls Through the Princess-Obsessed Years* (Naperville, IL: Sourcebooks, 2014); Shirley R. Steinberg, "The Bitch Who Has Everything," in *Kinderculture: The Corporate Construction of Childhood*, ed. Shirley R. Steinberg and Joe L. Kincheloe (Boulder: Westview, 1997), 207–218.
2. Hains, *The Princess Problem*, 109.
3. Valerie Tripp, in discussion with author. February 1, 2017.
4. Ien Ang, Watching *Dallas: Soap Opera and the Melodramatic Imagination* (New York: Methuen & Co. Ltd., 1985); Henry Jenkins, *Textual Poachers: Television Fans and Participatory Culture* (New York: Routledge, 2012).
5. Jenkins, *Textual Poachers*, 5–6.
6. Kathleen Ernst, *Captain of the Ship: A Caroline Classic, Vol. 1* (Middleton, WI: American Girl Publishing, 2014), 123.

7. As of the writing of this book, though Molly, Kirsten, and Cécile and Marie-Grace had been part of the historical collection, they had not been re-released as part of the re-branded BeForever collection.

8. Denise Lewis Patrick, *No Ordinary Sound: A Melody Classic Volume 1* (Middleton, WI: American Girl Publishing, 2016), 90.

9. Denise Lewis Patrick, *Never Stop Singing: A Melody Classic 2* (Middleton, WI: American Girl Publishing, 2016), 122.

10. Sarah Banet-Weiser and Roopali Mukherjee, "Introduction: Commodity Activism in Neoliberal Times," in *Commodity Activism: Cultural Resistance in Neoliberal Times*, ed. by Roopali Mukherjee and Sarah Banet-Weiser (New York: NYU Press, 2012), 2–3.

11. Study of the role of fathers in the experience of doll purchasing or doll play, the role of boys in doll play, and adult women involved in doll collecting or play was beyond the scope of this book but certainly deserves greater attention. Rebecca West (2014) has written about adult American Girl collectors.

12. I have not included, in this count, the best friend's stories which were limited to Elizabeth, Nellie, Ruthie, Emily, and Ivy because these were not central stories, were added later, and were available for limited time period.

13. Mary Pipher, *Reviving Ophelia: Saving the Selves of Adolescent Girls* (New York: Ballantine, 1994), 12.

14. "Pleasant: A Christmas Story," *Wisconsin State Journal*, December 1, 1996. https://www.highbeam.com/doc/1G1-69570428.html; Michael J. Silverstein, Neil Fiske, and John Butman, *Trading Up: Why Consumers Want New Luxury Goods—and How Companies Create Them* (New York: Penguin, 2008), 75.

15. Lisa Damour, "For Teenage Girls, Swimsuit Season Never Ends," *New York Times*, August 10, 2016. https://well.blogs.nytimes.com/2016/08/10/for-teenage-girls-swimsuit-season-never-ends/.

16. Peggy Orenstein, *Girls & Sex: Navigating the Complicated New Landscape* (New York: Harper Collins, 2016), 40–41.

17. Sharon Lamb and Zoë D. Peterson, "Adolescent girls' sexual empowerment: Two feminists explore the concept." *Sex Roles* 66, no. 11–12 (June 2012), 707.

CHAPTER 2

Branding the American Girl: The Making of Cultural Icons

If you had to imagine the story of the woman who launched American Girl you couldn't dream up anything more perfect than the true story of Pleasant Rowland. Even if you overlook the aptness of her given name, her story has all the makings of a Hollywood film. Rowland, the daughter of an advertising executive and a homemaker, graduated from a women's college, became an educator and curriculum writer, and then, at age forty-five, launched a doll company that made her one of *Forbes'* fifty Most Successful Self-Made Women in America and one of *Working Woman* magazine's Top 50 Women Business Owners for six years in a row. In 1986 American Girl was an independent start-up operating out of a rented warehouse with makeshift plywood packing stations; thirty years later American Girl is a subsidiary of toy behemoth Mattel, with twenty retail stores, facilities totaling over 1.8 million square feet, and $570 million in sales.[1]

Born in 1941, Rowland was raised in Bannockburn, Illinois, a wealthy and exclusive suburb of Chicago. Her mother, also named Pleasant, but known as Petty, stayed home and diligently kept the house running for Rowland and her three younger siblings while her father, Edward Thiele, served as president of the Leo Burnett advertising agency. As a child, Rowland was enamored of her father's advertising portfolio. She recalls that her father would often share his ideas with his family before he revealed them to clients; the portfolios of consumer products such as Campbell's soup and Green Giant vegetables seemed magical to Rowland and were the source of her belief that "great ideas need to be detailed and beautifully executed."[2]

© The Author(s) 2017
E. Zaslow, *Playing with America's Doll*,
DOI 10.1057/978-1-137-56649-2_2

After graduating in 1962 from Wells College, a women's college in upstate New York, Rowland worked as a teacher in public and private schools along the East Coast and in California.[3] Finding that the curricula she was assigned were lacking in creativity, and in the attention to detail and beautiful execution she had learned from her father, Rowland began to develop her own educational materials.[4] After six years in the classroom Rowland shifted careers and began to work on-camera as a television news reporter in San Francisco. This new career direction was cut short by a fortuitous on-camera interview for a news segment in which Rowland profiled the author of a bilingual reading curriculum. The two bonded over their mutual interest in writing lessons for children. Sharing the materials she had created for her own classes, Rowland impressed her interviewee so much that the author connected Rowland with the company that had published her bilingual curriculum.

In this highly unusual success story, Rowland was offered a position at the Boston Educational Research Company. She moved to Boston to join the company and over the next eight years worked on developing a reading curriculum, which is still used in classrooms today.[5] She rapidly rose through the company's ranks and in the capacity of Vice President she went to Madison, Wisconsin, to supervise the curriculum's printing. There she had another serendipitous meeting, this time with Jerry Frautschi, the owner of the printing company. Frautschi recalls, "There were problems with the film, and there was going to be a three- to four-day delay... So as a good salesman I felt I should take care of this customer."[6] The couple fell in love, had a whirlwind courtship, and were married six months later, writing romantic letters to each other until they could merge their lives in Wisconsin the following year.[7] Shortly after Rowland moved to Madison, she purchased *Children's Magazine Guide,* a small publication that indexed magazines for librarians.[8]

In 1984, Rowland, then forty-three years old, joined her husband at a convention at Colonial Williamsburg, the world's largest living history museum. Located in Williamsburg, Virginia, the museum recreates a revolutionary city through restored and historically accurate reconstructed homes, shops, and other community hubs. In the historical city, Rowland became "inspired by the sights, scents, and sounds" that were punctuated by interactions with tradespeople and actors who took on the roles of colonial townspeople. She was excited by the immersive experience including the homes, the churches, the costumes, and the everyday paraphernalia she discovered as she walked the grounds. An educator by trade and a ready entrepreneur, Rowland wondered what mechanisms were in place to help children better understand their Williamsburg experience.[9] She proposed the development of an information packet for children and secured a contract with Colonial Williamsburg to write it.[10]

Later that same year, Rowland became frustrated with her options as she shopped for a Christmas doll for her eight- and ten-year-old nieces. Finding the most popular dolls at the time, the Cabbage Patch Kids, or as Rowland called them "the scrunchy vegetable dolls," to be ugly, Rowland continued down the toy aisles.[11] She rejected the next doll she happened upon, an American classic, because she felt that the buxom Barbie, garbed in her tight mini dresses and high heels, was too sexual for young girls and rushed them into a pre-mature adolescence.[12] Explaining her thought process, Rowland is explicit about her interest in reimagining the doll market and in her understanding of dolls as communicative objects. "Here I was," she has said, "in a generation of women at the forefront of redefining women's roles, and yet our daughters were playing with dolls that celebrated being a teen queen or a mommy."[13] Rowland knew that she could not be alone in seeking new role models for girls. She says that the two experiences—her visit to Colonial Williamsburg and her Christmas shopping trip—"collided and the concept [of American Girl] literally exploded in [her] brain."[14]

On a wintery weekend in front of the fireplace in her Wisconsin cabin, Rowland began to conjure up the vision of American Girl.[15] In a letter to her friend and former co-worker, Valerie Tripp, who would later become the author of over thirty American Girl books, Rowland dreamed of a doll that could teach American history, moral and ethical values, and independence.[16] She wrote out her concept for the first three dolls—Kirsten, Molly, and Samantha—as well as her entire business plan including retail stores, musical theater programs, and matching girls' clothing.[17] Recalling this moment, Rowland recounts, "I have done a lot of writing in my life but never before, nor since, have words flowed so easily and so quickly."[18] Two years later Rowland launched the eponymous Pleasant Company.

The concept of this eighteen-inch doll was not immediately well received. At the time, the commonly held belief in the toy market was that girls stopped playing with dolls after the age of six. The idea that a doll business could target seven to twelve year olds was deemed absurd. But Rowland was lucky; she had saved $1.2 million from her textbook royalties and was able to start the company without backers.[19] Knowing how to get books published was her forte but Rowland had no experience in fiction writing or doll production and she wasn't even sure what the doll should look like. She called on Tripp, with whom she had shared many conversations about the books they'd loved as girls, and asked her to sketch out a concept for the stories. She sent another friend to Chicago to find a doll they could use as a model. The friend found a cross-eyed but beautiful doll in a dusty box in the Marshall Field's department store. When she brought it to Rowland they undressed the doll and discovered that it was manufactured by the Götz company in Germany. After many phone calls and letters, Rowland headed to Germany to work with the company on the production of the first three American Girls.[20] Eventually Pleasant Company would source out production of dolls, clothing, furniture, and accessories to factories in China, Taiwan, Sweden, Russia, Spain, and the United States.[21]

Although Rowland had a vision and wanted to push it through, she agreed to conduct focus groups as suggested by some of the fifteen employees she had hired to aid her in the start-up. Early focus groups with mothers proved to be very informative and cemented the lessons she had learned as the daughter of an advertising executive; Rowland's success would lie in her ability to execute her idea. As toy industry executives had predicted, mothers in the focus groups who were told about Rowland's doll idea said that their daughters would not play with the doll. In fact, Rowland remembers feeling that the mothers absolutely hated the idea of historical dolls. However, when these same mothers saw the prototypes of the books, dolls, and furniture they started to become intrigued and quickly fell in love with the product.[22] Rowland believed that she had something special to contribute to girls.

Recognizing that the company did not have the capital to compete for shelf space with major doll companies such as Hasbro and Mattel, Rowland opted to keep the American Girl dolls off the toy store shelves. Even if she did manage to secure a spot in the toy market, Rowland feared that the "neon frenzy of discount toy stores" and television commercial advertisements would cheapen the image of her quality dolls. She did not want to see the young faces of her American girls on lunch boxes or sleeping bags. As a witness to the explosion of the Cabbage Patch Kids, their market saturation, and the subsequent loss of their popularity, Rowland initially refused to license out her characters. Further, Rowland said that she did not want to be a party to making "kids and parents victims of [the] commercial hype" that was associated with ads that played during the era's Saturday morning cartoons and afterschool television programming.[23]

Eschewing mainstream marketing, Rowland chose only print ads in upscale magazines such as the *Smithsonian* and *Yankee and Child* as well as direct marketing and word of mouth. Her market was clear; she was after what she called the "thinking girl," the well-heeled girl with educated parents who could afford her upscale doll.[24]

COMPANY MISSION

In interviews and speeches Rowland has often stressed her role as nurturer rather than her role as entrepreneur. She establishes her connection to girls not only as an aunt searching for a doll for her nieces but also through her indirect maternal care for all girls. In 1991, the childless doll maker told a newspaper reporter, "It doesn't take a Freudian genius to figure out that in some ways I was making all eight-year-old girls my child. And what other women invest in their own children, I was going to invest in girls at large."[25] In 1996 she expanded on the connection between her maternal sense and her doll design, "I began to think what I would have wanted to give a daughter... I would want her to have a sense of the wonderful traditions of girlhood, the legacy that mothers have passed to daughters for generations in answer to the age-old question, 'Mommy, what was it like when you were a girl?'"[26]

Rowland's story is well situated within a long history of doll makers whose creations sprung forth out of maternal concern for children. In the early part of the twentieth century, Martha Chase and other New England businesswomen created soft, durable, and realistic dolls in their opposition to both fragile fashion dolls from Europe and gimmicky dolls made by American businessmen. Arguing that those molded dolls were neither safe nor educational, Chase sought to give girls dolls that would help them to develop what she considered their natural ability to nurture; she saw herself as much a social reformer as a businesswoman.[27] Likewise, the creative mind behind the world's most popular doll, Barbie, also claimed maternal concern as a source for her inspiration. In interviews about her design of Barbie, Ruth Handler talked about how her daughter's play with paper dolls moved her to create a doll through which "every little girl" could "project herself into a dream of her future."[28] She claimed that the doll's large breasts were designed to help girls adjust to the changes they experienced in their own bodies.[29]

Rowland's intention was always to work within the toy industry to produce counternarratives that challenged traditional representations of American girls throughout history. Tripp understands the brand as "the embodiment of Pleasant's respect for, enchantment with, and delight in girlhood."[30] Though Rowland never publically identified the brand as feminist, Tripp says that a feminist politics was fundamental to the brand's identity because it was focused on empowering girl readers and also the women who worked for the company.[31] Instead of using the term feminist, Rowland used various phrases to define the brand's values. Her oft-quoted phrase, "We're not in the doll business, we're in the business of little girls" frames not only the expanse of the business but also the company's value-laden mission. Early on she called the products "chocolate cake with vitamins" which was a metaphor for her blend of entertainment and education.[32] Later, she stressed teaching "goodness" as the company's objective. Rowland says that she wanted girls to know that they could "trust in goodness" and she often ended company meetings with a quote from the Yeats poem, *To a Wealthy Man*, that captured her goal of providing girls with the right tools they needed to find and trust in goodness:

> Look up at the sun's eye and give
> What the exultant heart calls good
> That some new day may breed the best
> Because you gave, not what they would
> But the right twig's for the eagle's nest![33]

Nina Diamond and a team of marketing scholars who have studied the American Girl brand concept argue that Rowland positioned herself as the "moral salve" for a girl culture that promotes early sexual development.[34] Whether her goal was to teach morality, goodness, history, or female empowerment, Rowland always imagined American Girl as more than a consumer product and her mission was always more than just to grab a larger market share.

If Rowland's public image is one of concern for girls, her private image is that of a marketing genius. Past employees describe her as a brilliant, creative, and guiding force.[35] Says Tripp, "Working with Pleasant was—and still is—exhilarating, demanding, heady, unpredictable, hilarious, rewarding, and fun, just like Pleasant herself."[36] Many agree that her intense involvement in the company extended down to the most minute details—even the selection of the salt and pepper shakers in the employee dining room. One former co-worker describing Rowland, whose middle initial is T, said, "Do you know what her initials, P.T.R., stand for? Prepare to Redo! She's demanding!"[37] Aware of reports by former employees that she can be difficult to work for, Rowland has countered: "Am I finicky? Yes, my name is on the company."[38] As a social entrepreneur, Rowland combined business acumen with a mission to empower contemporary children with stories of brave girls throughout American history. Rowland retired in 2000 shortly after she sold the company to Mattel. Her vision and leadership shaped the company from 1986 to 2000 and remain a legacy today.

THE ORIGINAL DOLLS: KIRSTEN, MOLLY, AND SAMANTHA

From the start Rowland followed through on her vision that each doll would be sold with a story that brought her to life. The story served to situate the girl within her family, her cultural environment, and her historical time period. It focused on family lives, friendships, education, history, adventure, and the struggles of growing up as a girl. In each story, the girls were spunky take-charge characters who were active agents in their own lives. Rowland argued that authenticity was paramount and that everything, from the type of school a girl would attend in a specific time period to what kind of lunch sack she would carry, was researched before anything was finalized in the books or catalog. This attention to historical accuracy, initially overseen by Rowland and a full-time historian, made future character development a three- to four-year process.[39] In 1983, Rowland asked Tripp, whom she had previously hired to work on the SuperKids curriculum, to outline stories for the first three characters. Tripp, a young writer who was part of the first co-educational graduating class at Yale, shared Rowland's excitement about producing history for girls.

Two years later, in 1985, Kirsten Larson, Samantha Parkington, and Molly McIntire dolls were released. Kirsten Larson was a Swedish immigrant growing up in Minnesota in 1854; Molly McIntire was a white, suburban, middle-class girl whose father was a medical officer in the Army during World War II; and Samantha Parkington was a white orphan living with her wealthy and conservative grandmother in the Victorian era. Each doll was sold with her first story for $82.

Sold separately were a series of six books narrating a year in the fictional girl's life as a nine- to ten-year-old, six dresses, and a collection of miniature replicas of historic accessories profiled in the books. Although written by different authors, each of the series' books for the three original girls, and all American Girl series produced before 2002, followed the same pattern in theme and title. Using Kirsten as an example, each series included:

- *Meet Kirsten: An American Girl*
- *Kirsten Learns a Lesson: A School Story*
- *Kirsten's Surprise: A Christmas Story*
- *Happy Birthday, Kirsten! A Springtime Story*
- *Kirsten Saves the Day: A Summer Story*
- *Changes for Kirsten: A Winter Story.*

Each *Meet* book introduced the girl, her family, and other important people in the girl's life. It situated her within a historical time period and often within a socio-historical conflict. The *School* stories provided an opportunity for readers to follow the girl to school and observe the kind of education she received in her time period; the stories often contained a moral tone as the lessons learned by the girl were value driven and not solely academic. The *Christmas* and *Birthday* stories allowed for gifts to be exchanged (and thus replicas of these gifts to be sold via catalog) and generally included parties and celebrations for which girls needed new dresses. The *Saves the Day* books presented the girl in the middle of an adventure and as the ultimate heroine in the solution of a conflict. Finally, the *Changes* books were about new events in the girl's life and how she faced the challenges of change. The series' books also included a non-fiction addendum entitled "Looking Back," later renamed "Peek into the Past," which offered additional non-fictional information about the character's historical era.

Each book within the series used both illustration and prose to present the protagonist with at least one new seasonal dress as well as several new accessories. Authors employed to write American Girl series books have reported that they were directed to include specific details in their prose about items that would be sold in the catalog. Of his experience writing the Girl of Today series for a doll named Marisol Luna in 2005, for example, author Gary Soto wrote,

> I … listened to the parent company (Mattel) about elaborating details so that Marisol would be hip—she needed a cell phone, for instance. She could also use a carrying case for her dance costumes; so could I, then, mention the carrying case once or twice in the narrative? I was getting the picture. I also dutifully added a purse and necklace—merchandise in other words.[40]

This way, the dolls, books, and accessories could work synergistically. For example, if girls sought to recreate the English tea party Molly had for her birthday in the fourth book of her series they were able to purchase replicas of Molly's drop leaf table and chairs, the china set she used to serve the tea, the new dress she wore to her party, and a toy birthday cake. The books then can be conceptualized not only as narratives but also as marketing tools for the dolls and their accessories.

Girls were addressed as consumers and agents of play within the catalogs where prose spoke directly to them. In early catalogs, each American Girl took up ten pages of the catalog including an initial two-page spread (requiring the consumer to turn the catalog vertically) which displayed the doll in her *Meet* outfit and eight subsequent pages highlighting the doll posed with her additional accessories while clad in her other dresses. Historically accurate doll beds sold for between $40 and $60; trunks or dresses to store the dolls' $22 dresses ranged from $150 to $175 and parents who were able to purchase the whole collection at once shelled out nearly $1000.

Enticing descriptions of the products, many beginning with imperative verbs, instructed girls to buy accessories to enhance their play; "Pack a lunch for Kirsten in this charming oval wooden box" or "Set the table for Kirsten's birthday," suggested the catalog copy. Girl consumers were also reminded to satisfy their doll's needs with protective clothing. Samantha owners, for example, were reminded to buy the $24 *Travel Duster & Hat* so they could "Tie her scarf around her neck to keep out the chilly ocean breezes!" and Molly's fans were told to buy her *Slicker & Rain Hat* to "Keep Molly warm and dry." In addition to protecting them from the elements, it was suggested that girl owners could satisfy their dolls' needs—or even save their lives—with the right products. Molly owners discovered that they could improve their doll's mathematical skills when they paid $65 for her school desk because, "Molly loved everything about school except Miss Campbell's horrible multiplication bees. And she might like those if you sit her straight and tall in her desk and help her practice her flashcards." Kirsten's fans could "imagine how proud she'll feel and how beautiful she will look" when they adorned their doll with her $16 *Saint Lucia Wreath*, a traditional Swedish crown worn during the Christmas celebration. Samantha's life was on the line because "In 1904, bathing suits were heavy when wet" so purchasing Samantha's $28 *Bathing Costume* included a buoy or "life save" that girls were told to keep "close at hand – just in case!" There was a seamless connection, then, between the stories, the accessories, and the catalog where girl owners were promised that the books' scripts could come alive with the acquisition of accessories.

Rowland's attention to detail paid off; during the 1986 Christmas season, their first as a company, Pleasant Company sold $1.7 million worth of products. In their second year, sales increased to $7.6 million. In the third year, the company faced a potential setback when Rowland was diagnosed with breast cancer just after moving the company's operations into an expanded warehouse. She says, "I cut the ribbon on the new warehouse in the morning and went into the hospital that afternoon to have surgery." Though the tumor was large and the prognosis poor, Rowland attributes her survival to the work she did at Pleasant Company where "throughout chemotherapy and radiation [she] never missed a day of work."[41] Her dedication paid off in her health as well as in the company's growth.

Purchase by Mattel

By 1991 Pleasant Company had already reported sales of over $50 million and had developed a loyal customer base.[42] When Pleasant Company sent out invitations to a tea party at Colonial Williamsburg where its newest doll Felicity would be unveiled, Rowland received an overwhelming response and was encouraged to add an additional fifteen sittings for the tea to accommodate 6000 girls and 5800 parents from forty-nine states.[43] Despite the cost of travel for many families, and the admission fee of fifty dollars for adults and thirty dollars for children, fans flocked to the tea party demonstrating the brand's growing popularity with upper-middle-class families and Rowland's masterful ability to synergize.

The company expanded rapidly, adding new historical dolls every few years, a baby doll collection in 1990, a magazine in 1992, a contemporary doll collection in 1995, living history experiences in 1997, and a retail store in 1998. By 1998, Pleasant Company was the nation's second most popular doll, worth $300 million. That year, a little over ten years after she began the company, Pleasant Rowland sold her empire to toy giant, Mattel. Best known for Barbie, the enemy against which American Girl was marketed, Mattel purchased the company for $700 million. Defending the hypocrisy of selling her company to the makers of the very doll she resisted buying for her nieces in the early 1980s, Rowland cited her connection with then Mattel CEO, Jill Barad, who had raised the Barbie profile and expanded the aging brand. Rowland says, "The ironies did not escape me, and many were critical of my decision, but I saw in Jill a blend of passion, perfectionism, and perseverance with real business savvy. During the same thirteen-year period that I built American Girl from zero to $300 million,

Jill built Barbie from $200 million to $2 billion. An amazing feat."[44] For Mattel, acquiring American Girl meant that it could expand its reach to older girls beyond the Barbie years, which start at two or three years of age and begin to dwindle thereafter until generally ending at about age eight.[45]

Under Mattel's umbrella, the name Pleasant Company was officially dropped and rebranded as American Girl. Rowland was named Vice Chairman of Mattel, a position in which she remained until her retirement in 2000. American Girl has been fully absorbed into Mattel and is considered one of its core brands, but maintains its headquarters in Middleton, Wisconsin, nearly two thousand miles from the Mattel corporate headquarters in El Segundo, California. Following Rowland's retirement, three women have had positions at the helm of the brand; Ellen Brothers (2000–2012) who had extensive direct marketing experience, Jean McKenzie (2012–2016) whose experience included prior oversight of the Barbie brand as well as professional experience at both Disney and the English language arts curriculum, *Hooked on Phonics*, and Katy Dickson (2016–present), who had served in various capacities at the General Mills cereal company and as Global Chief Marketing Officer at News Corp's News America.

HISTORICAL DOLL DEVELOPMENT

Both before and after the sale of the company, American Girl expanded its collection of historical dolls. The historical collection was renamed BeForever in 2014 at which time each of the girls' six story collections were re-bundled into two illustration-free volumes, all of the original *Meet* outfits were replaced with new versions, and many of the original accessories and outfits produced by Pleasant Company were retired or revamped. The list below details the historical dolls, in the order that they have been released. It includes both those that have been "archived" (permanently or temporarily discontinued) and those currently in production, and exhibits the extensive social history explored in the collection.

- Kirsten Larson, introduced in 1986, represents a girl from 1854. Written by Janet Shaw, Kirsten's story focuses on her experience leaving Sweden and making a new life in the Minnesota Territory. This story explores an immigrant experience and the hardships of a pioneering life on the plains. The Kirsten doll was archived in 2010. Kirsten's biggest dream is "to build a new home with her family."[46]

- Molly McIntire, introduced in 1986, represents a girl from 1944. Written by Valerie Tripp, Molly's story focuses on life in Jefferson, Illinois, during World War II. With Molly's father caring for wounded soldiers in the field, her mother taking a job outside of the home, and Emily Bennett, a girl from England coming to live with the family for safe harbor, Molly's life is filled with change. The Molly doll was archived in 2013. An Emily doll was sold as a companion for Molly from 2006–2013. Molly's biggest dream is "to do her part to help end the war."
- Samantha Parkington, introduced in 1986, represents a girl from 1904. Written by Susan Adler, Maxine Rose Schur, and Valerie Tripp, Samantha's story focuses on gender roles and social class in New York City at the turn of the century. Her aunt protests with the suffragists for the right to vote while Samantha protests the feminine etiquette that is expected of her. Her story also focuses on her friendship and aid to Nellie O'Malley, the girl who is hired to work as a servant in a home next to Samantha's. The Samantha doll was archived in 2009 and re-released in 2014. A Nellie doll was sold as a companion for Samantha from 2004–2009. Samantha's biggest dream is "to help those in need."
- Felicity Merriman, introduced in 1991, represents a girl from 1776. Written by Valerie Tripp, Felicity's story focuses on an independent, spirited girl living in Williamsburg during the start of the American Revolution. Felicity is challenged by the social expectations of her time; she would prefer to ride horses and help at her father's store than to do needlepoint and take lessons on tea service. The Felicity doll was archived in 2011 and re-released in 2017. An Elizabeth doll was sold as a companion for Felicity from 2005–2011. Felicity's biggest dream is "to stand up for what she believes in."
- Addy Walker, introduced in 1993, represents a girl from 1864. Written by Connie Porter, Addy's story focuses on a girl who is born into slavery but escapes with her mother to live as a free girl in Philadelphia. The story explores her escape, her new life, school, home, the reunification of her family, and the challenges of living in a racist and segregated Northern state. Addy was the brand's first African American doll. Addy's biggest dream is "to help her family stay close."
- Josefina Montoya, introduced in 1997, represents a girl from 1824. Written by Valerie Tripp, Josefina's story focuses on the company's first Latina doll. Along with her three sisters, Josefina is trying to

maintain family traditions after her mother's death and aids in the development of a blossoming romance between her father and her mother's sister. Her story takes place in New Mexico when the land was actually a part of Mexico and not the United States and Josefina helps her father to avoid conflict with an Anglo trader. Her biggest dream is "to be a healer."

- Kit Kittredge, introduced in 2000, represents a girl from 1934. Written by Valerie Tripp, Kit's story focuses on a white girl growing up in Cincinnati, Ohio, at the height of the Great Depression. Kit's story highlighted both the challenges experienced by families during a failing economy as well as the power of journalism. A budding reporter, Kit exposes the struggles of the era's homeless children. Kit's biggest dream is "to turn hard times into good times."

- Kaya, introduced in 2002, represents a girl from 1764. Written by Janet Shaw, Kaya's story focuses on life in the Nez Perce tribe prior to the invasion by white Europeans. On the land that is now part of the United States' Pacific Northwest, Kaya cares for her animals, participates in her tribe's harvest, and bravely escapes from another tribe by whom she has been taken captive. Her biggest dream is "to be a leader for her people."

- Julie Albright, introduced in 2007, represents a girl from 1974. Written by Megan McDonald, Julie's story focuses on life in San Francisco after her parents' divorce. Julie has to negotiate her relationships now that she no longer lives with her father, nor nearby to her best friend, Ivy Ling. It also explores her fight to gain a spot on the boys' basketball team, because there is no equivalent for girls, and her work with an organization that rescues eagles. An Ivy doll was sold as a companion for Julie from 2007–2014 which was significant as she was the collection's only Asian American doll. Julie's biggest dream is "to stand up and fight for what's right."

- Rebecca Rubin, introduced in 2009, represents a girl from 1914. Written by Jacqueline Dembar Greene, Rebecca's story focuses on growing up as the child of Russian Jewish immigrants on New York City's Lower East Side. Rebecca's family has to negotiate traditional customs and American ways as they consider how to assimilate into a new, and mostly Christian, country. Rebecca maintains her appreciation for the rituals of Shabbat and Hanukkah while also learning to love modern cinema. Rebecca loves to act, help out at her father's shoe store, and also speaks out against the horrible factory conditions in which some of her family members work. Rebecca's biggest dream is to keep "shining bright for others."

- Marie-Grace Gardiner and Cécile Rey, introduced in 2011, represent two girls from 1853. Marie-Grace's story was written by Sarah Buckey and Cécile's story was written by Denise Lewis Patrick. These two girls, representing best friends living in New Orleans, were simultaneously released. Cécile, a Creole girl born to a wealthy, free black family, is homeschooled, and gives her time and her voice to helping the children in her community who have been orphaned by the Yellow Fever epidemic. Marie-Grace, a white girl who has recently moved back to New Orleans after the death of her mother and brother, becomes Cécile's best friend when they meet at vocal lessons. The girls' friendship blossoms over their interest in singing but also in helping the orphans. Marie-Grace's biggest dream is "to make a difference to others" and Cécile's biggest dream is "to share her gifts with the world."
- Caroline Abbott, introduced in 2012, represents a girl from 1812. Written by Kathleen Ernst, Caroline's story focuses on her display of bravery as she defends her family's Lake Ontario shipyard and saves her father from British captivity during the War of 1812. Caroline, who identifies as adventurous, dreams of having her own boat. She loves to ice skate and finds herself at odds with her cousin and friends who would prefer to do each other's hair than be active. Her biggest dream is "to be a courageous captain of a ship."
- Maryellen Larkin, introduced in 2015, represents a girl from 1954. Written by Valerie Tripp, Maryellen's story focuses on an open-minded, inventive girl who is interested in STEM (science, technology, math, and engineering) fields. Maryellen, a survivor of polio, has one weak leg and cold-sensitive lungs. She is conflicted about her desire to both be her own unique, individual self and to simultaneously fit into the crowd. Valerie Tripp has said that part of the inspiration for Maryellen's disability were the letters she received from girls with disabilities asking for stories of girls like them.[47] Maryellen's biggest dream is "to inspire others to stand out from the crowd."
- Melody Ellison, introduced in 2016, represents a girl from 1964. Written by Denise Lewis Patrick, Melody's story focuses on life in Detroit, Michigan, during the Civil Rights movement of the 1960s. Melody fights social injustice and builds community through

performing in her church choir and civic organizing. With the support of her family and friends, she finds immense courage to carry on with her activism after she learns of the Birmingham church bombing. Melody's biggest dream is "to use her voice to stand up for equality."

BRAND EXPANSION: CONTEMPORARY GIRLHOOD

Even before its acquisition by Mattel, Pleasant Company had begun to develop a line of products that represented contemporary girlhood but it has certainly been expanded under Mattel's ownership. In 1992 the company began to grow its library to include *American Girl* Magazine with a mission to "encourage young readers' self-confidence, curiosity, and dreams."[48] Each issue of the newly launched bimonthly *American Girl* magazine featured a story from the American Girl historical collection as well as stories about contemporary girls' lives, craft ideas, recipes, an advice column, and play scripts based on the historical characters. Until 2000, every magazine featured a paper doll with historical and contemporary clothing based on a real modern girl who had researched her family's ancestry. However, after Mattel purchased Pleasant Company, the focus of the magazine shifted away from historical characters and featured more articles on contemporary girls.

Girl of Today, renamed Just Like You in 2006, My American Girl in 2010, and finally Truly Me in 2015, a collection of dolls sold without stories and meant to represent contemporary girls, now occupies the greatest amount of catalog and retail floor space. These dolls were initially sold with a set of six blank books in which a girl consumer was encouraged to follow a Valerie Tripp-created writing guide to create her doll's story. The company's connection between dolls and stories was deemphasized when it stopped packaging the contemporary dolls with blank books and writing guides. Furthermore, the name change and the increased options in this collection for variations of hair, skin, and eye color, originally only twenty, and now as high as fifty, entice consumers to purchase dolls that look like themselves rather than characters from whom they may learn history or with whom they may share similarities across time, space, and physical identity markers. In 2016, Mattel announced that for the American Girl brand, its "number one priority is really to provide more access to more girls and accomplishing that objective is best served through distribution expansion."[49] This development includes plans for a franchise licensing agreement to expand the brand into the Middle East and a deal with Toys R Us to sell Truly Me dolls in stores across the country. The amplified fiscal imperative of getting dolls into a greater number of girls' hands, certainly challenges an element of the brand's original mission which was value-laden even as it was commodified.

It is not unusual to read lamentations about the change in mission which adult writers claim no longer focuses on history and now offers girls a bland self-empowerment message and focuses on buying.[50] Reminiscing about the Samantha doll her grandmother gifted her, Adrienne Raphel writes in *The New Yorker*, "the problem with the huge cast of characters today is that it creates an American Girl world that—rather than allowing girls to identify with the lives of others (fictional as they may be) and thereby helping them understand the shared history that links us all together—teaches girls about little other than their own burgeoning personalities."[51] Similarly, Amy Schiller argues that while the original dolls' stories revolved around important historical conflicts, look-alike dolls "offer blander avatars who reflect only the present time period and appearance of contemporary girls… [or historical dolls that have] a greater focus on appearance, increasingly mild character development, and innocuous political topics."[52]

American Girl says that its mission has not waivered too far from Rowland's original one; it seeks "to champion and celebrate girls and who they are today, while giving them the tools to be strong, compassionate, resourceful, and independent women tomorrow."[53] In an attempt to maintain the original focus on storytelling, American Girl has released Girl of the Year dolls since 2003, which tell the story of a modern-day character, launched Wellie Wishers, a line of dolls for a younger market, whose stories focus on friendship, imagination, and outdoor play, and hinted at a new line of contemporary characters with its 2017 announcement of Tenney Grant, Suzie "Z" Yang, and its first boy doll, Logan Everett, all of whom will be featured in narratives. In addition, by the time Nanea Mitchell greets the shelves in August 2017, the company will have released three additional historical dolls in the past three years. American Girl counters the claim that it is betraying its mission; Stephanie Spanos, a public relations executive at American Girl states, "We've definitely evolved [but]…We are deeply committed to our historical collection. It remains what we feel is the foundation of our company."[54]

Experiences and Retail

Rowland's business savvy led her to imagine American Girl not only as a doll and book set but also as an immersive experience. The American Girl Fashion Show in partnership with 250 Junior League chapters around the country was launched in 1996 and billed as a way to raise money for child-serving organizations. Each sponsoring fundraising organization had to pay Pleasant Company several thousand dollars to produce a show with the fashion kit the company sent to them. The sponsoring organizations kept all proceeds from tickets and raffles and were also entitled to 5 percent of any sales resulting from catalog distribution at the event, thereby encouraging the organizers to push sales. These fashion shows served three purposes according to Rowland: to raise money, to provide an educational and entertaining experience for attendees, and serve as an advertisement for the girls' companion clothing collection.[55] For a brief period, Pleasant Company also offered character-specific fundraisers such as Samantha's Ice Cream Social where guests paid an entry fee that was donated to charity in return for the chance to dress in Victorian styles, learn how to set Victorian tables, make their own sundaes, and watch a video about the life and times of Samantha Parkington.[56] Similar fundraisers were launched along with the release of several dolls including Kit's Care and Share Party and Josefina's Fiesta.

In 1997, four living history exhibits were created around the country including Felicity's tour in Colonial Williamsburg, Kirsten's tour in Scandia, Minnesota, Samantha's tour in Washington, D.C., and Molly's tour in Portsmouth, New Hampshire. However, just before the purchase by Mattel, these experiences transitioned into wholly commercial ventures with the opening of the company's first retail store on Chicago's magnificent mile. After twelve years of success as a direct mail brand that sold through catalog only, Rowland's early vision of a retail store came to fruition. The company claimed that the store was built to offer families an experience rather than a shopping trip. Some floors featured a typical layout while others looked more like a museum featuring dioramas of each historical character against a contextual backdrop. In addition, the dolls were said to come alive through experiences that girls could have at the retail locations: at the café girls could sit with their families and their dolls who were given special doll chairs; at the in-store theaters girls could watch their dolls' stories come alive; and in the doll salon, added later, girls could get their dolls' hair styled, ears pierced, or more recently, have their dolls receive a facial, have nail decals applied, or have hearing aids installed.[57]

From the start, the store was a tourist destination; in 2006 *Fast Company* reported that most visitors traveled three to six hours to get to the store and spent an average of four hours once there.[58] One mother told an Arizona newspaper that her family planned their summer vacation around a visit to the Los Angeles store for their nine-, twelve-, and thirteen-year-old daughters and added, "I don't know if I had more fun or my girls had more fun. ... I don't know how many hours we spent there, and we could have spent longer."[59] The retail division's focus on intergenerational consumption and bonding—grandparents and parents buying for and dining with their grandchildren—allows the company to be "old-fashioned without being old," and to celebrate respectability and morality beside female empowerment and spirited leadership.[60] Discussing the retail space's ideological function in the lives of consumers, Stefania Borghini and colleagues argue that the museum-like displays, themed food, dining rituals, and memory-building activities promote a message that both the store and the family that visits it support the notion of decency and goodness, which rests in part on American Girl's opposition to other popular dolls such as Bratz and Barbie, whose sexual personae brand them as amoral. In addition, as discussed in Chapter 4, the brand reifies a beauty culture that emphasizes the importance of appearance and self-disciplining beauty work. Describing the experience, Borghini et al. write,

> Moral and social values are enacted throughout the store. Beauty and perfection characterize the dolls' appearance and display, suggesting a feminine emotional energy that energizes *American Girl Place*. This energy marks [the store] as a place where intergenerational ideologies can be materialized, purchased and customized. In the Museum area, perfect reproductions of domestic spaces belonging to different, American Girl-brand associated historical periods create learning opportunities for girls. Motherhood and femininity are at the heart of conversations and activities performed in the Salon venue. The professional service delivered by salon attendants, who style doll's hair, emphasize how grooming is a serious component of girls' identity projects.[61]

Though the retail experiences have varied over the years, American Girl Place has continued to be a destination shop where girls learn specific meanings of girlhood and family that focus on consumption, morality, personal grooming, and sharing memories. Within ten years there were six additional stores and one additional flagship location in New York City. To date there are three flagship stores and nineteen smaller Boutiques and Bistros in fifteen states as well as seven locations in Canada and three stores in Mexico City.

As the new millennium chugs on, American Girl is evolving. The company is working on its digital presence capitalizing on the popular homegrown AGSM (American Girl Stop Motion) YouTube genre that began in 2013, in which girls create stop motion videos using their American Girl dolls as the film's characters. Noting that by 2015 the genre had become so popular that it surpassed thirty million views on YouTube,[62] American Girl has launched its own stop motion program, Z. Crew, which focuses on a vlogger character named Z who offers lessons on how to make stop motion films.

STUDYING AMERICAN GIRL

In 1986 a forty-five-year-old woman independently launched a doll company that was advertised through 500,000 catalogs. Twenty-five years later, celebrating the company's anniversary, American Girl announced a seven-day branded cruise from Miami to the Caribbean, that included movie screenings, crafts, author signings, and dinner with your doll. The cruise, for 500 girls and their families, sold out in forty-eight hours. Today, American Girl dolls and stories are a major part of the play landscape for millions of girls.

This chapter has laid out the history of American Girl as well as the corporate language surrounding its products. The remainder of the book provides a critical analysis of American Girl, specifically the BeForever historical collection. From its onset, American Girl has generally received praise from families, librarians, and educators. Rowland herself has been praised for her business acumen as well as for producing a doll that does not rely on her sexuality for identity. Moreover, the dolls' stories present girls with role models who are kind, courageous, adventurous, and committed to a better world. In this way, American Girl celebrates girlhood and resists positioning girls as demure, quiet, and sweet. It further seeks to counteract the cultural pull toward early sexual display by young girls. At the same time, criticism has reflected a concern over the cost of the dolls and the collection's celebration of consumption, sanitization of history, representations of race and ethnicity, and (re)production of traditional notions of femininity. This book unpacks these arguments, beginning by situating the analysis of American Girl within a discussion of why we study dolls and books, as well as by exploring the cultural environment in which American Girl emerged and came to popularity.

Notes

1. "Fast Facts," American Girl, accessed on February 15, 2017, http://www. americangirl.com/corporate/fast-facts; Sarah Halzack, "American Girl's Pint-Size Antidote for Its Multi-Million Dollar Problem," *The Washington Post*, July 21, 2016; Julie Sloane with Pleasant Rowland, "A New Twist on Timeless Toys," *Fortune Small Business*, October 1, 2002, http://money. cnn.com/magazines/fsb/fsb_archive/2002/10/01/330574/index.htm.
2. Kay Miller, "Dolls Are a Pleasant Surprise," *Star Tribune*, November 19, 1991, E1.
3. Shortly after college she entered into her first marriage with Richard Rowland.
4. Pleasant Company, "Background Information: Pleasant T. Rowland Biography," Pleasant Company, press release, received by mail December, 1996.
5. Miller, "Dolls Are a Pleasant Surprise."
6. Sara Freeman, "Jerry Frautschi and Pleasant Rowland: Who Is Jerry Frautschi?" *Isthmus*.com. April 7, 2011, http://isthmus.com/archive/from-the-archives/jerry-frautschi-and-pleasant-rowland-who-is-jerry-frautschi/.
7. Ibid.
8. Pleasant Company, "Background Information: Pleasant T. Rowland."
9. "Pleasant Company," accessed December, 1996, www.pleasantco.com.
10. Elizabeth Mehren, "Playing with History," *Los Angeles Times*, November 28, 1994, E1.
11. Ibid.
12. Sharon Stangenes. "Barbie Backlash," *Chicago Tribune*, January 4, 1990, C1.
13. Sloane with Rowland, "A New Twist on Timeless Toys."
14. Ibid.
15. Pleasant Rowland, "AG 25th Birthday Tribute Speech," uploaded November 29, 2011, https://www.youtube.com/watch?v=_ltX5W6eZYw.
16. Brian Dumaine, "Pleasant Co.: How to Compete with a Champ," *Fortune*, January 10, 1994, 106.
17. Sloane with Rowland, "A New Twist on Timeless Toys."
18. Pleasant Rowland, "AG 25th Birthday Tribute Speech."
19. Ibid.
20. Sloane with Pleasant Rowland, "A New Twist on Timeless Toys."
21. "Rejecting Barbie, Doll Maker Gains," *New York Times*, September 1, 1993, D1.
22. Sloane with Pleasant Rowland, "A New Twist on Timeless Toys."
23. Molly Neal, "Cataloger Gets Pleasant Results," *Direct Marketing Magazine* 55, no. 1 (May 1992): 33.
24. Sloane with Pleasant Rowland, "A New Twist on Timeless Toys."

25. Miller, "Dolls Are a Pleasant Surprise."

26. "Changes for Pleasant," *Wisconsin State Journal*, December 1, 1996, A7.

27. Miriam Formanek-Brunell, *Made to Play House: Dolls and the Commercialization of American Girlhood, 1830–1930* (New Haven: Yale University Press, 1993).

28. Robert Lindsey, "A Million Dollar Business," *New York Times*, June 19, 1977, 91.

29. "Interview with Ruth Handler," *Barbie Nation*, directed by Susan Stern (San Francisco, CA: Bernal Beach Films, 1998), DVD.

30. Valerie Tripp, e-mail message to author, February 17, 2017.

31. Valerie Tripp, in discussion with the author, February 1, 2017.

32. Pleasant Company, "Background Information: Pleasant T. Rowland."

33. Pleasant Rowland, "AG 25th Birthday Tribute Speech."

34. Nina Diamond et al., "American Girl and the Brand Gestalt: Closing the Loop on Sociocultural Branding Research," *Journal of Marketing* 73, no. 3 (2009): 122.

35. Tripp, e-mail; Leanna Landsman, "Induction Speech for Pleasant Rowland to Association of American Publishers Hall of Fame," 1990, http://publishers.org/2009-pleasant-t-rowland#leanna.

36. Tripp, e-mail.

37. Leanna Landsman, "Induction Speech."

38. "Meet Pleasant," *Wisconsin State Journal*, December 1, 1996, A6.

39. Julia Prohaska, e-mail message to author, April 1, 1997.

40. Gary Soto, "Why I've Stopped Writing Children's Literature," *Huffington Post*. September 25, 2013, http://www.huffingtonpost.com/gary-soto/childrens-literature-writing_b_3989751.html.

41. Sloane with Pleasant Rowland, "A New Twist on Timeless Toys."

42. Suzanne Alexander, "Doll Line Is History – a Pleasant Hit," *Wall Street Journal*, August 22, 1991, B1.

43. Felicity Wright, "American Girls to Treasure," *The Washington Post*, August 27, 1991, C5.

44. Sloane with Pleasant Rowland, "A New Twist on Timeless Toys."

45. Dana Canedy, "Takeovers Are Part of the Game; Any Hot Toy Can Grow Up to Be a Unit of Mattel or Hasbro," *New York Times*, February 9, 1999, http://www.nytimes.com/1999/02/09/business/takeovers-are-part-game-any-hot-toy-can-grow-up-be-unit-mattel-hasbro.html.

46. All quotes about the character's dreams in the following section are from: Carrie Anton, Laurie Calkhoven, and Erin Falligant, *American Girl: Ultimate Visual Guide* (New York: DK Publishing, 2016).

47. Tripp, in discussion with author.

48. Pleasant Company, "Background Information: American Girl," Pleasant Company, press release, received by mail December, 1996.

49. Chris Sinclair, "Mattel Inc. Analyst Day – Final," (Speech), November 3, 2016. http://files.shareholder.com; Martin Gilkes, "Mattel Inc. Earnings Call – Final," (Speech), October 19, 2015, http://files.shareholder.com.

50. Christina Drill, "2012: The End of the American (Girl Doll) History," *verbicide*, January 24, 2012, http://www.verbicidemagazine.com/2012/01/24/end-of-the-american-doll-history/; Abby W Schachter, "Could Today's 'American Girl' Be Any Blander?" *Acculturated*, February 27, 2013, http://acculturated.com/could-todays-american-girls-be-any-blander/; Amy Schiller, "American Girls Aren't Radical Anymore," *The Atlantic*, April 23, 2013, http://www.theatlantic.com/sexes/archive/2013/04/american-girls-arent-radical-anymore/275199.

51. Adrienne Raphel, "Our Dolls, Our Selves," *The New Yorker*, October 9, 2013, http://www.newyorker.com/business/currency/our-dolls-ourselves.

52. Shiller, "American Girls Aren't Radical Anymore."

53. Susan Jevens, e-mail message to author, March 10, 2017.

54. Kara Morrison, "American Girl Dolls Are No Fad Toy: Popularity Continues to Grow After 30 Years," *The Republic*, August 21, 2015, http://www.azcentral.com/story/entertainment/kids/2015/08/21/american-girl-dolls-popularity-continues-grow-scottsdale-store/32119301/.

55. Molly Neal, "Cataloger Gets Pleasant Results," *Direct Marketing Magazine* 55, no. 1 (May 1992): 33.

56. Annette Arnold, "Samantha's Ice Cream Social," *NWI Times*, September 30, 1998, http://www.nwitimes.com/uncategorized/samantha-s-ice-cream-social/article_87ac3ace-fdf9-5249-9763-2de0a6147a24.html.

57. Experiences at the various stores change periodically.

58. "American Girl," Fast Company, September 1, 2006, https://www.fastcompany.com/57754/american-girl.

59. Morrison, "American Girl Dolls Are No Fad Toy."

60. Diamond et al., "American Girl and the Brand Gestalt."

61. Stefania Borghini et al. "Why Are Themed Brandstores so Powerful? Retail Brand Ideology at American Girl Place," *Journal of Retailing* 85, no. 3, (2009): 375.

62. Anne-Marie Tomchak, "#BBCtrending: The Secret World of Animated Doll Videos," *BBC News*, March 31, 2015, http://www.bbc.com/news/magazine-32042509.

CHAPTER 3

Situating American Girl: Tools of Socialization in a Changing Culture

When American Girl released the 2005 Girl of the Year, Marisol Luna, many residents of Chicago's Latino community were angry and insulted. In her story, written by Gary Soto, Marisol's family of Mexican American descent moves from the Pilsen neighborhood of Chicago to a less "dangerous" one in the suburbs because her parents want their daughter to have a safe place to play. Some members of the real Pilsen community felt that this was a racist story line, suggesting that Marisol needed to move out of a largely Latino community and into a whiter one in order to be protected. In addition, the narrative clashed with their own experiences because, as Latino Studies scholar Jennifer Rudolph points out, the idea that Marisol's family would be leaving Pilsen because they were concerned about crime and safety was factually inaccurate during the early 2000s when the Pilsen neighborhood was being gentrified and Latino families were being driven out because of skyrocketing housing costs. If the story was more reflective of the experiences of real Latino girls living in Pilsen, writes Rudolph, Marisol would have been moving either because her family could no longer afford to pay their soaring rent, because of the failing neighborhood schools, or because of the neighborhood's high levels of pollution. Three hundred community residents met at the local library to discuss their outrage, and some called on American Girl to re-write the story and/or to set up internships for Pilsen youth as reparation for the offense.[1] Close to seventy high school students protested outside of the American Girl Place asking the company to apologize, cease publication of Marisol's books, provide college scholarships and

© The Author(s) 2017
E. Zaslow, *Playing with America's Doll*,
DOI 10.1057/978-1-137-56649-2_3

jobs for young adults from the Pilsen neighborhood, and donate a percentage of the doll's sales to Pilsen youth programs.[2]

While American Girl articulated their regrets "that the comments of one of the fictional characters in the story have caused any community members to feel misrepresented," it also suggested that protesters read the books so that they can "see a community that is vibrant, charming, warm, caring and immersed in Latin culture and tradition," as Soto intended. This soft apology was not enough for activist and cultural critic Anne Elizabeth Moore who saw the Marisol issue as emblematic of bigger concerns about the brand. She planned and executed her own act of civil disobedience against the company. In what she labeled "Operation Pocket Full of Wishes," Moore developed a series of cards that mimicked the store's own "pocket full of wishes cards," and planted them in the store. Unlike the store's real wish cards, Moore's were filled not with images of desired dolls and accessories but with what she wrote were "the wishes of real girls that I had actually spoken to: equal pay for equal work, domestic partnership benefits; self-confidence; healthy body images; safe and effective birth control; ample career opportunities; safe, legal abortion access; and free tampons."[3]

Eight years later, recalling the aftermath of Marisol's publication, Soto defended his narrative choices; he argued that the book was fiction and therefore entitled him to take liberties, but that Chicago, and the area surrounding Pilsen, was at the time of his writing "statistically dangerous."[4] He felt that protesters overlooked the fact that Marisol moved from Pilsen to Des Plaines, a suburb heavily populated by Latino families.[5] Soto ended his reflection emphatically claiming that he would no longer write children's literature because "the genre is too dangerous."[6] Soto might have been playing with words here, but he was also noting the power society ascribes to children's culture.

Children's literature is rarely as innocuous as the children's librarians' adage, "The right book for the right child at the right time." The rise of children's consumer culture, including multicultural fiction and branded fiction, has also given rise to a scholarship that explores issues of ideology and authenticity in children's literature and toy culture.[7] The questions surrounding whose stories are being told, by whom, and with what underlying message are paramount in this research.

In the 1970s, researchers began to argue that girls were underrepresented in children's literature and that this had the potential to shape children's social values and perceptions of self.[8] Studies of women's and girls' cultures gained traction a decade later when feminist scholars, particularly those influenced by Cultural Studies, began to insist that women's texts be considered worthy of analysis. Soap operas, romance novels, teen magazines, and other forms of media that gave women and girls pleasure were now accorded the respect required to move them from being considered trivial objects to being taken seriously as cultural forms.

In the 1990s, both Miriam Forman-Brunell and Ann duCille helped to spotlight dolls as cultural texts that not only served as loving playthings but as tools of gender socialization that embody and shape meaning about what it means to be a girl and a woman.[9] Today, dolls are understood as complex texts that "represent layered versions of realities, mediated by the often-contradictory ideologies, values, or worldviews of doll creators, producers, consumers, and players."[10] More recently, Robin Bernstein has suggested that dolls be studied as scripts that encourage certain kinds of play behaviors and invite children to participate in particular ideological performances.[11] Although it is still underdeveloped, the study of dolls has begun to explore the playthings' cultural transmission of discourses around sex, race, ethnicity, class, sexuality, history, and memory.[12]

It is instructive, then, to analyze one of our most popular contemporary doll collections, their stories, and the social climate in which they were imagined and ask what they communicate to their owners about femininity, racial identity, social class, and what it means to be an American. This chapter explores the research on children's literature and play culture in shaping children's values. I also explore the changing social environment in which American Girl was conceived, and the impact this environment had on the collections' stories, dolls, and marketing strategies. Finally, this chapter explores the ways in which mothers discuss American Girl as a product that can be trusted in this changing environment.

Children's Literature as a Tool of Socialization

R. Gordon Kelly argues that children's literature "constitutes one important way in which the adult community deliberately and self-consciously seeks to explain, interpret, and justify the body of beliefs, values, and practices, which taken together, define, in large measure a culture."[13] Until the middle of the sixteenth century parents primarily gave only religious books to their children but, by the nineteenth century, as Puritanism waned, the didactic and religious tone of books intended for children softened and included a variety of themes.[14] Still, children were seen as incomplete projects who had to be trained in social etiquette and morality, so that the books produced and marketed to them continued to be understood as teaching tools rather than forms of entertainment. For girls, in particular, children's literature of the nineteenth century reified traditional gender roles supported by the ideology that heterosexual marriage was the key to identity completion. Girls were expected to tame their wildness as well as suppress their passions, educational achievements, and professional skills in order to "find their place in life by making others happy."[15] Through these books, girls were taught the lesson that domestic servitude was their destiny and that it would be fulfilling.

John Newbery turned books for children into a commodity in the eighteenth century, advertising children's literature in catalogs and in the backs of children's magazines. In 1774, Newbery was at the forefront of marketing, pairing *A Pretty Little Pocket-Book* with small toys and encouraging children not only to identify as readers but also as consumers. Not surprisingly, Rowland, who was once called Newbery's "true spiritual heir," paid homage to Newbery by including a copy of *A Pretty Little Pocket-Book* in Felicity's Nighttime Necessities accessories.[16]

The mass marketing of children's books expanded when series books, dominated by the Stratemeyer Syndicate, took the market by storm. The Stratemeyer Syndicate produced eighty-one distinct series between 1894 and 1930 including *The Hardy Boys, Nancy Drew,* and the *Bobbsey Twins.* Many who worked with children and policed their development feared the explosion of the series book market. Campaigns against series books were mounted by the American Library Association, the American Bookseller's Association, the Boy Scouts of America, and the era's most well-known child psychologist, G. Stanley Hall. They feared the loss of art and the principles of literature in the age of commodification. They also worried about possible injury to children's moral development that they believed would result from the adventuresome and unrealistic tales, and an onset of discontent in girls who now had greater access to boys' series. This cultural anxiety may also have been attributable to the era's shift in children's literature featuring girl characters that reflected the changing roles of women in society. Gertrude Lehnert finds that "even in the early 1900s ideals of feminine autonomy and individuality had begun to infiltrate girls' literature" even though it was often blended into a tale of female conformity to mask its ideological resistance.[17] Despite the multifaceted attacks on series books, their popularity did not wane.[18]

Prompted by the Great Depression, the Second World War and the introductions of film, radio, and television, there was a hiatus in public discussion regarding the ideology of children's literature. By the 1960s, however, two significant discussions about the role of children's literature resurfaced. After a mid-sixties memo produced by the American Library Association suggested that small libraries eliminate outmoded and poorly written series books, some educators, librarians, and parents pushed back insisting that the quality of literature should be based upon children's enjoyment rather than adults' desires and that focus on classics was anathema to the love of reading.[19] The debate inspired by these two opposing arguments was timely in an era that challenged the supremacy of high culture over people's culture but also in an era that saw rates of illiteracy rising in sync with the amount of time children spent in front of the television.[20] Worry about children's illiteracy surged again in the 1980s following the Department of Education's release of *A Nation at Risk* that suggested that American students were falling behind and that one remedy was for parents to instill the habit of reading in their children. There was certainly a case to be made in the 1960s, and again in the 1980s when Rowland launched American Girl, that series books which developed storylines over the course of many books and many years could be seen as habit-forming and therefore positively impact literacy rates.[21]

The second discussion that emerged in the late 1960s focused on whose stories were being told, in what way, and by whom, in children's literature. The era's social movements for equality saw the political education of children as an ideological investment in a more equitable future.[22] The Council for Interracial Children's Books (CIBC), founded in 1965 by writers, editors, illustrators, teachers, and parents, was determined to establish children's literature as a "tool for the conscious promotion of human values that will lead to greater human liberation" because, they argued, current children's books, "reflect the needs of those who dominate society... to maintain and fortify the structure of relations between dominators and dominated"[23] Nancy Larrick, a member of the CIBC, documented the symbolic annihilation of black identity in children's picture books in a *Saturday Review* article demonstrating that of the thousands of children's books published between 1962 and 1964 less than seven percent included any image of an African American. This figure included those that had just one black face in a crowd as well as those that depicted black characters as slaves, servants, and sharecroppers. Only one percent of the books published in this two-year period actually told the story of contemporary black life, leading her to maintain that there is "an all-white world of children's books."[24] The CIBC worked with writers, publishers, librarians, and parents to write, publish, catalog, and seek out books with diverse, positive representations that promoted social justice and gender equality. The council published bulletins highlighting diverse children's literature and organized writing contests for new writers of color.[25] In 1975 the CIBC published *Guidelines for the Future: Human and Anti-Human Values in Children's Books* which included a rating instrument that appraised books' racist, sexist, elitist, materialist, ageist, individualist, and conformist plots or images.

As cultural critics, feminists, and civil rights activists found voices within universities, academic examinations of ideology in children's literature proliferated.[26] It may have "seemed obvious that repeated exposure to [gender stereotypes in children's books] was likely to have detrimental effects on the development of children's self-esteem, particularly on that of girls, and on the perception children have of their own, and others' abilities and possibilities," but scholars began to conduct social scientific studies of children's literature to provide evidence.[27] Lenore Weitzman working with three colleagues produced a groundbreaking study in 1972 that found that women were underrepresented and poorly represented in children's picture books. Depicted as passive, as followers, and as in the service of others, women were routinely sex-role stereotyped in books for young children.[28] Research in this area continued in the academy and had an impact on the publishing industry. Studies suggested that children who read books with non-traditional, non-stereotyped images of women and books about those who successfully fought gender discrimination were less likely to have gender bias.[29] These studies influenced the children's publishing industry to create "guidelines for eliminating sexist bias" and to understand its role in shaping perceptions of gender in young minds.[30] Despite this awareness, recent studies demonstrate that women and girls are still underrepresented in children's literature, particularly women and girls of color and women and girls in non-traditional roles.[31] Likewise, although the later part of the twentieth century saw an increase in children's books written by and about people of color, these books represent only a very small percentage of those published.[32]

American Girl sought, in part, to fill this void in an increasingly consumer-oriented book market. If those who studied and catalogued books that promoted social justice and gender equality feared that such books might be too alternative, published in such small runs, and too poorly distributed for children to find,[33] American Girl's wide distribution and adroit marketing guaranteed that most girls would find these girl-centered series that highlighted the experiences of spunky girls whose voices were demanding to be heard. American Girl books can now be found in bookstores, public and school libraries, American Girl retail stores, and even airports where they may be sold with miniature dolls.[34]

The particular genre of historical fiction also requires some attention because of the centrality of the BeForever collection to the brand's identity. Focused on the social histories of common peoples, historical fiction in general, and American Girl in particular, has been shown to aid children in the development of intellectual curiosity about historical eras, understanding how people lived in history, and discussions of controversial events.[35] At the same time, historical fiction can often raise red flags as it comes under scrutiny for its use as an ideological tool.[36] American Girl historical fiction might better be understood as neo-historical, blending the old and new, and creatively and critically engaging "with cultural mores of the period it revisits."[37] In neo-historical fiction, by nature a contradiction within itself, there is an entanglement with the past but also the addition of a revisionary flavoring so that "it strives for accuracy while conscious of the limitations of that project."[38] And, for American Girl, there is also the awareness of the limited marketability of a purely historical project; neo-historicism allows the brand to be "characterized as old-fashioned without being old."[39] As Joel Taxel has argued, the consolidation of the publishing and bookselling industries has led to an increased focus on profit margins and risk management rather than interest in publishing books that may be experimental or target an underrepresented audience.[40] Neo-historical fiction is well suited to respond to this market because the genre is as much about highlighting the stories of bygone eras as it is about "answering the needs and preoccupations of the present."[41] From its inception, American Girl has sought to encourage girls to understand both that things were different in the past *and* that there are common experiences of girlhood. In her earliest catalogues, Rowland wrote,

> Read on and meet Kirsten, Samantha, and Molly. You'll learn what growing up was like for them….You'll see that some things in their lives were very different from yours but others—like families, friendships, and feelings—haven't changed at all. These are the important things that American girls will always share.[42]

Over twenty-five years later, in 2016, the language has been updated to reflect the incorporation of a popular feminism, but the message stays the same:

Through the BeForever characters, girls today can find out what it would have been like to grow up during key moments in America's past. Each character's timeless story encourages modern girls to follow their hopes and dreams, and to draw inspiration from the past to build a better tomorrow.[43]

For some critics, this suggestion of universality means that a kind of sameness supersedes historical accuracy, creating a history defined less by its social and cultural norms and conventions and more by its style and aesthetic.[44] Similarly, others argue that the universality of girlhood leads to the suggestion of a multiculturalism that feigns to value difference and disregards the cultural specificities and historical realities that shape identity.[45] In the next three chapters I engage with these critiques, exploring the complexity of this neo-historical collection that exists within the contradictory and complementary nexus of a social change project that relies on the capitalist imperative of market success.

DOLLS AS TOOLS OF SOCIALIZATION

In her ground-breaking book, *Made to Play Dolls and the Commercialization of American Girlhood,* Miriam Forman-Brunell demonstrated that the inscription of social values on the bodies of dolls has a history as long as the doll industry itself. From the start, dolls have often been created with the intention of serving a purpose deeper than play and entertainment. According to most American and European doll histories, girls began playing with dolls in fourteenth-century France. Designed as miniature mannequins, these dolls were first manufactured for adult women to admire couture, not for child's play. Life-sized fashion dolls pre-dated fashion plates as the most common mode through which to display Parisian fashions to those in high society, such as the Queens of England and Spain, who could not see the new styles first hand.[46] Once the adult women were finished examining the mannequins they gifted them to their daughters or younger sisters who used them as playthings.[47] The handing down of these mannequin dolls, intentional or not, positioned girls as consumers; further, they were learning about beauty, fashion, and the body as they played with dolls whose ideal bodies were constructed to display high-end fashions.

While we do not know if mothers were aware of this cultural transmission in the fourteenth century, by the late nineteenth century when dolls were increasingly purchased as playthings for middle-class girls who were taught to mimic adult social norms, a *Harper's Bazaar* article recognized that dolls held a utility for mothers who chose them "with a view to giving their girls correct ideas of symmetry and beauty."[48] In addition to teaching girls about the aesthetics of normative femininity, dolls have long been understood as tools to prepare girls for their roles within the domestic sphere. Forman-Brunell's analysis of doll culture in nineteenth-century America found that as post-Civil War consumer culture emerged, doll play increasingly focused on simulating "the new rituals of high society" including dressing dolls in fancy garb to attend tea parties or go visiting with miniature calling cards.[49]

The role of the doll in training a girl was taken as common sense but the specifics of what she would learn was contested. Social critics worried that the European fashion dolls' expensive wardrobes, focus on appearance, and sexualized adult bodies would corrupt young girls and, worse, promote their active participation in a consumption-oriented society. As recognized "technologies of gender," dolls embodied the cultural anxieties of changing definitions of modern womanhood.[50] Writing in the late 1860s, one English journalist, as quoted in Juliette Peers' study of nineteenth century French fashion dolls, quipped,

> If you buy a doll in Paris now-a-days you must...furnish for her a luxurious boudoir in the Pompadour or Empire style. She must have a carriage. She must have a saddle-horse....She must have a grand piano...She must have 72 petticoats...She must bathe in milk of almonds...[She] would eat you out of house and home, mortgage your lands, beggar your children, and then present you with a toy revolver to blow your brains out withal.[51]

Female doll makers also began to question the role of the doll in girls' lives and how the body of the doll would influence their social learning.[52] Like the journalist cited above, New England doll manufacturer Martha Chase and her fellow "maternal feminists" believed that "overdressed French and German bisque dolls represented a culture of luxury, fashion, and other *bêtes noires* of the bourgeoisie at odds with domestic values."[53] These maternal feminists saw their role as cultural guardians protecting girls from the messages of consumption and greed embodied by fragile European dolls dressed in high fashions. Rather than have their daughters play with those dolls and learn upper class social conventions, they sought out or made dolls that would teach girls how to nurture and take on the domestic operations that would be expected of them as middle-class women.[54] By the late nineteenth century, it was commonly believed that doll play could "cultivate taste in dress," but equally importantly train girls to be moral, to sew, to be tidy, and to model good behavior.[55] Dolls embodied the timely questions about the role of women in society; Should girls learn to be consumers, domestic agents, beauties, and/or mothers? What would femininity become and how should it be taught?

Only recently have scholars begun to examine the intersectional cultural learning of doll play in the nineteenth century. Bernstein's pivotal book, *Racial Innocence*, explores the ways that dolls "provide especially effective safe houses for racial ideology because [they] are emblems of childhood that attach, through play, to the bodies of living children."[56] As the use of dolls in the moral training of white girls was underway in the late nineteenth century, it included racist scripts of violence against black dolls. Supported by fiction, nonfiction, theater, and the dolls themselves, white children were encouraged to play with black dolls by positioning them in acts of servitude as well as beating, throwing, and hanging them. These scripted doll bodies, on which pretend pain was inflicted, served as cultural texts on which girls and their adults sustained racist logics. In response, African American leaders of the late nineteenth and early twentieth centuries suggested that African American girls be given black dolls to cultivate self-love and racial pride. This movement increased after the doll tests conducted by the Clarks in the 1930s became widely publicized in the 1954 *Brown v. Board of Education* Supreme Court case, which successfully challenged segregated schools. These studies demonstrated that African American children had a preference for white dolls and identified white dolls as being "nicer" and less "bad" than black dolls.[57]

Dolls continued to be understood as educational throughout the twentieth century and taught many of the same lessons about domesticity and beauty as they had in the previous century. In the 1920s and 1930s, advertisers and magazine editorials developed the concept of "Toys that Teach" as one of their broad strategies to motivate parents to purchase.[58] Advertisements, and the parental magazines that supported them, attempted to sell parents—primarily mothers—on the idea that toys, books, dolls, and other consumer goods could pinch hit where parents failed. Magazines such as *Parents* instructed their readers to buy ever more in order to stimulate children's minds. For girls, doll and toy ads throughout the decade, and well into the 1960s, emphasized domestic and appearance work and the joy that those labors could bring them.

When women began to enter the workforce in greater numbers after World War II, market persuaders responded and adjusted their strategies to this new reality. Between 1950 and 1986, the percentage of American women who worked outside of the home rose to fifty-five percent and of those who were married, more than half had children under the age of six.[59] Advertisers capitalized on the change in women's roles, targeting the population of white middle class women who were entering the formal economy for the first time. Knowing that these women had begun to leave their children in the care of others for greater periods of time, and were spending less time directly interacting with their children, advertisers renewed their emphasis on the importance of giving children toys that prepared them for their future roles. Advertisements depicted girls alone or with their mothers in domestic spaces or in front of the dressing table gazing at their own image in the mirror. For girls, this still meant that toys were largely limited to caring for children, the home, or their appearance.[60]

Despite the second wave feminist movement of the 1970s, television commercials for dolls in the 1980s and 1990s still took place "well inside the domestic space" with depictions of play that invited "girl's participation in homemaking and childcare as unchallenged spheres of feminine power."[61] Even if these girls followed in their mothers' footsteps and joined the paid workforce, they would be well-prepared to take on the responsibilities of child care and housework that still fell unevenly on mothers' shoulders.[62] Further, throughout the century, doll advertisements continued to showcase a Western European blond-haired, blue-eyed whiteness with visual emphasis on white girls playing with white dolls. Girls of color featured in ads were either relegated to background shots or depicted as marveling over blond hair.[63]

Unlike baby dolls, Barbie, who hit the toy shelves in 1959, allowed girls to deviate from household responsibilities, despite the lure of the doll's dreamhouse. As a teenage fashion model, Barbie was not responsible for childcare, cooking, or cleaning. She represented a departure from domestic duties and a movement toward a more public womanhood. When she took on the roles of fashion designer, nurse, college graduate, astronaut, and surgeon throughout the sixties and seventies and ultimately President of the United States in 1991, Barbie presented a challenge to the toy industry which had continuously placed dolls in the realm of the home.

Still, Barbie with her endless wardrobe, normatively feminine appearance, oversized breasts, and mandate of slimness was the object of ideological analysis by scholars and parents alike. If she could be celebrated for leaving the familial home, she could be feared for her possible entrance into the world of adult sexuality, the shopping mall, the eating disorder clinic, or the cosmetic surgeon's office. In an anthropometric study that scaled Barbie's body to that of an average American woman who measures five foot four, researchers found that beneath the many professional costumes in which Barbie can be dressed, a real life Barbie would be clinically anorexic and have a body that is nearly unattainable.[64] Psychologist Barbara Mackoff warned parents that Barbie is "passive, an invitation to anorexia, a clotheshorse—a symbol of perfection no girl can match."[65] Barbie reflected the changing definition of feminine that was no longer located in the domestic sphere; the feminine ideal was shifting from home-maker to beauty queen. This critique was materially addressed by Mattel in 2016 when it introduced "curvy," "petite," and "tall" Barbies to join the original, thereby acknowledging the social learning that emerges not just from doll stories, or uplifting slogans such as "I Can Be," but also from the logic produced in the doll's plastic body.

Furthermore, studies of Barbie's artifice have explored its relationship with diverse racial representations and its construction of an unproblematized whiteness. Most notably, Ann duCille's work explores the history of African American Barbies starting with the 1967 "Colored Francie" who had the same mold as a white Barbie but was dipped in brown dye. In the 1990s Mattel released Shani and her friends, Asha and Nichele, each of whom had a "realistically sculpted body," and facial features meant to reflect African American identity. While each had her own unique tone of brown skin and hair, Shani and friends' racial identity was largely reduced to their "fuller lips, wider noses, wider hips, and higher derriere," which harkened back to the eugenics movement that used measurements and body typing to support the notion of white supremacy.[66] Analyzing the promotions and construction of the 1990s dolls, duCille argues that despite the fact that the marketing rhetoric surrounding the doll communicates a message of black pride, the dolls do nothing to disrupt the ideological position of Barbie's value as tied to her appearance nor that of an essential black female identity. The dolls, though varying in tone, share the same body mold because of Mattel's and girls' practical need for all Barbies to share clothing, and all have long hair because of the company's finding that girl-consumers desire to comb and style hair. This raises the question of how a company can ever fabricate racial or ethnic authenticity on the body of a doll, especially if these identities are aesthetically driven by market imperatives.

White privilege is also scripted on doll bodies through their manufacturing processes, which remain largely invisible. Approximately 20,000 people in China, Thailand, Indonesia, Malaysia, and Mexico are working on Mattel's Barbie and American Girl products for low wages and in poor working conditions. Sally Edward's analysis of the literature surrounding Mattel and its Chinese factories finds that, according to activists, Mattel is one of the toy companies that takes corporate responsibility and workers' health and safety most seriously, but there are still major concerns about the living and working conditions of its factory employees.[67] It is very difficult to document the environments of these factories, but *China Watch*, a non-profit organization that advocates for the rights of Chinese workers, launched an undercover investigation of Mattel toy factories and found that workers were often forced to stand for over ten hours, were housed in dirty congested dormitories, and worked in factories where emergency egresses and fire escapes were blocked or locked.[68] The whiteness of the dolls and the consumers, the normative femininity that their privilege allows, and in the case of American Girl, the middle- to upper-class status of doll owners, contrasts starkly with the identities of the low-wage, poorly treated Mattel workers of color. This inequity, although often unacknowledged, is also a racial logic encoded on the body of the doll.

THE MARKETING OF AMERICAN GIRL IN A CHANGING CULTURE

From the start, Pleasant Rowland was aware that dolls functioned as ideological tools. The creation of the doll as a nine-year-old girl with round full cheeks implied a pre-sexual status that Rowland saw as the antithesis of Barbie and of the youthful sexuality that was becoming typical of the era. This was the 1980s. Cyndi Lauper was singing about female sexual pleasure in "Girls Just Want to Have Fun," and Madonna was "burning up for love." Female sexual agency was being discussed at universities, where academics were debating the role of sexual objectification, prostitution, pornography, and female sexual desire in women's lives. For Rowland, it seems, it was a defining moment, and the dolls she produced responded to it directly; reflecting on the collection, she said, "Our whole essence is holding off that onslaught of mass culture trying to sexualize little girls too early."[69] Rowland believed that her dolls, with their anatomical incorrectness, their young age, and their historical clothing, served to protect girls in their tween years.

A spring 1991 catalog insert, serving as an advertisement, shared letters that were supposedly written to the company. Their veracity is irrelevant, but their message is significant. Part of Rowland's sales technique was to convince parents and grandparents that the doll was not just a beautiful treasure but also an ideological tool. A parent from Providence, RI, is quoted as being "very pleased to see a toy which helps [her] girls enjoy their childhood rather than pushing them too fast into adolescence and adulthood." To sell to girls as well as their parents, it was important that this holding off of adolescence was not just a parental desire but something sought by children as well. This is why D.K. from Takoma, Maryland, is quoted in the same catalog as writing, "I'm thirteen and the other kids at school think I'm pretty immature because I like Molly and not make-up or boys. I don't care and the main reason I wrote this letter was to thank you for giving me a new best friend."[70] A central element in the American Girl marketing plan was the positioning of the company as protectionist; American Girl, associated with innocence and history, could counter the modern sexual messages that were increasingly pervasive in American culture.[71]

By the mid-1990s, thanks to developmental and educational psychologists, the conversation about girls began to expand and focus not only on protecting girls against early sexuality but also protecting them from the larger impacts of growing up in a patriarchal society. Rhetoric surrounding the ideological purpose of toys and dolls, including that of American Girl, evolved with this shifting discourse. Inspired by Carol Gilligan's *In a Different Voice,* which documented the uniqueness of women's identity formation and moral development, considerable scholarship on girls' psychological and social development started being produced in the early 1990s. These studies uncovered evidence of girls' lack of self-esteem and gender inequity in schools, that resulted from growing up in a patriarchal culture.[72] They told the story of pre-adolescent girls who had "clear-eyed views of the world and their own right to be heard," spoke with direct voices, challenged authority, and formed genuine relationships but became adolescents who shut themselves down and swallowed their emotions because they strove to be perfect girls. The need to appear nice and good took precedence over the quest for authentic communication.[73]

Carol Gilligan and Lyn Mikel Brown at the Harvard Project on Women's Psychology and Girls' Development found that as girls near adolescence they develop a gradually growing recognition that their experiences and feelings are not valued and that the social requirement to be 'nice' outweighs their emotional need for genuine relationships. These researchers found that, at ages seven and eight, the girls they studied were open to speaking honestly about friendship, emotional love, and pain and to challenging each other and authority figures when they felt issues of fairness were at stake. These girls had authentic conversations, strong relationships, and strong voices. Yet as they grew older these same girls came to realize that "it is better not to speak, to pretend things are fine when they are not, to act as if nothing happened" in order to maintain the image of the perfect girl.[74] The researchers found that the pressure girls feel to achieve perfection and niceness leads them to lose confidence in themselves, feel a growing confusion about their own emotions and desires, find their voices constricting, and lose the ability to articulate their experiences and thoughts.

As the members of the Harvard Project on Women's Psychology and Girls' Development shifted their focus to girls, other organizations and independent researchers were doing the same. In 1991 the American Association of University Women (AAUW) released *Shortchanging Girls, Shortchanging America* which demonstrated that girls in elementary school reported that they were happy with who they were at rates equal to boys but by the time they reached high school half of all boys surveyed reported "I am happy the way I am," while only thirty-three percent of girls could agree with this statement. The results of this study demonstrated that younger girls had confidence and self-esteem but were losing these qualities as they got older.

Based on her interest in the AAUW study, author Peggy Orenstein spent one year as an observer of girls in two California middle schools; one school was a mostly white suburban school and the other an urban school populated by working class and poor students of color. Her ethnographic research supported the findings that schools and families praise boys for their assertiveness yet recognize girls for their amenability. Further, she reported on the overwhelming number of girls she met who had eating disorders and/or negative body image. Well-received and widely reviewed, Orenstein's *School Girls: Young Women, Self-Esteem, and the Confidence Gap,* which received praise from the *New York Times,* the *Washington Post,* and the *Los Angeles Times,* was excerpted in the *New York Times* and in *Glamour* magazines.[75] This national attention in popular media created buzz around girls and the psychosocial corseting they experienced as they "begin to restrict their interests, confine their talents, [and] pull back on their dreams" for the sake of being the perfect girl.[76]

But if Orenstein raised a red flag, clinical psychologist Mary Pipher, sounded the alarm in her *Reviving Ophelia: Saving the Selves of Adolescent Girls,* which remained on the *New York Times* bestseller list for three years. Drawing on interviews and case studies from her clinical practice, Pipher argued that because they are growing up in "girl poisoning culture," girls learn to silence themselves, deny their feelings, and understand themselves as devalued. They learn that in order to be acceptable they must look, smell, dress, speak, and think in culturally approved ways; they learn that they are in need of repair by way of consumer products that will improve their looks, feelings, and selves. In addition, Pipher expressed concern over the rampant images of sexuality to which teen girls were exposed and the pressure to be sexual at a young age. Writing about the experiences of girls in the "halls of junior high," Pipher warned that contemporary girls were becoming sexually active at a younger age and with more partners than girls in earlier eras.[77] Ultimately, Pipher argued, American girls will become "causalities of our cultural chaos" due to the mixed messages and pressures they experience in the family, in schools and through their engagement with mass media.[78]

Reviving Ophelia, rightly criticized for its thin evidence and lack of scholarly rigor, was largely responsible for the national spotlight that began to shine on girls' experiences of coming of age in patriarchal society during the 1990s. It paved the way for mainstream conversations about how gender bias impacts girls and spawned a protectionist discourse that played out in parenting, news, and entertainment journalism; a twenty-five page "Special Report: For Our Daughters" ran in *Parenting* magazine, "Surviving Your Teens: For Troubled Adolescent Girls and the People Who Love Them" graced the pages of *Time,* and "Teen Tumult: Why It's Harder on Girls" was published in *People.* These reports created a market for girl power, a cultural discourse that shrink-wraps feminist messaging with feminine styling.[79] No fewer than twenty advice books that focused on how to raise daughters without their falling into the pitfalls of a gender biased culture—from *Growing a Girl: Seven Strategies for Raising a Strong, Spirited Daughter* to *Any Girl Can Rule the World*—were published in the five years after the release of *Reviving Ophelia,* fueling the public obsession with saving girls.

Many of these books helped to promote an industry of girl power media products—from television shows and music to dolls such as American Girl—suggesting that parents could help their daughters by ensuring their interaction with narratives about strong, independent, active girls.

In *Celebrating Girls*, for example, psychotherapist Virginia Beane Rutter, whose work has since been published by American Girl, suggested that parents could reverse the cultural trajectory of female adolescence by ritualizing everyday activities such as bathing, hair combing, and storytelling with the goal of empowerment. In her chapter on the importance of narratives, Rutter recommended that parents share stories that feature active, confident, competent, and brave girl heroines in order to "directly influence a girl's self-esteem."[80] Jeanne and Don Elium wrote in *Raising a Daughter*, that parents should carefully seek out books with positive female role models and provide a broad selection of toys but also "support a girl's femininity" by allowing daughters to engage in traditional "girl stuff [such as] tea parties, knitting, setting a proper table, social etiquette, dancing and all the fine graces we associate with femininity."[81] Following suit, Barbara Mackoff also suggested that parents inventory their children's rooms to make sure that girls are playing with a diverse collection of toys that teaches a range of skills. Still, she insisted that parents not dismiss dolls because they give girls the chance to engage in loving care and to role-play complicated relationships in their lives. Further, like the other authors of books on raising daughters, she suggested that parents provide girls with books that tell the stories of positive female role models who are self-reliant, active, messy, and risk-taking.[82] One could not imagine a better environment for American Girl to thrive.

Rowland capitalized on this messaging. She saw a symbiosis between her own desire to protect her young nieces from Barbie's sexuality and the national discourse on the dangers of raising a girl in a sexist culture. In 1997, one American Girl public relations officer told me that she believed the company to be successful in part because baby boomer moms who "want their daughters to have positive role models and playthings that encourage a healthy self-esteem" are drawn to the doll that is "unlike some of their dangerously lean and physically 'mature' counterparts [which]…often encourage girls to aspire to be older, more beautiful, more mature."[83] The American Girl pre-sexual dolls, with healthy bodies and backstories that celebrate their failures, their curious and spunky attitudes, and their places in history, fit the bill for parents who sought out a toy or story that could help their girls from falling down the frightening rabbit hole of contemporary adolescence. One mother of four girls captures this sentiment, telling a newspaper reporter, "There are so many things telling them that they're not pretty enough or smart enough or skinny enough, and the whole American Girl brand is (about) empowering girls … showing girls their importance and showing girls they can do anything."[84]

The innocence Rowland claimed to protect in the eighties seemed even more in jeopardy a decade later when girls' vulnerabilities were front-page news. If teen girls were growing up too fast and were victims of a world in which their sexuality was being exploited and used as a sign of empowerment, one thing parents could do to fight a powerful consumer market was to keep their children as young as possible for as long as possible. In 2002 Abercrombie and Fitch was marketing its smallest thong to the very same demographic as American Girl was selling its dolls and parents were faced with making consumer decisions about what to teach their daughters. At this critical time in their daughters' lives many parents embraced American Girls' embodiment of innocence and play.

VALUES INSCRIBED ON THE BODY OF THE DOLL

Each of the BeForever and Girl of The Year dolls in the American Girl collection has her own social location yet their bodies are all the same, with slight differences between their face molds. The doll bodies, accompanied by their accessories and their stories, embody the discursive frames in which the brand was produced and evolved as well as script the play that is intended with them. That is, the dolls overtly or by implication prompt certain behaviors, imaginative acts, and child-doll interactions.[85]

Embodied in the American Girl doll's prepubescent body is Pleasant Company's original mission "to prolong and protect childhood for an audience of young girls who are constantly being pressured by mass media and pop culture to grow up too quickly."[86] Not only does the doll's story tell us that she is nine years old, but her physical form reveals her young age and her lack of physical and sexual maturity. The American Girl doll body is soft, squeezable, and chubby. Although some fans have noticed that "the bodies were slimmed down overall in the Mattel era," the doll has no visible eating disorder.[87] Additionally, despite the fact that a girl of this age may be at the very early stages of puberty, the doll's eighteen-inch soft torso does not have breast buds, her hips are straight with no clear waist, and she has no defined nipples or genitalia. Recent doll accessories have included glasses, hearing aids, insulin testing kits for diabetic dolls, and a wheelchair, yet there have been no bras, menstrual pads, or tampons, despite the fact that the company's best-selling book, *The Care and Keeping of You: The Body Book for Girls*, states that girls can get their periods as early as nine.

American Girl dolls have little make-up; the Pleasant Company dolls were paler than those produced under the Mattel umbrella, sporting only a hint of blush and lip color, but currently produced American Girl dolls, with a pop of color on their lips and eyes, still do not represent a girl in make-up as do Barbie or Bratz. One American Girl public relations manager told me that the dolls were explicitly intended to "reflect the nine year-old girls playing with them."[88] The dolls' soft, rounder bodies and lack of sexuality are intended to ease the minds of parents and professionals like Virginia Beane Rutter who worries that Barbie's impossible thinness will inspire her daughter to acquire an eating disorder or Mary Pipher who documents the early sexual behaviors of adolescent girls.[89] Indeed, as one journalist observed, "Unlike Barbie, who is busty and glamorous, the American Girls ooze innocence."[90] Rowland's dolls with huggable bodies may give girls a sense of confidence in themselves, in some ways, but their lack of anatomical correctness may also stifle girls' natural curiosity about sexuality and the changes that will take place in their bodies as they reach adolescence.

Many young women remember acting out romantic and sexual fantasies with their Barbies, but American Girl dolls' bodies and collections do not typically inspire such play.[91] To start, for heterosexual fantasy, where Barbie had Ken, American Girl has been, until the 2017 release of its first boy doll, missing a male counterpart doll. While American Girl stories often include boys and young men, these male characters are never considered to be the romantic interests of the protagonists, although as I discuss in the next chapter, older secondary characters in these series books often have romantic interests. Lesbian sexual play is also made less likely because of the dolls' childlike, undeveloped bodies. American Girl does not have the adult body that girls may be more likely to sexualize at a very young age and through which girls can explore the anxieties and curiosities they have about adult sexuality.[92]

Furthermore, in spite of some parents' worry that sexual dolls can lead to the early sexualization of their daughters, psychologist Sharon Lamb argues that giving a girl "the permission to explore, to educate herself, or even to lose control for a bit in a safe place" is important for a girl to "grow into an adult who has and gives pleasure without shame or fear" and to have a healthy sense of herself as erotic and in control of her own body and pleasure.[93] Certainly not every doll must serve the same function, but parents who entirely deny girls this opportunity to explore may find that they are suppressing a necessary part of healthy sexual development.

While possibly shielding girls from an early sexualization, this erasure of the dolls' adolescent development may also signify a passive femininity in which girls—with no doll body parts to name or touch—do not have agency of their bodies or their sexuality.

Selling the American Girl Doll
in a Neoliberal Economy

Contributing to the creation of a climate ripe for a doll that celebrated nostalgic wholesomeness, were the neoliberal ideology and backlash against feminism that emerged during the Reagan–Bush era of the 1980s, and continued throughout the 1990s and into the new millennium. Whereas we often understand the term liberal to be synonymous with left-leaning or aligned with the Democratic party, neoliberalism is a conservative concept based on a right-wing Republican economic theory. Summed up eloquently by David Harvey, neoliberalism is an approach to political economy that

> proposes that human well-being can best be advanced by liberating individual entrepreneurial freedoms and skills within an institutional framework characterized by strong private property rights, free markets, and free trade.[94]

Neoliberalism supports not only an economics that favors an unregulated free market and privatization of social programs, but also an ideology of heroism and personal responsibility in which social problems can be solved by individuals who work hard and pull themselves up by their proverbial bootstraps.[95] This approach to economic and social problems led to a cultural shift in which attention was turned away from the protections and supports a government could provide citizens and on to the self-improvement and personal success a person could achieve on their own. Neoliberalism helped to advance American Girl and make it the perfect brand for the era because of its support of social stratification, the backlash against feminism, and the focus on individual empowerment.

In the 1980s, cuts to social welfare programs and tax codes that favored the wealthy through a model of trickle-down economics led to an increasing social disparity. Over the next two decades, those who benefitted from these economic policies grew wealthier and had an increasing amount of disposable income, which they often used to purchase luxury products that highlighted their status. This accelerated economic divide between the "haves" and "have nots" created a market for a high-end $82 doll who was meant to be loved and played with rather than left gathering dust on a collector's shelf.[96] Because they also wanted to demonstrate a degree of status, the middle class, who did not benefit from the growing economic divide, increasingly drew on consumer credit to participate in this conspicuous consumption.[97] With consumption and credit card debt on the rise, and government supports on the decline, the responsibility to keep the family afloat resided in the ideal-worker, whose commitment was primarily to their work and secondarily to their family. In this economy, women, often more than men, face the conflicting demands of a workforce that expects both a flexible worker who can stay late, travel for work, or relocate for more lucrative employment and simultaneously a culture that expects her to be responsible for the maintenance of family and the domestic flow.[98] In this incongruous ideological environment, women learned that good mothers should be focused on their children's growth, good workers should be focused on their company's growth, and good citizens should be focused on personal gain and individual achievement. The persuasion industry was aware of this challenge and the anxiety women felt about the requirements demanded of them by their multiple roles.[99]

Like other industries, the toy market sought to profit from women's "double bind: a desire [or social pressure] to work hard, achieve and make money and an equally strong desire [or social pressure] to be with their families."[100] One way that the market responded was in the identification of a new type of consumer who sought empowering toys for their daughters. These toys, it proposed, could fill the void in teaching girls about gender equality while their mothers were busy bringing equality to the workforce.[101] American Girl was an early adopter of this approach; the collection, marketed to girls generally considered beyond the years of doll play, offered innocence (in the form of round-faced, round-bellied dolls representing pre-pubescent girls), female empowerment (in the form of narratives of spirited and active girls), nationalism (through tales of American history that sanitized some of the nation's shameful actions) and safety (in the form of nostalgic, asexual fashion). With American Girl, parents could give their daughters something special that promised to protect them against early sexualization, celebrate girlhood, model care, and tell the stories that had always been shared within families (but which parents were now too busy to tell).

BACKLASH AND FAMILY VALUES

Neoliberalism also contributed to a cultural focus on "family values" and a backlash against feminism, blaming multiple social ills on the movement for women's rights. In neoliberalism, families, not social institutions, bear the responsibility for the development, protection, and training of children. The family is reimagined as a "powerful and autonomous yet acculturated entity that serves the nation through its support of the free-market and of 'traditional' American values."[102] At first, it was only conservative evangelicals who spoke of "family values," which was code for maintenance of traditional gender norms, a pro-life agenda, and Christian morality, but this rhetorical coalescence of "personal agency, nationalism, and marketplace" soon became pervasive and impacted popular discourse throughout the 1980s and 1990s.[103] As government withdrew social support for education, the eradication of poverty, and youth development programs, it claimed that rather than government support, human rights or social justice, increasing private wealth and traditional conservative family values would be the salve for disparity and for the social impacts of oppression.

This ideological turn supported the burgeoning of a doll company built on nostalgia, morality, and the stories of families. Just as it had become popular with working mothers, American Girl became popular with politically and socially conservative families. This rhetoric elevated cultural anxieties about the stability of the nuclear family, claiming it was under attack and needed to be restored, and it blamed women for the breakdown. Feminism did make work outside the home a possibility for a greater number of women but the neoliberal economy made it a necessity for middle- and working-class women who were on the losing end of the economic divide. This shift in the economy and in social norms challenged the family structure, taking mothers out of the home and farther away from the domestic sphere for longer periods of time. Politicians and news media linked mothers' absence from the home to reports of increasing juvenile delinquency, declining educational test scores, and the rise in teen sexual activity.[104] In this "undeclared war against women," feminism, rather than neoliberalism, was accused of disrupting social norms.[105] In essence, the backlash against feminism held the social change movement, and all women who benefitted from it, responsible for a supposed national collapse in traditional values.

To support the backlash, the ideology of intensive mothering, or "new momism," emerged. Intensive mothering maintained that the best mothering put a mother's needs and desires behind those of her children. A good mother, women were told, should spend her "time, energy, and income on children's activities, consumer goods, education, and enrichment rather than on those that would contribute to her self-actualization."[106] Douglas and Michaels, powerfully connecting neoliberal ideology, the backlash against feminism, and new momism, argue that:

> The new momism is the result of the combustible intermixing of right-wing attacks on feminism and women, the media's increasingly finely tuned and incessant target marketing of mothers and children, the collapse of governmental institutions...that served families in the past (imperfectly, to be sure), and mothers' own, very real desires to do the best job possible raising their kids in a culture that praises mothers in rhetoric and reviles them in public policy.[107]

The backlash, and its emphasis on martyrdom motherhood, had an emotional impact on women who were accused of wrongdoing and made to feel guilty.

Faced with the cultural contradictions of neoliberalism (which called for the ideal-worker) and intensive new momism (which called for the ideal-mother), women could not succeed. Often narrowly characterized by post-feminism rather than activist feminism, the women of this era increased their workforce participation, exited unhappy marriages in unprecedented numbers, grew their involvement in government, and built awareness campaigns against sexual assault and sexual harassment. These mothers might not have been able to make their daughters' world free of gender oppression, but they could buy a doll that would engage their daughters with an empowerment discourse that they had adopted in their own lives. Better yet, this doll—with her youthful character, nostalgic innocence, and domestically situated narratives—could embody the empowerment discourse but also the wholesome family values they were accused of tarnishing.[108]

A Girl Power Doll

Although many feminists critiqued the Reagan–Bush social programs, neoliberalist ideology also permeated mainstream feminism and the ways in which its messages were reproduced and coopted by popular culture. Media worked, sometimes unconsciously, to reimagine feminism; rather than representing it as a social change movement that required coalition, hard work, and collective struggle, media represented feminism as a trendy individual lifestyle that could be performed at will.[109] Popular culture embraced the neoliberal ideology of choice and attributed lack of success and gender-based oppression only to poor decision-making rather than inequitable social institutions shaped by patriarchy, sexism and inequality.[110] Women were encouraged to believe that their ongoing struggles— inequity in the workplace, rampant sexual violence, the high costs of childcare and healthcare—were the result of individual failures rather than systemic oppression.[111] Obscuring the ways in which power relations limit individual choices, neoliberalism pledged that personal empowerment, and not structural change, would be the key to women's emancipation.

This new empowerment politics was supported and promoted by the 1990s' consumer market. By the late 1990s *Adweek, Brandweek, Fortune,* and *Time* magazines had all declared this the era of girl power. Branding a social movement as a consumer commodity, girl power media culture borrowed convenient elements from feminist discourse, such as sexual empowerment and self-determination, while retaining the core values of normative femininity.[112] The girl of girl power

> believes that she should be treated as an equal to her male peers, that she should be in control of her own body, that she is entitled to play tough and be smart, that she can, and will, support herself financially, and that her future should be self-determined. Furthermore, she believes that she has a core of inner (girl) power on which to draw as she combats oppression and directs her own life. But the girl of girl power culture also feels she has a right to enjoy her sexuality, to revel in the desire she elicits, and to have a future in which the care of a child, and sometimes a husband, is of central importance. The girl of girl power shifts our conceptualization of femininity so that the cultural narrative about what it means to be a girl is upset and re-written.[113]

Girl power emphasized the neoliberal ideology of choice where celebration of an individual's right to choose, rather than a struggle for a collective's social justice, became the sign that feminism had arrived.

American Girl was launched on the precipice of this girl power era and demonstrates a clear example of girl power's mingling of feminist sensibilities with feminine styling. Whereas much of popular culture called upon the trope of sexual empowerment as a tool to promote feminism-lite, American Girl, culling a younger audience, drew heavily upon the language of individual empowerment and choice but avoided rhetorics of sexuality. Their early catalogs used words like "strength," "spirit," "free," "adventure," "independent," "spunky," "lively," and "courageous" to advertise their girls and their worlds. Carefully targeting mothers through messaging that recalled a "lost era" and a simple but beautiful childhood, American Girl played to parents who sought to protect girls from the sexual expressions of girl power in popular media.[114] As one of the first to appeal to this market, Pleasant Company anticipated the cultural anxiety about the over-sexualization of girls' culture. By creating a doll that was designed to "show girls that it's important to appreciate who they are right now," rather than who they will become, Pleasant Company intentionally created products that would counteract a culture that equated female power with sexual expression. It was to the mothers who sought to celebrate and protect girlhood that American Girl was marketed.

By the early 2000s, when American Girl had already created eight historical dolls and had twenty combinations of Just Like You dolls in production, fear that popular culture was trying to lure girls into a premature sexuality had spiked again. In 2007, the American Psychological Association released its *Report on the APA Task Force on the Sexualization of Girls*, which declared that the media environment in which girls were growing up put them at risk of body dissatisfaction, eating disorders, depression, diminished cognitive ability, lower educational and occupational achievement, and sexual passivity. Increasingly connected on social media, teen girls were growing up not only in a media culture saturated with sexualized images but also in a world to which their parents had limited access. Sue Jackson and Tiina Vares have demonstrated how books like *So Sexy So Soon*, *Girls Gone Skank*, and *The Lolita Effect* ushered in a new era of alarm about the detrimental effects of a sexually saturated media.[115] The sexualization of dolls, like Bratz and Monster High, had become so worrisome that some parents cited Barbie as the more wholesome of the mass-market dolls.[116] In fashion, too, girls' clothing began to incorporate girl power's sexual empowerment motif. Identifying this as porn-chic, raunch, or evidence of "corporate pedophilia," parents and experts sought to protect girls from a culture that they believed could be detrimental to their physical and mental health as well as their sexuality and their sexual presentation.[117] Although some scholars suggest that we must acknowledge that protectionist discourse limits the voice of the girl in her own agency, they also acknowledge that even when girls think critically about media images of sexuality and recognize the ways in which these images are constructed to elicit certain responses, the images may still produce negative feelings of self-hate, lack of confidence, and shame in young girls.[118]

Indeed, many of the mothers I interviewed expressed their willingness to spend more money than they desired on high-priced American Girl products rather than on products like Barbie or Disney Princess dolls because of what they consider to be the brand's positive messaging. These mothers seek to protect their daughters from a culture that they feel is giving their daughters the option of being a mother or being a sex object. Believing that mass consumerism is "out of their control," they turn to American Girl as a product they can entrust to teach their girls about independence, diversity, and having a range of interests.

Jessica who has two daughters, explained that her nine-year-old daughter, Riley, had not had much interest in dolls until recently. When Jessica saw Riley tucking in her new American Girl doll every night, she was happy to see that her daughter was engaging in imaginative play and caring for a doll. She was equally happy that it was an American Girl and not a baby doll because she says,

> everything in our society tells women that that's what we're born to do. And I want her to know that that isn't a requirement of being a woman. And I don't want her to feel the pressure of that from such a young age that to be a woman is to be a mommy. And if she wants to one day, God bless her. And if she doesn't, more power to her. I will support whatever decision she makes. But I don't want to push that.... Boys aren't pushed to nurture and take care of baby dolls.

Similarly, mothers expressed that the brand—its stories and doll bodies—could be trusted to be "wholesome." Even those who were initially daunted by the price tag and the commercialism, like Karen, Libby, and Suzanna, were eventually willing to "get behind" American Girl. Karen recounts that when her fourteen-year-old daughter, Nora, was young the mom said to herself,

> I don't do Disney. I don't do Barbie, and I don't know what the hell this American Girl doll thing is, but I'm not going to do that either. It's a big business. I believe that it takes advantage of people, and only a certain level of economic status can even afford a doll.

But, she says,

> The minute I saw the books I'm like, "Okay. We're in." I'm like, "We'll do whatever we need to do." I like that they have historical value…. I love that they have an accompanying book. I love that they have strong female characters. I love that they teach her about independence. I love that they help her live out fantasies. I love that they help her process her emotions. I think it's phenomenal.

Suzanna went through a similar process first thinking that "the whole thing was a huge money pit" but then found that "I do like the messages. I guess I would say that they are wholesome. I would much rather buy her that than make-up or all the devices." Libby agreed, "When I first heard about it, I didn't realize the books were attached to it and I was very much anti-purchasing things but then I started learning about what they teach girls about self-esteem and strength." She continued,

> Barbie's so outrageously inappropriately sized, and not really representative at all of a girl. And American Girl dolls, their bodies are a lot more like a girl would be and their experiences are a lot more like a girl would be. Not like stewardess Barbie or something like that. These are little girls who have experiences that little girls have. Adventures that little girls have.

Other mothers agreed, "I mean you know when [your children] are going to watch [an American Girl] movie you don't have to give it a second thought. There is not going to be swear words, it's not oversexed, it's not over gender stereotyped. It's age appropriate."

Jessica concurs and ties this into the lessons her Afro-Latina daughter can learn about gender as well as race through playing with her Cécile doll and the Truly Me doll that has a skin tone similar to hers,

> I feel like [American Girl] is in line with how I feel about kind of being modest and conservative for as long as you can be. I want to put a limit to Barbie because I feel like Barbie's oversexualized so much about the way she looks, and her curves, and her body. And what if you don't have that body, and you don't have that look, then what is that…? My mom thinks I overthink it. She's like, "I didn't have a black doll growing up. I only played with the white Barbie and I'm fine." But I think that it's different now with all of the information that our kids are getting, I think it does send a message. And I just want her to be—life is hard enough to grow up being confident in who she is.

For Jessica, American Girl products can support her value system as she tries to navigate the media messages that threaten her daughter's confidence, self-love, and future aspirations. Marcy also identifies the significance of the empowerment message for her daughter Olive, who is one of two girls who plays football with the boys during recess. She explains,

> I think even though Olive is really like this dance girl and she loves piano and crafting and all that stuff, she's seeing this other side of herself, too. Like [the American Girl doll] Julie, like how she plays on the boys' basketball team. That's part of [why I like American Girl brand]. It's about not being afraid to be who you are and being able to experience different things.

Some parents express desire for a more racially diverse cast of dolls as well as stories that show a wider range of interests, but those I spoke with overlook this because they feel that American Girl offers something that is different from other available toys. Karen who raves about her appreciation for the dolls in the life of her daughter also laments, "I don't believe as a company they embrace the full diversity of what America is and what America is becoming. I think that's where the big business takes over and what will sell. I think the title American Girl is a façade." She adds that "they do not embrace her [ethnicity] by any stretch of the imagination." Discussing her experience trying to find a Truly Me doll that looked like her daughters who are mixed race Kimberly said, "I think they could expand that a little bit. I don't think [my daughters'] hair is unusual or their skin is unusual" but she still bought them American Girl dolls because they elicited a different kind of play than Barbie who she called "trashy." Unlike their Barbie dolls who would go to "cocktail parties" and get married, their American Girl dolls went to school and were each like a "person in their lives."

Heather also expressed a need for diversity in the American Girl stories expressing, "I feel like they get very trapped in the same few things [like dance and art] over and over again" but "they are empowering to my daughters." Similarly, members of an online fan community remarked, "How about something medical (nurse, dr, vet, even a missionary medical worker) or just something completely different. I'm tired of dancers and music" and "Something like a girl wanting to be a scientist or doctor would be awesome. A story about the girl wanting to win the science fair." But Jessica argues, "I mean, they could add more and do other things that are more empowering to girls, like a doll that's in a place of power but I mean it's a complicated thing. I think they embrace a variety of things that a girl can do. Playing basketball and playing tennis or being into horses. And I think these dolls give more choice than other dolls." Similarly, Libby appreciates that the girls in the American Girl stories are "really good with problem-solving without the help of men and boys."

Overall, while some of the mothers in this study are concerned with the consumerism that accompanies the dolls' ever expanding collection and seek more diverse racial and gender representations, they continue to believe that the brand successfully counteracts what they perceive to be a culture that threatens the healthy development of their daughters. Fearing a culture that objectifies their daughter's bodies and may lead to early sexual activity, mothers embrace American Girl's protectionist discourse. Furthermore, these mothers express the significance of the brand's empowerment ideology, especially as it relates to girls taking pride in their racial and gender identities and in embracing their diverse interests.

UNPACKING AMERICAN GIRL NARRATIVES

For decades, both books and dolls were used as tools of socialization to help girls understand their role in the maintenance of the home as caregivers and in domestic servitude. Early dolls also positioned girls as consumers of fashion and located them within a culture of beauty. During and following the social change movements of the 1960s and 1970s activists began to understand the potential of books and toys to counter internalized sexism and racism as well as to socialize children to have more egalitarian world views.

American Girl was created and marketed in the mid-eighties and early nineties as a girl power commodity that served as an antidote to a changing culture. In the political, economic, and cultural environment in which the brand was launched and forming its identity, women's participation in the paid workforce had increased, female sexual display and desire was a common theme in mainstream popular culture, and researchers were claiming that young women were in psychological jeopardy. At the same time, the conservative backlash against feminism and social change was blaming women, rather than the consequences of neoliberalism, for social ills and calling for a return to conventional family values. In addition, the neoliberal economic culture led to a conflicting position for women who were expected to simultaneously fill the role of good mother and good citizen-worker. American Girl was an ideal product for the era; it successfully and comfortably blended messages of empowerment and girl power with innocence and tradition.

NOTES

1. Jennifer Rudolph, "Identity Theft: Gentrification, Latinidad, and American Girl Marisol Luna," *Aztlán: A Journal of Chicano Studies* 34, no. 1 (2009): 65–91.
2. Kevin Pang, "Doll Tale Sets Off Student Protest: American Girl Book Lies, Pilsen Teens Say," *Chicago Tribune*, March 30, 2005, http://articles.chicagotribune.com/2005-03-30/news/0503300334_1_american-girl-place-marisol-luna-student-protest.
3. Anne Elizabeth Moore, "Operation Pocket Full of Wishes: Cultural Intervention at American Girl Place," *In These Times*, March 15, 2005, http://inthesetimes.com/article/2006/operation_pocket_full_of_wishes.
4. Gary Soto, "Why I've Stopped Writing Children's Literature," *Huffington Post*, September 25, 2013, http://www.huffingtonpost.com/gary-soto/childrens-literature-writing_b_3989751.html.
5. Ibid.
6. Ibid.
7. Cross, Gary, *Kids' Stuff: Toys and The Changing World of American Childhood* (Cambridge, MA: Harvard University Press, 2009); Ellen Seiter, *Sold Separately: Children and Parents in Consumer Culture* (New Brunswick, NJ: Rutgers University Press, 1993); Diane Carver Sekeres, "The Market Child and Branded Fiction: A Synergism of Children's Literature, Consumer Culture, And New Literacies," *Reading Research Quarterly* 44, no. 4 (2009): 399–414.
8. Lenore J. Weitzman, et al., "Sex-Role Socialization in Picture Books for Preschool Children," *American Journal of Sociology* 77, no. 6 (1972): 1125–1150.
9. Miriam Formanek-Brunell, *Made to Play House: Dolls and the Commercialization of American Girlhood, 1830–1930* (New Haven, CT: Yale University Press, 1993); Ann duCille, "Dyes and Dolls: Multicultural Barbie and the Merchandising of American Culture," *differences* 6, no. 1 (1994): 48–68.
10. Miriam Forman-Brunell and Jennifer Dawn Whitney, *Dolls Studies: The Many Meanings of Girls' Toys and Play* (New York: Peter Lang, 2015), x.
11. Robin Bernstein, *Racial Innocence: Performing American Childhood from Slavery to Civil Rights* (New York: New York University Press, 2011).
12. Forman-Brunell and Whitney, *Dolls Studies.*
13. R. Gordon Kelly, *Mother Was a Lady: Self and Society in Selected American Children's Periodicals, 1865–1890* (Westport, CT: Greenwood Press, 1974), xiii.
14. Paul Deane, *Mirrors of American Culture: Children's Fiction Series in the Twentieth Century* (Metuchen, NJ: Scarecrow Press, 1991), 5; Sheila

A. Egoff, *Thursday's Child: Trends and Patterns in Contemporary Children's Literature* (Chicago, IL: American Library Association, 1981), 4.

15. Gertrud Lehnert, "The Taming of the Shrew: Socialization and Education of Young Women in Children's Literature," *Poetics Today* 13, no. 1 (1992): 113.

16. Jan Susina, "American Girls Collection: Barbies with a Sense of History," *Children's Literature Association Quarterly* 24, no. 3 (1999): 130.

17. Lehnert, "The Taming of the Shrew," 114.

18. Peter Soderbergh, "The Stratemeyer Strain: Educators and the Juvenile Series Books, 1900–1980," in *Only Connect: Reading on Children's Literature,* eds. Sheila Egoff, GT Stubbs, LF Ashley (Toronto: Oxford University Press, 1980), 68–69.

19. Ibid., 70–71.

20. Nancy Tillman Romalov, "Children's Series Books and the Rhetoric of Guidance: A Historical Overview," in *Rediscovering Nancy Drew,* eds. Carolyn Stewart Dyer and Nancy Tillman Romalov (Iowa City, IA: University of Iowa Press, 1995), 119.

21. Susan B. Neuman, *Literacy in the Television Age: The Myth of the TV Effect* (Norwood, NJ: Ablex, 1995).

22. Jack Zipes, "Taking Political Stock: New Theoretical and Critical Approaches to Anglo-American Children's Literature in the 1980s," *The Lion and the Unicorn* 14 (1990): 8.

23. Council on Interracial Books for Children, *Guidelines for the Future: Human and Anti-Human Values in Children's Books: A Content Rating Instrument for Educators and Concerned Parents* (New York: Council on Interracial Books for Children Racism and Sexism Resource Center for Educators, 1976), 1.

24. Nancy Larrick, "The All-White World of Children's Books," *Saturday Review* 48, no. 11 (1965): 63–65. Julia L. Mickenberg, *Learning from the Left: Children's Literature, the Cold War, and Radical Politics in the United States* (New York: Oxford University Press, 2005).

25. Mickenberg, *Learning from the Left,* 274.

26. Joel Taxel, "Multicultural Literature and the Politics of Reaction," in *Stories Matter: The Complexity of Cultural Authenticity in Children's Literature,* ed. Dana L. Fox and Kathy G. Short (Urbana, IL: National Council of Teachers of English, 2003), 143–164.

27. Sharyl Bender Peterson and Mary Alyce Lach, "Gender Stereotypes in Children's Books: The Prevalence and Influence of Cognitive and Affective Development," *Gender and Education* 2, no. 2 (1990): 186.

28. Weitzman et al., "Sex-Role Socialization in Picture Books for Preschool Children."

29. Peterson and Lach, "Gender Stereotypes in Children's Books."

30. Peterson and Lach, "Gender Stereotypes in Children's Books," 185.
31. Melanie D. Koss, "Diversity in Contemporary Picture Books: A Content Analysis," *Journal of Children's Literature* 41, no. 1 (2015): 32–42; Janice McCabe, Emily Fairchild, Liz Grauerholz, Bernice A. Pescosolido, and Daniel Tope, "Gender in Twentieth-Century Children's Books Patterns of Disparity in Titles and Central Characters," *Gender & Society* 25, no. 2 (2011): 197–226.
32. Rudine Sims Bishop, "Evaluating Books by and About African-Americans," in *The Multicolored Mirror: Cultural Substance in Literature for Children and Young Adults*, ed. Merri V. Lingren (Fort Atkinson, WI: Highsmith Press, 1991), 31–44.
33. Julia Mickenberg and Philip Nel, "Radical Children's Literature Now!" *Children's Literature Association Quarterly* 36, no. 4 (2011): 446.
34. Diane Carver Sekeres, "The Market Child and Branded Fiction."
35. Sarah Lewis Philpott, "'Those Events Really Happened!' How Elementary Students Transact with History and Historical Fiction While Reading the American Girl Series" (PhD diss., University of Tennessee, 2013).
36. John Stephens, *Language and Ideology in Children's Fiction* (New York: Longman, 1992).
37. Elodie Rousselot, "Introduction: Exoticising the Past in Contemporary Neo-Historical Fiction," in *Exoticizing the Past in Contemporary Neo-Historical Fiction*, ed. Elodie Rousselot, (New York: Palgrave Macmillan, 2014), 2.
38. Ibid., 4.
39. Nina Diamond et al., "American Girl and the Brand Gestalt: Closing the Loop on Sociocultural Branding Research," *Journal of Marketing* 73, no. 3 (2009): 123.
40. Taxel, "Multicultural Literature and the Politics of Reaction," 143–164.
41. Rousselot, "Introduction," 4.
42. 1989 American Girl catalog.
43. Carrie Anton, Laurie Calkhoven, and Erin Falligant, *American Girl Ultimate Visual Guide* (New York: DK Publishing, 2016), 32.
44. Jeanne Brady, "Reading the American Dream: The History of the American Girl Collection," *Teaching and Learning Literature* 4, no. 1 (September/October 1994): 3.
45. Angharad Valdivia, "Living in a Hybrid Material World: Girls, Ethnicity and Mediated Doll Products," *Girlhood Studies* 2, no. 1 (2009): 73–93.
46. Antonia Fraser, *Dolls: Pleasures and Treasurers* (New York: G. P. Putnam's Sons, 1963/1967).
47. Leslie Daiken, *Children's Toys Throughout the Ages* (London: B.T. Batsford, 1953); Wendy Lavitt, *Dolls* (New York: Knopf, 1983).
48. Formanek-Brunell, *Made to Play House*, 16.

49. Ibid., 20.
50. Teresa de Lauretis, *Technologies of Gender: Essays on Theory, Film, and Fiction* (Bloomington, IN: Indiana University Press, 1987).
51. Juliette Peers, "Adelaide Huret and the Nineteeth-Century French Fashion Doll: Constructing Dolls/Constructing the Modern," in *Dolls Studies: The Many Meanings of Girls' Toys and Play*, eds. Miriam Forman-Brunell and Jennifer Dawn Whitney (New York: Peter Lang, 2015), 170.
52. Formanek-Brunell, *Made to Play House*, 62.
53. Ibid., 64–65.
54. Ibid.
55. G. Stanley Hall and Alexander Caswell Ellis, *A Study of Dolls* (New York: E.L. Kellogg & Co., 1897), 44.
56. Robin Bernstein, *Racial Innocence: Performing American Childhood from Slavery to Civil Rights* (New York: New York University Press, 2011), 19.
57. Robin Bernstein discusses recent challenges to the widely-held conclusion of this study. See Robin Bernstein, *Racial Innocence*, 196–201.
58. Seiter, *Sold Separately*, 67.
59. Ibid., 18.
60. Ibid., 80.
61. Ibid., 129.
62. Arlie Hochschild, *The Second Shift: Working Parents and the Revolution at Home* (New York: Avon, 1989).
63. Seiter, *Sold Separately*, 136.
64. Jacqueline Urla and Alan C. Swedlund, "The Anthropometry of Barbie: Unsettling Ideals of the Feminine Body in Popular Culture," in *Deviant Bodies: Critical Perspectives on Difference in Science and Popular Culture*, eds. Jennifer Terry and Jacqueline Urla (Bloomington, IN: Indiana University Press. 1995), 277–313.
65. Barbara Mackoff, *Growing a Girl: Seven Strategies for Raising a Strong, Spirited Daughter* (New York: Dell Publishing, 1996), xix.
66. Ann duCille, *Skin Trade* (Cambridge, MA: Harvard University Press, 1996), 50.
67. Sally Edwards, *Beyond Child's Play: Sustainable Product Design in the Global Doll-Making Industry* (Amityville, NY: Baywood Publishing Company, 2010), 55.
68. Jillian Sequeira, "A Tale of Two Barbies: Did Mattel's Labor Law Violations Fly Under the Radar?" December 1, 2015, http://lawstreetmedia.com/issues/business-and-economics/tale-two-barbies-mattels-labor-law-violations-fly-radar/.
69. Susan Stiger, "Hispanic Doll Embodies an Era Unique Collection a Hit Among Girls," *The Denver Post*, August 24, 1997, D2.
70. Spring 1991 Catalog Insert.

71. Julia Prohaska (Public Relations Manager, American Girl,) e-mail message to author, April 1, 1997.
72. Mary Pipher, *Reviving Ophelia: Saving the Selves of Adolescent Girls* (New York: Ballantine, 1994).
73. Lindsy Van Gelder, "The Importance of Being Eleven: Carol Gilligan Takes on Adolescence," *Ms.* (July/August 1990), 77.
74. Lyn M. Brown and Carol Gilligan, *Meeting at the Crossroads* (New York: Ballantine Books, 1992), 81.
75. Janie Victoria Ward and Beth Cooper Benjamin, "Women, Girls, and the Unfinished Work of Connection: A Critical Review of American Girls' Studies," in *All About the Girl: Culture, Power, and Identity*, ed. Anita Harris (New York: Routledge, 2004), 15–27.
76. Myra Sadker and David Sadker, *Failing At Fairness: How Schools Cheat Girls* (New York: Touchstone, 1994): 77. Significantly, both the Harvard and AUUW researchers found that many of the working-class girls and girls of color were able to resist these cultural pressures but mainstream media rarely reported these findings and produced a narrative of the universal crisis in the lives of teen girls.
77. Pipher, *Reviving Ophelia*, 207.
78. Ibid., 210.
79. Emilie Zaslow, *Feminism, Inc.: Coming of Age in Girl Power Media Culture* (New York: Palgrave Macmillan, 2009).
80. Virginia Beane Rutter, *Celebrating Girls: Nurturing and Empowering our Daughters* (Berkeley, CA: Conari Press, 1996), 137.
81. Jeanne Elium and Don Elium, *Raising a Daughter: Parents and the Awakening of Healthy Woman* (Berkeley, CA: Celestial Arts, 1994), 303.
82. Mackoff, *Growing a Girl*.
83. Prohaska, e-mail message to author.
84. Kara G. Morrison, "American Girl Dolls Are No Fad Toy: Popularity Continues to Grow After 30 years," *The Republic*, August 21, 2015, http://www.azcentral.com/story/entertainment/kids/2015/08/21/american-girl-dolls-popularity-continues-grow-scottsdale-store/32119301/.
85. Bernstein, *Racial Innocence*, 77.
86. Pleasant Company, "*At A Glance!*" Pleasant Company, public relations materials, received by mail December, 1996.
87. "Basic Doll Anatomy," http://americangirl.wikia.com/wiki/Basic_Doll_Anatomy.
    Prohaska, e-mail message to author.
88. Ibid.
89. Pipher, *Reviving Ophelia*, 207–218; Rutter, *Celebrating Girls*, 52.
90. "Barbie, Meet American Girl of Today Doll," *The Arizona Republic*, December 25, 1995, B17.

91. Tracie Egan Morrissey, "Growing Up, Everyone Did Dirty Things with Their Barbies," September 12, 2007, http://jezebel.com/299195/growing-up-everyone-did-dirty-things-with-their-barbies; Sharon Lamb, *The Secret Lives of Girls: What Good Girls Really Do—Sex, Play, Aggression, and Their Guilt* (New York: Free Press, 2001).

92. Lamb, *The Secret Lives of Girls*.

93. Ibid., 228.

94. David Harvey, *A Brief History of Neoliberalism* (New York: Oxford University Press, 2005), 2.

95. Anthony Giddens, *Modernity and Self-Identity: Self and Society in the Late Modern Age* (Cambridge, MA: Polity, 1991).

96. Juliet Schor, *The Overspent American: Why We Want What We Don't Need* (New York: Harper Perennial, 1998), 12; In 2016 the cost of a doll was $115.

97. Christine Page, "A History of Conspicuous Consumption," in *SV—Meaning, Measure, and Morality of Materialism*, eds. Floyd W. Rudmin and Marsha Richins (Provo, UT: Association for Consumer Research, 1992), 82–87.

98. Hochschild, *The Second Shift*; Joan Williams, *Unbending Gender: Why Family and Work Conflict and What to Do About It* (New York: Oxford University Press, 2000).

99. Allison J. Pugh, "Selling Compromise Toys, Motherhood, and the Cultural Deal," *Gender & Society* 19, no. 6 (2005): 729–749; Brad Edmondson, "The Demographics of Guilt," *American Demographics* 8 (1986): 33–35, 56; Betty Holcomb, *Not Guilty! The Good News About Working Mothers* (New York: Scribner, 1998); Leah Rosch, "Sugar Daddies," *Folio: The Magazine for Magazine Management* 23 (1994): 52–56. Susan Douglas and Meredith Michaels, *The Mommy Myth: The Idealization of Motherhood and How it Has Undermined Women* (New York: Free Press, 2004).

100. Edmondson, "The Demographics of Guilt," 33.

101. Douglas and Michaels, *The Mommy Myth*, 270.

102. Rebecca Dingo, "Securing the Nation: Neoliberalism's US Family Values in a Transnational Gendered Economy," *Journal of Women's History* 16, no. 3 (2004): 175.

103. Ibid., 174.

104. Susan Faludi, *Backlash: The Undeclared War Against American Women* (New York: Crown Publishers, 1991).

105. Ibid.

106. Emilie Zaslow, "GFCFSF: Mothers Challenge Evidence-Based Medicine & the Privatization of Motherhood," in *Mothers and Food*, eds. Tanya Cassidy and Florence Pasche Guignard (Branford, ON: Demeter Press), 250.

107. Douglas and Michaels, *The Mommy Myth*, 24.

108. Nancy Duffey Story, "Pleasant Company's American Girl Collection: The Corporate Construction of Girlhood" (PhD diss., University of Georgia, 2002), 108.

109. Zaslow, *Feminism Inc.*; Bonnie Dow, *Primetime Feminism: Television, Media Culture, and the Women's Movement Since 1970* (Philadelphia: University of Pennsylvania Press, 1996).

110. Eva Chen, "Neoliberalism and Popular Women's Culture: Rethinking Choice, Freedom and Agency," *European Journal of Cultural Studies*, 16, no. 4 (2013): 440–452.

111. Marnina Gonick, "Between 'Girl Power' and 'Reviving Ophelia': Constituting the Neoliberal Girl Subject," *NWSA Journal* 18, no. 2 (2006): 1–23.

112. Zaslow, *Feminism, Inc.*

113. Ibid., 4.

114. Rebecca Joan West, "Some of My Best Dolls Are Black: Colorblind Rhetoric in Online Collecting Communities" (PhD diss., University of Loyola Chicago, 2014), 15.

115. Sue Jackson and Tiina Vares, "Media 'Sluts': 'Tween' Girls' Negotiations of Postfeminist Sexual Subjectivities in Popular Culture," in *New Femininities*, eds. Rosalind Gill and Christina Scharff (New York: Palgrave Macmillan, 2011), 134–146.

116. Judy Schoenberg in discussion with author.

117. American Psychological Association, Task Force on the Sexualization of Girls. *Report of the APA Task Force on the Sexualization of Girls* (Washington, DC: American Psychological Association, 2007), http://www.apa.org/pi/women/programs/girls/report-full.pdf; Ariel Levy, *Female Chauvinist Pigs: Women and the Rise of Raunch Culture* (New York: Free Press, 2005); Emma Rush and Andrea La Nauze, *Corporate Paedophilia: Sexualisation of Children in Australia* (Manuka: Australia Institute, 2006).

118. Sue Jackson, Tiina Vares, and Rosalind Gill, "'The Whole Playboy Mansion Image': Girls' Fashioning and Fashioned Selves Within a Postfeminist Culture," *Feminism & Psychology* 23, no. 2 (2013): 143–162.

CHAPTER 4

"Baby Doll, You Made the World a Little Bit Better by Speaking Out for What You Believe In": Narratives of Femininity and Political Action in the BeForever Collection

Meet Rebecca begins with the protagonist being called to set the table for Shabbat dinner. She would prefer to keep playing with her dolls but Rebecca does what she has been told. Even though she would rather participate in the weekly religious ritual by lighting the candles, arguably a more significant role, Rebecca takes "special care setting the table" and folding "the linen napkins so that the crocheted edges [are] lined up neatly."[1] Rebecca does have a rebellious streak, but in many of the series' scenes, she swallows her personal interests or desires in order to make others happy. In this way, Rebecca's story supports the claim made by some scholars that the American Girl BeForever collection reifies a "good girl" feminine identity that has plagued girls for centuries and privileges a work ethic where labor is valued over play and creativity.[2]

Yet, Rebecca's story is also emblematic of a different kind of representation of femininity and American identity that is infused throughout the BeForever series of which she is a part. Beside a normative femininity, the BeForever narratives promote a girlhood that values citizen engagement, using one's voice to stand for justice, and a recognition of the need for institutionalized and policy-based social change. Early in her series, Rebecca's uncle, aunt, and cousins immigrate to the United States. After they get settled, the elder male newcomers start work at a garment factory. One day, when Rebecca goes there to deliver to them the dinner they forgot, she is overwhelmed by the deplorable conditions in which they work:

© The Author(s) 2017
E. Zaslow, *Playing with America's Doll*,
DOI 10.1057/978-1-137-56649-2_4

The sour odors of sweat and machine oil blended into one foul smell.... Inside the huge loft, men with curved knives leaned over wide tables. Endless rows of young women in long-sleeved shirtwaists bent over clattering black machines. Everyone worked silently, unable to talk over the room's deafening roar.... The windows were covered with a layer of grime, shutting out the sunlight.... Thick dust clung to every surface, and fine particles of lint floated in the sticky air.[3]

Knowing she will be able to leave as soon as she drops off the food, Rebecca feels miserable for all the workers who are "trapped" inside because they need the work, even if the conditions are dangerous and the wages are unfair. Rebecca's sadness quickly progresses to political awareness. She writes a letter to the newspaper editor believing that if "people realize how awful it is inside the factory, then surely the city will change the laws." Her cousin, however, convinces her not to send it, reminding her that there have been many letters to the editor with no change in workplace practices.[4]

When Rebecca learns that the factory workers have gone on strike, she feels moved to "do her part."[5] Rather than stay home to finish the laundry, as instructed by her mother, who fears violence at the rally, Rebecca runs down to be with the protesters. Although she experiences a sense of power in the unity displayed by the workers, she also witnesses the violence and chaos that ensues when "thugs" hired by the bosses and protected by the city's police force, infiltrate the crowd. She is further stunned when she sees the police arresting the peaceful strikers.

In a climactic scene, Rebecca listens to Clara Adler, a young union organizer, who is giving a speech on a soapbox.[6] Suddenly, the bosses' goons knock Adler off the soapbox and Rebecca discovers she is right next to the makeshift stage. Pulling her letter to the editor out of her pocket, ten-year-old Rebecca steps on to the soapbox and takes up where the union leader has left off, giving a speech in support of fair pay, shorter workdays, and safer working conditions.

Rebecca's resistance to normative femininity, including her use of her voice and her participation in public life, and her resistance to accepting the power structures that create an unjust environment for workers, exist beside her participation in the feminine familial roles of the early twentieth century. Furthermore, these narratives of defiance exist beside the commercial realities in which her accompanying products are marketed. Rather than selling a soapbox as one of Rebecca's accessories, or having a podium set up in the American Girl Place retail locations through which girls could play-act giving powerful speeches and imagine taking on leadership roles, Rebecca's accessories include a bed "adorned with golden medallions" and topped with a "white lace bedspread," a hat, necklace, purse, dolls, games, and toy menorah while the retail locations' interactive experiences consist of lunch with dolls, a hair salon, and T-shirt design studio. Rebecca's narrative demonstrates American Girl's commitment to stories about girls' leadership, the power of girls' voices, standing up for strong beliefs, and working with others to make change. Paired with the collection's material consumer goods, it also exemplifies the contradictory portrayal of girlhood that is constructed in the American Girl BeForever series which requires both participation in and acts of opposition to normative femininity.

One could easily claim, as does Elizabeth Marshall, that American Girl has coopted rhetorics of resistance and employed them to "play on feminist and/or educative aspirations of parents, teachers, girls and young women" but I resist drawing this conclusion.[7] Rather than arguing that BeForever is "less about strong girls, diversity, or history than about marketing girlhood," I argue for a "yes—and" position that challenges the notion that a product cannot both market female identity *and* also generate a social justice message. As Julia Mickenberg and Philip Nel have demonstrated in their study of children's literature, politically progressive books "may be published by the very powers that such books arguably undermine."[8] Resistive ideological messages become complicated, though not necessarily impotent, when coupled with capitalism.[9] Sarah Projansky, focusing specifically on the commodity activism of girl power texts, has wisely suggested we move beyond simplistic analyses that repeatedly define such pop culture texts as having resistive feminist potential that is always ultimately deflated by a commodification of feminism. Calling this the "disruption-containment" argument she lays out a model in which scholars make the case for a popularized feminism that breeds—or has the potential to breed—girls' resistance, anger, and transformation but that is inevitably mitigated or contained by a feminism that is watered-down and depoliticized in its commodified state.[10]

It is not instructive, then, to ask if American Girl is feminist or if it is a commodity that has absorbed feminism. It is certainly neither "an ideal form of social action for 21st century consumers," nor an expression of a grassroots, anti-racist, anti-capitalist, intersectional feminism. This does not mean, however, that American Girls' political narratives are simply "a clever hoax intended to bring in greater profits" for Mattel.[11] Rather, this chapter seeks to explore the brand's contradictory embrace of resistive ideologies in its fictional construction of American girlhood and its simultaneous reification of normative femininity in its material representation. This chapter also seeks to understand the act of reading American Girl texts as a site of negotiation where consumers, both girls and their mothers, are not duped by the incorporation of political messages but are aware of and make compromises within the contradictions, tensions, and slippages of the neoliberal era in which commodity goods are produced.[12] While there may be a concern that girl consumers do not yet have the skills to negotiate these contradictions, research has demonstrated that young people engage critically and thoughtfully through commodity and story selections, play experiences, and social interactions with their cultural texts.[13] To this end, this chapter concludes by exploring mothers and daughters' interactions with these contradictory representations of American girlhood.

REJECTING THE DEVALUATION OF THE PRIVATE SPHERE: SIGNIFICANCE OF FAMILY WORK

Girls in the BeForever series often participate in traditionally feminine activities such as crafting and food preparation. For many of the protagonists in these series, particularly those whose stories take place before the first half of the twentieth century, planting, harvesting, and other means of producing food that will be consumed by their families is an integral part of their lives. These fictional accounts resist the devaluing of care and also depict it as one of many activities in which girls engage. Even as the girls in these books sometimes bemoan their workload, especially when it takes them away from doing something they love, readers are also led to understand the significance of their participation in the domestic sphere.[14] Kit, whose family turned their home into a boarding house to provide income after her father's business collapsed during the Great Depression, was frustrated that she could not spend time on the newspaper writing she loved to do, but she came to understand the realities of her time period when she discovered that her father had been secretly eating lunch at the local soup kitchen. Tripp writes,

> [Kit] thought about the chores waiting for her that absolutely had to be done. Mother needed her to set the table for dinner and scrub the potatoes and put them in the oven to bake. Then there was laundry to iron and fold and put away, all before dinner. *This is it*, Kit thought. *This is the truth of my life now. Maybe forever.*[15]

Kit never learns to enjoy her required housework nor to enjoy the garden parties that her mother likes to style impeccably, but she does come to understand how her role in maintaining her home for boarders allows her family to have shelter, heat, and food at a time when many of her neighbors do not. Still, she does not stop writing and uses her journalistic skills not only within her family to communicate her ideas for generating more household income but also within her community to share ideas about how to support homeless children.

Often the girls' work represented, not only their contribution to the sustenance of the family, but also served a secondary function. For Addy, laboring in her family's own plot of land represents freedom from toiling in the fields of the slave owner's planation. The imagery of her family gardening in Philadelphia contrasts starkly with a scene in the first book, before she has escaped the North Carolina plantation, in which an overseer forced Addy to eat worms because she had not carefully removed them from all of the plants. Moreover, the Walker family sells the vegetables to pay for Poppa to travel South in search of Addy's missing baby sister and older brother. For Molly, help in her family's victory garden represents one of her contributions to the war effort and Josefina's gardening helps sustain the family's memory of their deceased mother who originally planted the seeds.

In the more recent stories, that are written about life in the second half of the twentieth century, the girl protagonists and their mothers are less likely to be identified with the domestic sphere. In 1954, Maryellen's mother is a homemaker. However, shortly after meeting Mrs. Larkin, readers learn that she managed a factory assembly line during WWII. Although her mother says that she is now happily "managing" the family, it becomes clear that she enjoyed her work and only quit because, as Maryellen's sister, Caroline, tells us, "Lots of women quit working after the war... so the returning soldiers could have jobs."[16] Mrs. Larkin lets her children know that when her youngest is in full-day school she may be interested in pursuing a career again. Perhaps even more significant is the conclusion that Maryellen's oldest sister, Joan, comes to when she questions her own decision to get married to her sweetheart, Jerry. Having failed miserably in the cooking lessons her mother has offered her and enjoyed the adventures she experienced traveling in an RV camper with her family across the country, Joan muses:

I love Jerry… and I love the idea of living with him. Even though so far… a fire extinguisher seems to be the kitchen utensil I use the most, so we'll starve if he can't cook. [But] you made me think how I'd love to go to Massachusetts and see where my favorite poet, Emily Dickenson, lived. And I've always wanted to see the home of Louisa May Alcott, who wrote *Little Women*, and see Thoreau's Walden Pond. And then there's New York City. Lots of writers lived there, and London, and Paris…I want to travel and visit the places where all the writers that I love have lived. I want to go to college and study the books they've written. And I'd love to help other people love those books and writers as much as I do, maybe by becoming a teacher.[17]

After Joan does more soul-searching and has some conversations with her fiancé, she discovers that he supports her pursuit of an education and would be interested in traveling with her. Unlike her mother from a previous generation, Joan will not "have to choose" between family and work nor will her work have to be based within the domestic sphere.[18] A decade later, BeForever's Melody has a mother who is a school teacher and in 1974 Julie's mother owns her own business, Gladrags, a second-hand shop, and her role in the story rarely occurs in the home. In all of these stories, that are set in post-World War II America, while girls help at home with food preparation and other chores, their non-domestic interests are encouraged by their mothers.

Writing of the early series books, Sherrie Inness argued that the collection supported a stereotypical femininity that naturalized nurturing and caregiving as the "province of women" by telling the tales of girls who spent a lot of time "pursuing traditional girl activities" such as washing clothes and preparing meals.[19] However, throughout the series, the domestic sphere is not the only sphere in which girls' contributions are important to the family. In many of the series, girls are actively involved in two other primary forms of labor for the family: assisting with the family business and heroic rescue work.

In her story, Rebecca assists at her father's shoe store and even brings in money by selling her crocheted doilies. Melody helps out at her grandfather's flower shop, and Josefina takes a leading role in squashing a misunderstanding regarding a trade that could have ultimately been detrimental to her father's business. Like domestic work, work for the family business often has more significance than daily labor. Rebecca, for example, who starts to earn money at the shoe store with an eye toward buying candlesticks so that she can equally participate in her family's Shabbat rituals, ultimately decides to contribute her money to helping her Russian cousins emigrate out of a county in which they are facing persecution. Marie-Grace, who occasionally helps her father in the medical practice he operates from their house, encounters an instance in which this help takes on an importance that extends beyond ordinary assistance. When an enslaved woman leaves a light-skinned African American baby on her father's office doorstep in 1853, he explains to Marie-Grace that the baby's mother was probably trying to protect her son from a life of enslavement. Marie-Grace works with her father who wants to find the child a safe space in an orphanage rather than be returned to the plantation owner who has been nosing around. She and her free-born African American friend, Cécile, secure a fashionable outfit for the infant so that he looks like he has been abandoned by a wealthy family and is more likely to be accepted as white in the segregated orphanage. With her father's support, Marie-Grace determines that protecting the baby from the racist and oppressive institution of slavery is more important than telling the truth.

Another form of work in service of the family that is frequently depicted is rescue work, which often includes rescuing an adult male. Josefina sneaks off in the night to gather information that ultimately saves her father from a bad business decision, and Caroline gives her father a map with a secret code that helps him escape from the enemy's prison. Readers also encounter Samantha rescue her grandmother's love interest when he falls overboard and strikes his head on a rock, and Kirsten lead her father to safety when he is injured during a severe snowstorm. The girls also rescue their friends and siblings. Kaya rescues her blind sister who has fallen into river rapids, and Josefina saves a friend from a lethal snakebite and finds that her true calling is to be a healer. These narratives depict active girls who are thoughtful risk takers and who are integral to important aspects of their family lives, family businesses and communities.

REJECTING THE PRIVATE: USING VOICE IN THE PUBLIC

Because the BeForever series books are primarily located within pre-second wave feminist historical eras, in large part these books portray mothers whose roles as caregivers frequently cut "them off from most of the social roles that offer responsibility and authority."[20] Some of these fictional mothers actively seek to train their daughters to continue this private social contribution.[21] Yet, even as the protagonists' domestic work is portrayed as significant, it is also generally represented as the work of a bygone era, and mothers who promote decorum and domesticity over professional and political aspirations are depicted as backward and unsupportive. While the mothers in the BeForever series books may be stuck in the domestic sphere—and often endeavor to train their daughters to succeed there as well—readers encounter a consistent framing of public voice and political action as cornerstones of girls' participation in US society. Readers are guided to celebrate the girls' political achievements through plot lines in which mothers ultimately recognize their daughters' successes or in which another adult woman character offers praise to the girl for using her voice publicly. Cécile's mother, for example, initially doubts her daughter's ability to effectively participate in public civic engagement. She is shocked by her daughter's plan to speak at a benefit to raise money for children who have been orphaned by yellow fever. Hearing of Cécile's plan, Maman stammers, "All by yourself? Public speaking. I don't.... You can do this?"[22] When Cécile beautifully recites an original poem in front of a large crowd, however, her mother must demonstrate her pride. When Rebecca's mother is unimpressed that her daughter has given a speech at the workers' strike, her uncle's fiancé, Lily, promises her, "Listen, baby doll, you made the world a little bit better by speaking out for what you believe in. Nobody can fault you for wanting to see more fairness in the world. Just remember that the best we can do in this life is follow our hearts."[23] In many of these stories, mothers who initially doubted their daughters finally come to see the ways in which their daughters can make social contributions.

This dynamic in which girls are straddling domestic and public life with conflicted support from their mothers allows the company to play with a neo-historical nostalgia for the past while celebrating the modern and to capture the audience that seeks traditional values along with those who are looking for a more counterhegemonic toy. This neo-historical genre that attends to the past and also satisfies the feminist interests of contemporary readers, and the adults who purchase books for them, allows the series to depict girls who resist their containment in the private sphere, even if in small ways. This genre also encourages the positioning of girls' political action as modern and in opposition to the lady-like and domestic behaviors their old-fashioned mothers often seek for them to perform.

During the first half of the brand's history, roughly 1986–2000, the political element in the collection was primarily filled with a courage that was exhibited through plucky heroism and care for the less fortunate. Steeped in a girl power feminism, this political identity was more performative than activist because it highlighted individual acts of bravery and personal change rather than community acts requiring collective political action. The narratives painted a neoliberal politic of self-help and individual courage. Very often the girls in these books acknowledged injustice but did nothing (or could do nothing) to change it. And, while these characters may attempt to overcome the gendered norms of their time they ultimately find them difficult to resist. For example, the African American seamstress, Jessie, who works in Samantha's mansion, lives in a small, dark house on the other side of the railroad tracks. When Samantha asks another girl why Jessie lives there, the response is "I don't know...it's just the way grownups do things."[24] Even when wealthy Samantha does not just accept the way grown-ups do things—as in her friendship with Nellie, an impoverished girl who works in the home next door and later in a thread factory—her methods for working toward change focus on individual gallantry paired with a kind of patronage of Nellie and her newly orphaned siblings.

First, Samantha, brazenly speaks out against the dangers of child labor for a local speech contest on the topic of "progress." Her speech initially celebrated factories because, she argued, they save companies' money and production time. Later Samantha talks to Nellie who has worked in a factory; Nellie shares her memories of standing on her feet for twelve-hour work days and being required to work without talking while the noise of the machines created a buzzing in her ears each night. She tells Samantha about the impact of the work on her body; "My back hurt and my legs hurt and my arms got heavy. The machines got fuzz and dust all over everything. It was in the air, and it got in my mouth and made it hard to breathe."[25] Upon hearing this Samantha decides to change her speech. In this new speech, our protagonist spotlights the jeopardies faced by youth working in the factories and concludes that America has not made real progress if "factories can hurt children."[26]

Later, she hides Nellie and her sisters from passage on the orphan train. Tucking them into a corner in her wealthy aunt and uncle's attic, Samantha gives the girls books, toys, and blankets until they are discovered by her aunt and uncle who soon decide to adopt all three sisters. Samantha's actions have been read by some critics as the initial development of political consciousness, but also as patronizing or custodial.[27] And while she has used her voice in the interest of social change, the ameliorative *Little Orphan Annie*-like conclusion offers the perspective that oppression is a temporary, individualized experience with personalized solutions.

Similarly, set in 1774, Felicity's story examines a hot tempered, defiant character with a "strong-willed struggle for independence" who challenges social norms and stretches the boundaries of girls' participation but ultimately accepts her gendered position.[28] When author Valerie Tripp introduces the reader to Felicity, as the protagonist enters her father's general store, we learn that her character represents a departure from the domesticity we expect from eighteenth-century girls. Felicity is experiencing a conflict between her prescriptive social role and what she wants to be. Our protagonist argues for the right to learn Latin and philosophy rather than tea-time etiquette and needlepoint. She wants to help out at her father's store rather than do housework with her mother. The Felicity we first meet feels trapped by her domestic responsibilities; when her father tells her that she cannot assist him at the store,

> Felicity sighed. She knew where she *should* be helping—at home. A pile of mending was waiting for her there. Felicity hated the idea of sitting straight and still, stitching tiny stiches, when all the while she was stiff with boredom. She would much rather stay at the store. But her father had already turned back to his work. There was nothing to do but go home.[29]

The conflict between Felicity's desire to be in the public sphere of work and society's expectation that she should be in the private sphere of the home continues throughout the series. Disappointed in the clothes she is required to wear, Felicity complains that her stays are too tight and lifts the hems of her petticoats to allow her to walk with greater ease. In conversation with Ben, her father's apprentice, Felicity declares,

> It's very tiresome to be a girl sometimes...There are so many things a young lady must not do. I'm told the same things over and over again. Don't talk too loud. Don't walk too fast. Don't fidget. Don't dirty your hands, Don't be impatient...It's very hard. You're lucky to be a lad. You can do whatever you like.[30]

If she originally rebels against her training as an upper-middle-class young woman, in many ways Felicity appears to have embraced her role as a girl of the gentry by the end of the series. As the daughter of a Williamsburg, Virginia, shopkeeper, with two slaves and an apprentice, Felicity is expected to follow her mother in becoming a gentlewoman. She begins to love the etiquette lessons she once repudiated and finds a great delight in being able to dress in a fancy ball gown for a dance lesson at the Governor's palace.[31] Still, Felicity stands up for her political convictions through her refusal to take tea during her lessons and declares her alliance with the American revolutionaries, as she bravely alerts her townspeople when she hears the British talking about stealing the patriots' gun powder. Similar to Samantha's help for Nellie, Felicity aids Ben, helping him to negotiate an early release from his apprenticeship. These mostly individual acts of bravery and political action were significant for a girl in the eighteenth century but do not challenge neoliberal politics which downplay the need for systemic change and collectivist struggle and highlight the individual as an agent of change who can self-regulate to overcome temporary barriers to her personal success.

THE WORK OF COMMUNITY BUILDING AND PROTEST IN THE BEFOREVER COLLECTION

Despite the fact that one might imagine that the purchase of American Girl by the Barbie-owning toy behemoth Mattel would yield more conservative stories, the opposite has been the case. Since 2000, these historical narratives have positioned political labor—in concert with others and with a goal of structural change—as a central defining element of girls' American identity. Capitalism has long absorbed the rhetoric, styling, and sometimes ideas, of social movements.[32] However, in the new millennium, in part due to a neoliberalist emphasis on individuals taking the onus for correcting social ills where government has vacated its responsibility, profiting from dissent and critique became a "key feature of contemporary capitalist culture," with girl power representing the specific appropriation of feminist potential.[33] The attention to gender equality was bolstered by employees with a genuine belief in the power of literature and toys as tools of political socialization. In this era, community building and social change actions have been fundamental to many of the plots in the series books written for the American Girl BeForever collection.

The work of community building occurs in many forms including traditional means such as fundraising, charitable work, and volunteering. For example, Addy raises money for newly freed African Americans so she can give to others the kind of support she and her mother experienced when they arrived in Philadelphia, and Julie works with her class to raise money to protect bald eagles from extinction and to release rescued and rehabilitated eagles back into the skies. Frequently, the girls' charitable work is more active than fundraising: Molly and her classmates sew a blanket for injured soldiers during WWII; Maryellen produces a play to raise awareness about the polio vaccine; and Julie teaches American Sign Language to class bullies who are making fun of their school's new deaf student.

However, many of the girls go well beyond raising money and even beyond suggesting reformative changes to take active, agentic roles in social change movements that advocate for structural change supported by government and/or corporate policy. Each of these girls becomes aware of an injustice—either to herself or others—and uses her voice, time, and energy to fight for its defeat. These stories capture the tension of a feminist commodity in a neoliberal era as well as the tensions inherent in the agency of cultural professionals (in this case, writers of the American Girl series books) and the structures that produce, distribute, market, and create commodities related to their work (in this case, Mattel). The neoliberal market in which these narratives are produced privileges individual change and achievement rather than social change and institutional support. The courageous dolls created by the American Girl company in the Mattel corporation embody this display of personal success and are purchased, in part, to deliver this message of a powerful girlhood to their specific girl owners. Yet, the accompanying books, written by individually motivated authors, frequently offer collectivist visions of struggle against policies and institutions that maintain hegemonic structures and may serve as tools of resistive cultural transmission. Their participation in these struggles is essential to their identity as American girls. Below, I analyze the stories of Kit, Julie, and Melody to demonstrate these counterhegemonic themes in the collection's books.

Growing up in the Great Depression, Kit loved to pretend she was a journalist and created playful newspapers about her family (Fig. 4.1). Kit loved her typewriter, its sounds, its smell, and the way she could use it to create a story. When Kit's mother redecorated her room in pink frills, Kit recognized that this might be another girl's dream room but she was particularly upset about the way her new "white and spindly legged [desk]....looked too delicate to hold the big black typewriter that crouched on it."[34] Kit's mother further demonstrated her lack of support for Kit's interests when she asked her to "keep the typewriter in the closet, please, and only take it out when she used it."[35] Despite the request, Kit does not put her typewriter away. She continues to write her own newspapers and works on various reporting techniques including interviewing and photojournalism. The adults in her life devalue her writing but despite her family's trivialization of her passion, Kit uses her skill, along with the knowledge she gained about journalism, as a political tool. When her uncle describes her work as "nonsense" and "childish," she thinks:

Fig. 4.1   Kit Kittredge doll

> She was rather proud of her newspapers. She never wrote nonsense. She loved writing, respected words, and tried hard to find the perfect ones to use, which was not the least bit childish to do.[36]

When Kit sees the living conditions of the homeless children who are camped out in the soup kitchens during the freezing cold Cincinnati winter, she knows that she must do something. First, she donates her old coat, but she realizes that this is not enough. Describing Kit's raised awareness, Tripp writes,

> Kit knew that only luck and chance separated her family from those she saw around her....Everything could change suddenly and she could find herself standing in line for soup, just like these children....It made Kit's heart hurt to see them.[37]

Kit's friend, Ruthie, romanticizes the donation remarking, "Kit, you were like the fairy godmother...You gave that girl your old coat and *whoosh*.... you changed her," but Kit knows this is not enough, either for the girl or any of the other children needing food and shelter.[38] Using her reporting skills, Kit returns to take photos of the children and writes a letter to the editor advocating for clothing donations and also supporting the use of public funds to re-open an empty hospital as a shelter for the homeless families. Kit is no longer satisfied to bring one coat to one child; she wants a broad discussion of injustice to begin and government support for those in need. Kit's mother, once critical of her daughter's desire to write and have a public voice, ultimately praises Kit for the persuasive letter to the editor about the conditions of impoverished children.

In the curricular resources developed to support teachers who use Kit's books in the classroom one lesson suggests that students, acting as Kit, write a letter to the president discussing how a specific issue—home foreclosure, hunger, or unemployment, for example—has impacted them. The curriculum guide states that the letter should also make "a plea for help for all Americans."[39] The move to ask the government for help is especially relevant in our neoliberal "lift yourself by your bootstraps," non-interventionist era. This language suggests that the book and the curriculum guide are recognizing that citizen engagement, collectivist politics, and government intervention are important for social change.

Like Kit, Melody is not satisfied to make ameliorative change nor to keep quiet when she sees injustice. Melody is shaped by the Civil Rights movement of the mid-1960s in which she comes of age. Unlike Kit who must resist her family, Melody lives within a community and family for whom justice is a core value. When Melody's sister, Yvonne, decides to go natural with her hair with the intention of "honoring [her] African heritage" no one in the family is sure what to think, but when Yvonne ignores the snickers she hears when they are out in public, Melody is proud because Yvonne "stands up for what she believes in."[40] Furthermore, the pastor of her church sermonizes about justice and fairness and her parents participate in a block association that discusses ways of resisting racially discriminatory housing practices.[41] When Melody does not sit back and accept the inequalities those in her community experience, she has role models to look up to and a belief system against which to measure her actions.

Melody is involved in many political activities, big and small. She closes her savings account at the bank that discriminates against her sister, she attends a local march at which Martin Luther King, Jr. speaks, and she sings "Lift Every Voice and Sing," often called the Black American National Anthem, at her church youth day service. Melody is not satisfied watching the adults organize all of the social change actions. She takes on a leadership position organizing a Junior Block Club whose mission it is to clean up the local community park that has been left to decay by a city government that underfunds black neighborhoods. In addition to learning leadership skills, Melody gets an education in grassroots organizing, navigating city agencies, and using local media to promote her campaign. She leads the neighborhood kids to paint, add hopscotch boards, and plant flowers and vegetables. Despite all the hard work, there is no fairy tale ending; the city does not spend money fixing up the park and Melody knows that she and her friends will be required to maintain it.

The curricular resource guide for Melody identifies leadership, racism, and activism as thematic of the text and recommends that students who read her story discuss different forms of activism including Yvonne's afro and the Walk to Freedom march. To expand the reach of the text, teachers are instructed to have the class create effective protest signs for Melody and to think about what Melody and her family would say about contemporary racial issues.[42] Though the series' formula requires an individualized story of triumph, readers are meant to understand that Melody is not just advocating for her own rights and her own needs, she is community-driven and understands the value of working with others to achieve social change. She also learns that oppression is not temporary and requires ongoing collectivist work.

Like Melody, Julie growing up in Berkeley, California in 1974, sees value in community activism (Fig. 4.2). She becomes aware of the benefits of structural policies and laws to support equality as well as the need for institutional power to be in support of fairness and justice. A skilled basketball player, Julie is denied access to the boys' team at her school. She learns about Title IX from a newspaper and tells the coach that he has no choice but to allow her on the team. Fighting the feeling of "her insides" going "all runny like the yellow belly of a breakfast egg," Julie tells the coach, "If there's not a basketball team for girls at this school, you have to let a girl play on the boys' team ... I read it in the newspaper ... It's the law!"[43] When the coach ignores the legal precedent for Julie's claim, the protagonist becomes inspired by her mother's friend, a Vietnam War veteran who in his fight for re-funding a Veterans' community center creates a petition and collects signatures. Though the nine-year-old wins the approval of the school board, Julie does not just focus on her own successes. She uses the skills she has learned from standing up to school administrators to lead her class in an awareness and fundraising project on endangered eagles for Earth Day. Moreover, Julie challenges a local housing development firm that has cut down the trees that served as

Fig. 4.2   Julie Albright doll

a habitat for the bald eagles and convinces them to compensate for their environmental injustice by donating materials to build a tower for the eagles' release to the wild.

Finally, in the last book of Julie's series, she runs for student body president against a popular older boy because of "something she believed in," a policy change that she thought would be beneficial to the community: students in detention would be required to do something to help the whole school, like clean up litter or wash graffiti off the bathroom walls.[44] Throughout the series, Julie's mother is supportive and even offers women's struggle for the right to vote as an example of how fighting for change can be arduous. When Julie is discouraged by the small number of signatures she has obtained on her petition, her mother reminds her, "Any time you try to change something it's going to be difficult....There was a time, only fifty years ago, when people didn't even think women should be allowed to vote. It took a lot of hard work for that to change."[45] Like Kit's and Melody's resource guides for teachers, Julie's recommends that students extend the narrative of political action. In Julie's case, the guide suggests that students learn about Title IX, Billie Jean King, and the Seneca Falls Convention as well as debate whether they think Julie's experience trying to get on the basketball team will make her care about women's roles and issues in the future.[46] With the backdrop of the American bicentennial, Julie's national identity is constructed in connection with her belief that she must use her voice to fight for change and her awareness that change requires a combination of collectivist practice, corporate reparation, anti-discrimination laws, and school policies.

The BeForever series cannot just be read as cooptation of a feminist discourse resulting in the weakening of counterhegemonic or resistive ideology as some have suggested.[47] While many of the collection's narratives written in the brand's first fifteen years position the girls as desiring lives with more opportunities than those presented to their mothers but ultimately accepting their gendered positions, those published in the last fifteen years celebrate and normalize civic engagement and having a political voice. Many of these later stories share activist strategies for change including raising awareness, petitioning, protesting, working collectively, and running for office rather than featuring a heroic neoliberal subject who can save the day. The issues that these girl activists address are not exhaustive of the many that feminists identify as crucial to gender justice but provide suggestive blueprints for readers that can be applied for use in other movements.

CONSTRUCTING THE IDEAL AMERICAN GIRL CONSUMER

One cannot explore the collection's narratives independently of the material culture that surrounds, supports, and is supported by them. During the same time that there has been an increased focus on unified social action, the collection of accessories has grown and become further imbricated into Mattel's synergistic culture. The company's horizontal and vertical integration encourages readers to learn about particular hair styles and outfits that adorn the protagonists and then buy replicas of these outfits both for themselves and their dolls, bring their dolls to the retail store salons to be given the same hairdo, or buy *The Hair Book* which offers instructions on how to create similar hairstyles. These tie-ins reinforce normative femininity and materialism, emphasizing beauty culture, clothing, and haircare, and craft a particular gender and national identity that is tied to consumption and entrepreneurialism.

Even as they are invited into a world of civically engaged and activist characters, girl consumers are invited into a world of consumption. Alexis and Octavia, two sisters I interviewed, offered me a detailed description of the process they go through once the visually rich catalog arrives in the mail. "When we see it on the table," they explained, "We just run toward it, push away our homework, and read it first. Before homework. First, there's a scan. And then there's a deep read. And then there's a circle, then there's a dissect, and then there's a decide what's final." Every girl I spoke with, except those who were over twelve, sought to add to her American Girl collection. They talked of engaging with American Girl marketing materials in a variety of ways including poring over the catalog, visiting the website and the store, and watching videos on YouTube.

The American Girl doll, like any commodity in a capitalist culture that has interwoven counterhegemonic politics into its identity, is "not only a tangible product" but has "intangible attributes that include cultural responsibility, moral virtue, political ethics, and social action itself."[48] It neither only urges, nor only decries, consumption. Yet the collection's ever-multiplying line extensions, and increasing focus on contemporary rather than historical accessories, scripts a specific model of girlhood that is steeped in the normatively feminine activities of grooming, dressing, styling, and consuming.

Many of the narratives tell the tale of a young girl who saves hard-earned money to buy a desired material good but ultimately uses the money to help her family or others. Addy, for example, does not use the money she makes delivering dresses to buy the lamp that she and her mother so desperately need, or the red scarf she longed to buy for her mother because she thought that her mother's hard work made her deserve to "have something pretty."[49] Instead, she contributes her money to the Freedman's Fund so that newly freed African Americans, including her father and her siblings, can be reunited with their families and decides to make her mother a scarf from scrap material. Likewise, rather than buy new clothes for herself Kit helps pay her family's electric bill with money she has earned assisting her ailing uncle.

In the BeForever universe, however, equally as important as giving is consuming. Consumption is also woven into American Girl stories, not only as integral to daily life, but as a fundamental part of the protagonists' identities. While many of the tales depict the protagonists making hand-crafted gifts for others, these characters also often participate in buying or receiving new dresses and other objects of desire which are frequently ascribed a glowing or magical quality and appear to be gratifying for the character.[50] When Felicity's mother surprises her with a new dress, for example, Felicity

stopped stock still. She could not believe her eyes. The beautiful gown was
spread out on her bed, glowing in the light of her candle. Every stitch was
perfectly finished. Was it magic?[51]

Similarly, Josefina enters her bedroom and feels that it is brighter than the
single candle that was left burning in it; "Josefina smiled when she saw
why. Someone had laid out [her] *mantilla*, comb, and her best dress on
top of the trunk. The pretty yellow dress brightened the whole room."[52]
This depiction of material goods perpetuates the brand's lessons in normative femininity and may teach girls to relate consumption to joy, which
serves the economic interests of the company but might not serve the
interests of girl consumers.

To aid in the character's consumption, industriousness and accumula-
tion of wealth are identified in the narratives as elemental to American
girlhood. Felicity helps at her father's mercantile, Caroline at her father's
shipyard, Josefina on her family farm, Rebecca at her father's shoe store,
Kit in her family home turned boarding house, Melody at her grandfather's
flower shop, and Julie at her mother's second-hand goods store. This participation in the family business does challenge the notion of girls' relega-
tion to domestic spheres and practices, but it also serves as a technique to
create characters who acquire money, which can be used for them to purchase new consumer goods. Furthermore, for the characters whose families
are struggling financially, these plots, contradicting the narratives of political action, rely on the American myth of social mobility that suggests economic oppression is temporary and easily overcome through hard work.

When Pleasant Rowland headed the company, she institutionalized the
lessons in consumerism by creating a game through which girl consumers
could learn to save for products. In 1996 she released the American Girl
Savings Game which was designed to "teach the values of hard work and
savings."[53] Available for free from the company, the Savings Game book-
let included quotations from mothers and daughters about how these
girls had saved money by working around the house, washing cars, and
baby-sitting. It suggested that girls find a "Savings Coach" who would
help guide them through the process and give them a sticker each time
they reached a fiscal goal. When a girl consumer completed a goal she
received one of twenty stickers and by the time she finished she would
have a sticker poster of all five American Girls that were in production at
the time and ostensibly enough money to buy one doll. In this way, the
Savings Game not only taught girls how to make and save money but also

how and where to spend it. Later this idea of savings was incorporated into the American Girl Library first through *MoneyMakers: Good Cents for Girls* and more recently in *A Smart Girl's Guide: Money: How to Make it, Save it, and Spend it,* although both of these books removed the focus on saving specifically for the company's own products.

CONSTRUCTIONS OF NORMATIVE FEMININITY IN THE BEFOREVER COLLECTION

During the collection's first ten to fifteen years, Pleasant Company concentrated its clothing and accessories on carefully researched furniture replicas and historically accurate clothing. With the acquisition of the company by Mattel, American Girl discontinued a great deal of antique replica furniture and accessory options from their offerings. Their public relations department attributes this change to "basic product lifecycle management" which includes the need to sell "what customers are asking for and buying" as well as the physical space limitations in the catalog and retail stores. These various constraints led the brand to stop production of a range of accessories that alluded to the characters' stories, the historically specific moments in which they lived, and their cultural heritage. Instead, it limited production of accessories to those that reflect a greater commitment to the trappings of normative femininity. Because the number of items in the collection has been reduced, and its total cost decreased from approximately $750 to $150, this change may have decreased a hyper-consumptive pressure girl consumers experienced to acquire a massive collection for each doll. Yet, it also leads to play scripted by the narrow collection of accessories that increasingly focuses on gendered objects that position the character within the private spheres of bedroom, beauty, and food culture.

Using Josefina's collection, for example, furniture and accouterments that were suggestive of a public life or which contained cultural references were eliminated between 2001 and 2012 so that only clothing, hair accessories, and bedroom furniture remain. Both Josefina's *Writing Desk and Stand* and her *Books and School Supplies* are discontinued accessories that brought Josefina out of the private culture of the bedroom and into the public life of the community. Tia Dolores brings these objects with her when she arrives at the Montoya farm. At first the family regards a woman involving herself in the family's business as inappropriate but they soon discover that her ideas and her business practices will benefit the family.

Josefina's books and school supplies which included a Spanish speller with English translations and a ledger with the Montoya's business and trade plans would have allowed consumers to play out the important moments in which Josefina learned to read and gained entrepreneurial skills. Also discontinued were Josefina's *Weaving Loom*, telescope, and piano that Tia Dolores brings all the way from Mexico City, all of which have cultural significance in her story or demonstrate her participation in a diverse range of activities. Finally, the now discontinued *Santa Fe Summer Set* included both Mexican and American flags. Despite the fact that an accessory featuring the two flags may signify a false ease between the two nations, it stills hold historical and cultural significance in Josefina's story which takes place in New Mexico.[54] While girls have reported that they do not often strictly reenact the narratives in their doll play, these discontinued items encouraged a scripted play that valued historical and cultural specificity which is no longer available in the current accessories' collections.

If the older larger collections were attentive to the passions and interests of characters and their inclusion in public life, today's collections highlight stereotypically feminine bedroom, food, and beauty culture. Each of the ten currently produced historical dolls has a bedroom set, clothing, a purse, and hair accessories. Most of the characters have toy food as well.[55] Bedroom culture, signified by the collection's bedroom furniture and bedroom accessories, has long been associated with girls and their containment as a tool of protection from the feared public sphere.[56] The food play contributes to the socialization of traditionally feminine activities such as food preparation and cooking, and the emphasis on clothing, hair, and accessories, such as purses, reinforces the mandate that femininity must be regulated and maintained through the consumption of fashion and beauty products. Though there are other accessories such as those that emphasize music, like Rebecca's phonograph and Maryellen's juke box, and those that assist girls in active play, like Kit's scooter, Samantha's bicycle, and Julie's newly released basketball hoop, most accessories that represent the girl protagonists' historical specificity and exemplify the character's passions and agency are no longer in production. With the exception of Kit's typewriter, there are not now, nor were there ever, accessories that alluded to the characters' social change activism; the accessories collections have not included protest signs, podiums, or eagle launches.

Given the smaller collections of each BeForever doll, consumers are invited to mix and match with accessories made for the contemporary Truly Me line. Truly Me paints a similar picture of girls as focused on fashion, hair, food, and bedrooms. Although at the time of this research, individuals could purchase clothing for volleyball, cheerleading, basketball, gymnastics, soccer, and tennis, the collection of sports accessories consisted only of items related to horseback riding and ice skating. The "hobbies" accessories collection included three items related to camping and one to gardening. None of these suggests a radical break from the stereotypical construction of femininity.

This generic femininity supports Molly Rosner's claim that the rebranding of the historical collection as BeForever in 2014 invites the consumer to attend not to historical specificity but to the universality of hegemonic femininity. She argues that the material objects in the collection encourage the consumer "to identify historical periods, not with important social, cultural or political events but with semiotic signifiers like hairstyles, clothing, and accessories associated with particular trends."[57] Concurring with this assessment, fashion historian Nancy Deihl, argues that while the clothing both pre- and post-rebranding is well-abstracted from actual historical styles, the increase in the use of "popsicle" colors for clothing and accessories in the new edition imbues it with a "presentist" rather than a historical bias.[58] Jo Paoletti, who has extensively researched the history of children's clothing, noted that the incorporation of highly saturated and pastel colors typically associated with contemporary girls allows the company to attend to history while still tempting consumers.[59] Further, the attention to universality is supported by the emphasis on generic or normative girlhood and the consistent themes of doll play scripted by current accessories.

Focus on fashion and hair is also supported by narrative attention to appearance and heterosexual couplings in the series books. Though the young protagonists in these stories rarely ever mention their own exterior presentation, their older sisters are often portrayed as being attentive to their outward physical appearance. Teens featured in stories throughout the BeForever collection, such as Josefina's sister Francisca in 1824, Molly's sister Jill in 1944, and Julie's sister Tracy in 1974, "suggest, no matter the time period or plot line, growing up means caring more about one's physical appearance."[60] This spotlight on older girls' appearance ties into the incorporation of heterosexual coupling in the books. As with beauty work, the work of romantic relationships is aspirational; the nine-year-old protagonists are not focused on boys but on adventure, friendship, and social change yet their older sisters (those of Molly, Maryellen, and Kaya) are coupling off or their uncles (those of Samantha, Marie-Grace, and Rebecca) are planning marriages to young women who the protagonists adore.

Molly's fourteen-year-old sister, Jill, for instance, is boy-obsessed and explicitly concerned with her appearance. Although Molly initially thinks, "If that's what happened to you when you got to be fourteen, she'd rather be nine forever," she, too, spends a lot of time at school daydreaming about her teacher's hair style and engagement ring. By the last book in the series Molly is mirroring her sister's behavior. Her desire to be grown-up and attractive becomes noticeable when Molly learns that her father will be returning home from his World War II post. Referring to Molly as "olly Molly," his nickname for her, he writes in his letter,

> I can tell from the pictures you sent that Ricky is probably a basketball star by now, and Brad isn't a baby anymore. And Jill! You look so grown-up and sophisticated in your prom dress! You've become a beauty just like your mother. And of course, I can't wait to see good old olly Molly and taste Mrs. Gilford's perfect pot roast.[61]

Molly, who becomes jealous that her father sounded proud of everyone but her, dreams of surprising him by starring in the tap dance show for war veterans so he can see how much she has grown, how her dance skills have improved and how she, like Jill, has become a beauty. For the audition Molly focuses on her appearance as much as her dance skills, believing that in order to get the part she must ditch her usual braided hair and wear it in curls instead. With the new hairdo, styled by Jill, Molly does get the role, but she experiences discomfort:

> Sleeping on pin curls was like sleeping on thorns. Molly tried putting her face in the pillow but then she couldn't breathe. She tried wadding up her pillow under her neck instead of her head but that made her neck hurt. The pins seemed to find a way to dig into her scalp no matter what she did.

Despite the pain and the "funny red wrinkles on her face" the next morning, she concludes, "it was all worth it because when Jill took the bobby pins out, Molly's hair was—NOT STRAIGHT...And at school, all the girls oohed and ahhed when she pushed back her hood on her jacket....[and] when Susan said, 'Gosh, Molly! You look like a movie star!'"[62] Though Molly ultimately learns that people, especially her father, will like her just as she is, readers learn that beauty play is integral to Molly's identity as a pre-teen girl and Jill's identity as a teen.

The uncle's fiancés, too, are described as aspirational not only because of their social, political, and cultural work but because of their beauty. Samantha's Uncle Gard marries Cornelia who is active in the women's suffrage movement but is first introduced as "pretty and dark haired." Madame Océane, who will marry Marie-Grace's Uncle Luc, is an opera singer who is painted in words as "slender" and "young," with "blue-green eyes the color of the ocean" and "fair skin and chestnut brown hair held back with a silver comb."[63] And Lily who will marry Rebecca's Uncle Max is a movie star who helps the protagonist take pride in her voice but the first thing Rebecca notices when she sees Lily is that she is "dainty" and has "the slimmest waist Rebecca had ever seen."[64] Although the protagonists of American Girl series are portrayed as active, engaged girls who do not spend a significant amount of time thinking about their appearance or about romantic relationships, beauty work and heterosexual romance is made aspirational through the portrayal of sisters and aunts.

Hair and fashion, then, are a site of importance in the series books as well as in retail stores' doll salons, the catalogs' fashion spreads, and the collections' play accessories, such as the Salon Chair or Julie's Vanity Set. Rather than producing material objects that represent the series' historical and culture specificity and narratives of resistance, American Girl relies on stereotypical tropes of femininity and doll play.

Mothers and Girls' Reception of Gender Representation in the BeForever Collection

Writing about the American Girl collection, Kim Chuppa-Cornell observes "Those who read the books first meet brave, smart, spunky, and adventurous girls, learning to conquer both everyday challenges (bullying) and potentially life-threatening situations as well (slavery). Those who meet the characters through the store, website, or catalog first will find pretty dolls with stylish clothes and accessories."[65] While I agree with Chuppa-Cornell's assessment of the contradictory nature of the books and doll/accessories, the girls I spoke with were at least familiar with, if not very knowledgeable about their dolls' backstories due to the wide availability of the series books and movies for many of the characters. Further, girls and their mothers appear to move seamlessly between their appreciation of the feisty girl narrative and the scripted feminine play.

Heather, a mother of two girls, says that the BeForever characters are "all kinds of brave and strong and just go for it when they see something that's wrong or when they want to make positive change...." She cites Samantha and Julie as examples of these positive characters. Samantha, she says, is "someone born into privilege who could have been very uppity, and snooty, and entitled" but is laudable because "she befriends Nellie, the servant girl who is of a different class than she is and she doesn't treat her like 'the help' when she very well could. She empowers her. She teaches her how to read. She helps her get out of the factory life and all that." Julie, she notes, is admirable because she encourages girls to "see that...the equal rights movement... was a real struggle and still is to some extent" and because "her whole storyline about helping the eagles is great because it's nice to fight for causes that you believe in and she's an activist that way." Other mothers, like Marcie, are less invested in the dolls' activism than they are in their pluckiness. She calls the characters' industrious spirit and sense of adventure "a confidence builder" and appreciates that the stories feature girls who "just go get it on their own." In addition, as discussed in Chapter 3, a great number of mothers are drawn to the brand because their political convictions direct them toward dolls that are invested in celebrating girlhood.

Still, these mothers also appreciate the more traditional feminine skills regarding care and social interactions they believe the brand teaches their daughters. It was not infrequent for mothers to describe and take pride in how their daughters put their dolls to bed. Libby, who applauded the way that the dolls' narratives represented girls who were able to problem solve independently, and is herself involved in progressive social change movements in her community, expresses this clearly when she notes of her two daughters, "The big thing in their world seemed to be making sure that these dolls had beds to sleep in. And they would make beds from nothing, from rags and pillowcases, make sure they were warm enough and cozy enough. So it was sort of a nurturing thing that they would always end up doing and I thought that was very sweet." (Fig. 4.3). Several of the mothers also mentioned their appreciation for the social skills girls encounter in the collection either through interacting with the doll who in some cases "becomes part of the family" or through the American Girl movies and books that explore friendship, jealousy, and team work.

Girls, too, are drawn to their protagonists' bravery and the way they can, as Octavia notes, "advocate for themselves and others." Nora shares her passion for the dolls' history and the way "they tell girls that you can make a difference in your community." She shares how Kit's story in which "she made a difference by writing an article in the newspaper making people view a different way of these people who are poor and don't have any homes" inspired her to write an article for her school newspaper

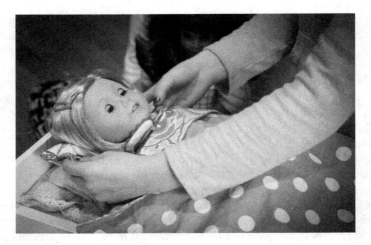

Fig. 4.3 Putting doll to bed

"about different people like blacks, lesbians, and gays to see that we're all the same people and that we don't dress a certain way to be different or anything. We're all the same person but just with a different liking or skin color, but we're all people." Alexis says she liked learning from Melody's story about "standing up for what's right, because she was in the Civil Rights movement" and Hannah explains that she likes to learn about "how girls didn't always have the rights that they do now." She says that when she reads the American Girl books she thinks, "Girls have the power to do whatever they want to do, and they can't let somebody stop them from doing it. So everybody should just be themselves and fight for what's right. Be your own person. Don't sit around and do nothing." Hannah, who has read the Addy and Melody series adds that the books have taught her that "girls in American history fought for their rights. And we can be strong and just fight for our rights and do what's best for us." Charlotte sums up, "I like American Girl dolls because they remind me of different kinds of stories that make me feel like we're powerful inside of our bodies."

It may be that the girls I interviewed simply answered the questions in a way that reflected what they believed a researcher would want to hear or that they were expressing honest feelings. Either way, when asked about their play experiences with the dolls, girls almost always talked about doing their dolls' hair, dressing their dolls, crafting clothing for their dolls, caring for "injured" dolls and putting their dolls to bed. Repeatedly girls identified bandages, slings, and the toy wheelchair as favorite or highly desired accessories. Girls who engage in imaginative play with their dolls typically do not base their play on the historical plots in the books but act out stories related to their own school, afterschool, or other contemporary experiences. Girls shared that, like themselves, their dolls sometimes went to karate classes, dance lessons, gymnastics team meets, Girl Scout meetings, shopping at the mall, school (where they sometimes ran for class president) or on nature walks through the park. Girls, then, easily articulate the narrative themes but either use the material objects to script play involving caregiving, hair styling, or fashion, or to reenact a familiar contemporary girlhood involving their own personal experiences.

American Girl claims that to construct an American identity it focuses on a girls' "drive to reach for her dreams despite great obstacles" and that "each girl is driven by hope and conviction that the world can be better—and that it's up to her (i.e. to each of us) to make it so."[66] What would girls' American Girl doll play look like if the accessories were true to this definition of American girlhood? American Girl doll play certainly is not currently emancipatory or counterhegemonic but would it be different if the accessories collection and retail experience reflected the fictional accounts of community, equality, justice and girls' public sphere work? Beyond Kit's typewriter and reporter set with a pretend camera, notebook, and pen, there is almost no material evidence of these values: Julie's collection has no eagle launching pad or a "How to Run for School President" set; Cécile has no podium to speak at, nor a guide on how to write a powerful poem or how to speak publicly; Rebecca has no soapbox, and Melody has no picket sign to boycott the store nor even tools to clean up her neighborhood park. Taking a look beyond the BeForever collection, the kind of activism and leadership displayed by the protagonists in the American Girl historical books is missing from the company's *Smart Girl's* advice book series. As of 2017, the series had books devoted to manners, relationships, and money management but where were the *Smart Girl's Guide to Leadership*, to *Giving Back to Your Community* or to *Using Your Voice for Change*? In the retail store, there was a salon for ear piercing and hairdos and a station to decorate a T-shirt but there was no letter writing station to communicate with elected officials, no area for a girl to get her picture taken on a soapbox or behind a podium, and no place for her to create her own newspaper.

Contradictions in Girlhood

Scholars have argued that the American Girl protagonists' activities reify a normative girlhood that is relegated to private domestic arenas and delivers conventional messages about girls' roles in American society. These critics claim that the books are filled with hegemonic ideas about how women should behave and that because many of the stories are situated in historical eras in which women lacked political, social and cultural agency they only offer a limited depiction of womanhood and girlhood.[67] Further, these critics express concern that a traditional conservative definition of femininity is naturalized by the BeForever mothers and daughters' engagement in the work of caring for the family and involvement in activities typically associated with girl culture, such as doll play and crafting.

While these narratives do feature domestic work, and girls are central players in the sustenance of their family lives, they also take their work outside of the home, often in spite of their mothers and the social institutions of their times. Work in the house is presented as valuable and significant and as only one aspect of a girl's labor. A femininity that is completely confined within the private sphere of the household is depicted as archaic and something against which to resist. Further, almost all of the BeForever characters make social contributions that are public and political and not just "faux empowerment" as at least one researcher has suggested.[68] These series profile girls who understand their location within a political and cultural system and often advocate against the injustices of these systems. Moreover, they frequently tell stories of girls with agentic voices who stand against oppression.

Susan Jevens of American Girl expounds on the role of activism in the BeForever series locating this narrative strand within the company's mission. She explains,

> Our mission is to empower girls and to give them a sense of their own ability and strength, and one way to do that is to depict other girls—girls whom they identify with and admire—standing up and speaking out for what they believe in....One of the best ways to do this is to tell stories that reflect the themes and situations people were faced with in the past, and to show how their actions and choices changed the world around them. Since our audience is girls, we show girls as the actors and agents of change. Our country was founded by people who did just that: took a situation that was unjust and intolerable, and changed it in an effort to make it better, just as our characters do. So it's fair to say that as a company, we do see this kind of activism or agency as a fundamental aspect of American identity. And we hope that by helping girls to understand that as Americans, they too have

this power to create change and improve their world, through our characters and stories we hope we are giving them the confidence to pursue their dreams, to be their best, and to do good in the world.[69]

The aplomb with which Jevens draws on the language of social movements demonstrates the way in which the agency of professionals, who were college-educated after the second (and sometimes third) wave feminist influence was present in American universities, interfaces with the capitalist imperative of the corporate structure. The tensions within these conflicting discourses of capitalism and social change are at the heart of the brands' contradictory embrace of femininity and feminism. American Girl represents not only the commodification of progressive political rhetoric but also a corporate attempt to negotiate feminism and capitalism.

The accounts of collectivist action are there to be read but they are not accompanied by any tools with which to perform them. There are nearly no accessories that reference public life or civic engagement and those that refer to historical or cultural specificity have been discontinued. Rather, BeForever accessories position girls within the bedroom, food, and beauty cultures to which they have long been confined. This is unlikely to change given that the company has announced that it is exploring several partnerships that "expand the brand into new segments of growth from fashion to wellness and health and beauty."[70] Since young people often use their engagement with media texts to aid in the construction of their life strategies, personal identities, and world views, these restrictive material constructions may impact their understanding of what it means to perform girlhood and American identity.

American Girl, then, is a girl power commodity. It is a product, of course, but with a meaningful counterhegemonic narrative. It is filled with the slippages of girl power commodity activism, of independent writers producing for a multinational corporation and of a collection produced for well-educated, wealthy, largely white mothers who turn to American Girl as a cultural intermediary positioned to protect their daughters from a girl-poisoning sexualizing culture. In every era, the American girlhood of BeForever characters is constructed as one that rebels against the domestic roles occupied by their mothers but also as immersed in traditionally feminine beauty and consumptive cultures. These narratives offer not only the embrace of a normative feminine appearance but also demonstrate various ways of engaging in political action in a way that challenges neoliberal discourse of strong private property rights and free markets. Rebecca rallies against the factory bosses and Julie against the construction industry. Both Kit and Melody ask for financial support for social change from the government. These girls are looking for strategic methods of change and are providing some roadmaps readers can follow as they think about the change needed in their own communities including lessons in how to be leaders, how to use their own voices for change, how to work collaboratively with others for common purposes, and how to think about oppression as having a structural, systemic foundation that requires structural, systemic change. This political work is elemental to the American Girls' identity building and citizenship; it codes the characters as the plucky, courageous girls that define the brand and as involved democratic participants. Yet the objects manufactured to support the play recast real American girls, the BeForever consumers, within the traditional spheres of normative femininity, in the bedroom and in front of the vanity. In American Girl, the cult of beauty is maintained and reinforced while a resistive feminist voice that participates in social change is promoted and presented as a model of ideal American girlhood.

NOTES

1. Jacqueline Dunbar Greene, *Changes for Rebecca* (Middleton, WI: American Girl Publishing, 2009), 5.
2. Nicole LeConte, "Not One That Looks Like My Daughter: How American Girl Makes History Hegemony" (Honors Thesis, Department of History, Connecticut College, 2011); Jennifer Miskec, "Meet Ivy and Bean, Queerly the Anti-American Girls," *Children's Literature Association Quarterly* 34 (2009), 157–171; Nancy Duffey Story, "Pleasant Company's American Girl Collection: The Corporate Construction of Girlhood" (PhD diss., University of Georgia, 2002).
3. Greene, *Changes for Rebecca*, 21–23.
4. Ibid., 32.
5. Ibid., 39.
6. Clara Adler is modeled after Clara Lemlich, a real union leader at the turn of the twentieth century.
7. Elizabeth Marshall, "Marketing American Girlhood," in *Rethinking Popular Culture and Media,* eds. Elizabeth Marshall and Özlem Sensoy (Milwaukee: Rethinking Schools, 2011), 133–134.
8. Julia Mickenberg and Philip Nel, "Radical Children's Literature Now!" *Children's Literature Association Quarterly* 36 (2011), 447.
9. Emilie Zaslow, *Feminism, Inc.: Coming of Age in Girl Power Media Culture* (New York: Palgrave Macmillan, 2009).

10. Sarah Projansky, "Mass Magazine Cover Girls: Some Reflections on Postfeminist Girls and Postfeminism's Daughters," in *Interrogating Postfeminism: Gender and the Politics of Popular Culture,* eds. Yvonne Tasker and Diane Negra (Durham, NC and London: Duke University Press, 2007), 66–68.

11. Sarah Banet-Weiser and Roopali Mukherjee, "Introduction: Commodity Activism in Neoliberal Times," in *Commodity Activism: Cultural Resistance in Neoliberal Times,* eds. Roopali Mukherjee and Sarah Banet-Weiser (New York: NYU Press, 2012), 13.

12. Sarah Banet-Weiser, "Free Self-Esteem Tools?: Brand Culture, Gender, and the Dove Real Beauty Campaign," in *Commodity Activism: Cultural Resistance in Neoliberal Times,* eds. Roopali Mukherjee and Sarah Banet-Weiser (New York: NYU Press, 2012), 52–53.

13. David Buckingham, *Children Talking Television* (London: the Falmer Press, 1993); Meredith Rogers Cherland, *Private Practices: Girls Reading Fiction and Constructing Identity* (London and Bristol, PA: Taylor and Francis, 1994); JoEllen Fisherkeller, *Growing Up with Television: Everyday Learning Among Young Adolescents* (Philadelphia: Temple University Press, 2002); Zaslow, *Feminism, Inc.*

14. Four of the girls—Cécile, Marie-Grace, Molly, and Samantha—have paid household staff (cooks, maids, etc.) and do not participate in much domestic labor.

15. Valerie Tripp, *Kit Learns a Lesson* (Middleton, WI: American Girl Publishing, 2000), 53.

16. Tripp, *The One and Only: A Maryellen Classic Volume 1* (Middleton, WI: American Girl Publishing, 2015), 23; Tripp told me that her own mother used to tell her five children the same thing about temporarily managing her own family.

17. Valerie Tripp, *Taking Off: A Maryellen Classic 2* (Middleton, WI: American Girl Publishing, 2015), 130–131.

18. Ibid., 131.

19. Sherrie Inness "'Anti-Barbies': The American Girls Collection and Political Ideologies," in *Delinquents and Debutantes: Twentieth-Century American Girls' Cultures,* ed. Sherrie A. Inness (New York: New York University Press, 1998), 178.

20. Joan Williams, *Unbending Gender: Why Family and Work Conflict and What to Do About It* (New York: Oxford University Press, 2000), 1.

21. In the case of Samantha, it is her grandmother who is the agent of socialization.

22. Denise Lewis Patrick, *Cécile's Gift* (Middleton, WI: American Girl Publishing, 2011), 23.

23. Greene, *Changes for Rebecca,* 49.

24. Susan Adler, *Meet Samantha* (Middleton, WI: American Girl Publishing, 1986/1998), 41.
25. Susan Adler, *Samantha Learns a Lesson* (Middleton, WI: American Girl Publishing, 1986/1998), 47.
26. Ibid., 51.
27. LeConte, "Not One That Looks Like My Daughter."
28. American Girl Catalog, Spring 1997.
29. Valerie Tripp, *Meet Felicity* (Middleton, WI: American Girl Publishing, 1991/2000), 5.
30. Ibid., 14.
31. Ibid., 34.
32. Thomas Frank, *The Conquest of Cool: Business Culture, Counterculture, and the Rise of Hip Consumerism* (Chicago: University of Chicago Press, 1997); Robert Goldman, Deborah Heath and Sharon L. Smith, "Commodity Feminism," *Critical Studies in Mass Communication* 8, no. 3 (1991): 333–351; Dick Hebdige, *Subculture: The Meaning of Style* (New York: Routledge, 1979); Luc Boltanski and Eve Chiapello, *The New Spirit of Capitalism* (New York: Verso, 2005).
33. Judith Taylor, Josée Johnston, and Krista Whitehead, "A Corporation in Feminist Clothing? Young Women Discuss the Dove 'Real Beauty' Campaign," *Critical Sociology* 42, no. 1 (2016): 123–144.
34. Valerie Tripp, *Meet Kit* (Middleton, WI: American Girl Publishing, 2000), 4.
35. Ibid., 4.
36. Valerie Tripp, *Changes for Kit* (Middleton, WI: American Girl Publishing, 2000), 24.
37. Ibid., 11–12.
38. Ibid., 14.
39. Pat Scales, *A Teacher's Guide to Read All About It: A Kit Classic* (Middleton, WI: American Girl, 2014), http://www.americangirlpublishing.com/marketing/teachers-guides/.
40. Denise Lewis Patrick, *No Ordinary Sound: A Melody Classic Volume 1* (Middleton, WI: American Girl Publishing, 2016), 61.
41. Ibid., 62.
42. Pat Scales, *A Teacher's Guide to No Ordinary Sound: A Melody Classic* (Middleton, WI: American Girl, 2016), http://www.americangirlpublishing.com/marketing/teachers-guides/.
43. Megan McDonald, *Meet Julie* (Middleton, WI: American Girl Publishing, 2007), 45.
44. Megan McDonald, *Changes for Julie* (Middleton, WI: American Girl Publishing, 2007), 35–36.
45. McDonald, *Meet Julie*, 65.

46. Pat Scales. *A Teacher's Guide to The Big Break: A Julie Classic* (Middleton, WI: American Girl, 2014), http://www.americangirlpublishing.com/marketing/teachers-guides/.

47. Angharad Valdivia, "Living in a Hybrid Material World: Girls, Ethnicity and Mediated Doll Products," *Girlhood Studies* 2 (2009), 73–93; Marshall, "Marketing American Girlhood."

48. Banet-Weiser and Mukherjee, "Introduction," 14.

49. Connie Porter, *Addy's Surprise* (Middleton, WI: American Girl Publishing, 1993; reprint, Middleton, WI: American Girl Publishing, 2000), 13.

50. Sonja Zepeda Pérez, "Mis(s)Education: Narrative Construction and Closure in American Girl," (PhD diss., University of Arizona, 2015), 102.

51. Pérez provides the example from Valerie Tripp, *Felicity's Surprise* (Middleton, WI: American Girl Publishing, 1991; reprint, Middleton, WI: American Girl Publishing, 2000), 52.

52. Pérez provides the example from Valerie Tripp, *Josefina's Surprise* (Middleton, WI: American Girl Publishing, 1997; reprint Middleton, WI: American Girl Publishing, 2000), 48.

53. "Pleasant Learns a Lesson," *Wisconsin State Journal*, December 1, 1996, A7.

54. The positioning of Josefina's story in pre-United States New Mexico is discussed further in Chapter 6.

55. Americangirl.com as of March 2016.

56. Angela McRobbie with Jenny Garber, "Girls and Subcultures," in *Feminism and Youth Culture: From 'Jackie' to 'Just Seventeen,'* ed. Angela McRobbie (Boston: Unwin Hyman, 1978), 1–15.

57. Molly Rosner, "The American Girl Company and the Uses of Nostalgia in Children's Consumer Culture," *Jeunesse: Young People, Texts, Cultures* 6, no. 2 (2014): 41.

58. Nancy Deihl (Director of Costume Studies MA Program, NYU,) interview by author, October 17, 2016.

59. Ibid.; Jo Paoletti, (Professor, American Studies, UMD) interview by author, October 24, 2016.

60. Kim Chuppa-Cornell, "When Fact Is Stranger than Fiction: Hair in American Girl Stories and Dolls," *The Lion and the Unicorn* 37, no. 2 (2013): 110.

61. Valerie Tripp, *Changes for Molly* (Middleton, WI: American Girl Publishing, 1986/2000), 9.

62. Ibid., 34–37.

63. Sarah Buckey, *Meet Marie-Grace* (Middleton, WI: American Girl Publishing, 2011), 18.

64. Jacqueline Dembar Green, *Rebecca and the Movies* (Middleton, WI: American Girl Publishing, 2009), 21.

65. Kim Chuppa-Cornell, "When Fact Is Stranger than Fiction."
66. Susan Jevens (Associate Manager, Public Relations, American Girl,) e-mail message to author, March 10, 2017.
67. Inness, "Anti-Barbies"; Lisa Mae Schlosser, "'Second Only to Barbie': Identity, Fiction, and Non-Fiction in the American Girl Collection," *MP: An Online Feminist Journal* 1, no. 4 (May 20, 2006); Sarah Eisenstein Stumbar and Zillah Eisenstein, "Girlhood Pastimes: American Girls and The Rest of Us," in *Growing Up Girls: Popular Culture and the Construction of Identity*, eds. Sharon R. Mazzarella, and Norma Odom Pecora (New York: Peter Lang, 1999), 87–96; Story, "Pleasant Company's American Girl Collection."
68. Marshall, "Marketing American Girlhood," 135.
69. Jevens, e-mail message to author.
70. Chris Sinclair, "Mattel Inc. Analyst Day—Final," (speech), November 3, 2016. http://files.shareholder.com; Martin Gilkes, "Mattel Inc. Earnings Call—Final," (speech), October 19, 2015, http://files.shareholder.com.

CHAPTER 5

From "This Where Freedom Supposed to Be At" to "She Knew She Would Never Stop Speaking Out for What Was Right": Racial Logics and African American Identity in American Girl

In 1993, Pleasant Company released Addy Walker, who wore a pink cotton dress and a cowrie shell around her neck. Addy was the company's first African American doll. Rowland told the press that she had envisioned Addy from the brand's inception and that she was no longer listening to market analysts who told her that an African American doll at this price point would not sell. The rise of the black middle class and the company's strong record had given her the leverage to take what the market considered to be a risk.[1] Rowland believed that Addy represented not only expansion into a new market but also a shift in how black dolls would be incorporated into white families; she remembers feeling that "… if I got hit by a car tomorrow, I could die knowing that we made toy history. We made a black doll the object of status and desire for white children."[2] She was thrilled, she said, to create a black doll that would be loved by white and black girls alike (Fig. 5.1).[3]

To bring Addy to market—to make sure that she was seen and purchased by African American families—the company advanced new marketing techniques including attending black expos and black Family Reunions organized by the National Council of Negro Women, organizing book donation programs with Delta Sigma Theta, the largest African American sorority in the country, and sending a promotional video out to African American families. If Addy's roll-out marked new territory for the

© The Author(s) 2017
E. Zaslow, *Playing with America's Doll*,
DOI 10.1057/978-1-137-56649-2_5

Fig. 5.1   Addy Walker doll

brand, so did her conception. To make sure that the company's first doll of color was well-received and "authentic," Pleasant Company assembled an advisory board of African American historians, psychologists, and educators headed up by Dr. Wilma King, author of a book on childhood in slavery.[4] Rowland told a reporter, "This advisory board recommended unanimously and in no uncertain terms that we must deal with the issue of slavery—that it was the seminal issue of black history in this country, and without understanding it, one cannot understand the significance of the civil rights movement in America and the issue of race that divides the country today."[5] Elaborating, Susan Jevens, an Associate Manager of Public Relations at American Girl explains that the advisory board was certain that Addy's "story *must* start in slavery—that anything else would be an abdication of our responsibility to tell not just the real history of African Americans, but the real story of *America itself.*"

While the advisory board may have been certain about its choice of the historical moment around which Addy's story would revolve, parents and cultural leaders in the African American community were divided in their response to Addy's status as an escaped slave. Children's author, Eloise Greenfield, whose work focuses on African American experiences, told the *Washington Post* that Addy's story did not fit with those of the other dolls; "How can you compare the horror of slavery with Kirsten's mother having a baby?" she pondered.[6] Notes another writer, "Other American Girls struggle, but Addy's story is distinctly more traumatic."[7] Further, Greenfield and others argued that focusing on slavery rather than a more hopeful period, such as the Harlem Renaissance, was stereotypical and, as the only African American doll in the collection, reduced the experiences of black Americans to oppression and pain rather than other more joyful experiences such as community building and artistic collaboration.[8] Writing in the *Paris Review*, African American author Brit Bennet reflects, "If you were a white girl who wanted a historical doll who looked like you, you could imagine yourself in Samantha's Victorian home or with Kirsten, weathering life on the prairie. If you were a black girl, you could only picture yourself as a runaway slave....She is a toy steeped in tragedy, and who is offered tragedy during play?"[9] Even contemporary parents who have discovered Addy more recently may be dismayed about the general tenor of her story. In 2012, blogger Jennae Petersen wrote a post entitled, "American Girl, Your Slave Doll is a Big, Fat Fail." Admitting that she had not read the story, Petersen admonished that a slave doll is offensive and "essentially forcing a heavy conversation with a child about slavery because [American Girl was] too lazy and culturally blind to come up with a less stereotypical depiction of African Americans in history."[10]

On the other end of the argument, Connie Porter, who authored the Addy series, has responded, "Some people don't want to see a character in slavery—that's ridiculous. You can run the risk of being so politically correct that you can lose whole periods of history."[11] She also points out the contradiction that Felicity's family owned slaves and that no one ever challenged *that* story. Nor did there seem to be any critique of the fact that Pleasant Company "had an opportunity in the Felicity books to talk about the issue [of slavery] before Addy came out and they didn't take it."[12] Although she signed on to the project after it was determined by the advisory board that Addy would be born into slavery, Porter remembers learning that the board had explored other time periods but that "slavery swept up millions of people" and that the transition from being an enslaved people to a free people was a story that needed to be told.[13] Adult women who reflect upon their Addy dolls often say that Addy was an important doll for them. In response to Petersen's negative reaction to Addy, one blog follower replied,

I had an Addy doll as a child and ALL of her books and other accessories. She was my favorite. I loved that she had skin and hair like mine and her books were so interesting to me as a child. I grew up in a home where my family was very honest about prejudice and racism I would face outside of my home and Addy served as a great tool for me to learn about it...I don't think it's ever too early for children to learn this part of American history.

Another respondent to this blogger wrote,

I'm a woman who's half black & I grew up with an Addy doll & love her dearly (she is still displayed on my doll shelf 20 yrs later). I never once saw her as an insult. I saw her as being a symbol of STRENGTH (she doesn't let anything stop her from escaping to freedom), LOVE (Addy's family & her love for them is everything important to her & is her strength) & HOPE (she never loses hope of reuniting with her family).[14]

Addy's story was generally well-received and garnered support and recognition from the National Council of Negro Women as well the African American organizations through which she was marketed.[15]

But the core of Addy's story was not the only debate surrounding the doll. The author and advisory board discussed whether they should include historically accurate racist epithets in a children's book, as well as other specific controversial plot details.[16] For example, they discussed the pragmatic reasons Addy would be taken with her mother when she escaped the plantation while her baby sister, Esther, might have been left behind. Based on the recommendation of an advisory board historian, it was decided that Esther, as a baby, would have been financially worth very little in the slave trade so it was likely that she would be relatively safe on the plantation with her elderly relatives. In addition, a baby's inability to control its crying or volume would have been too great a liability. But Addy's parents would have felt a sense of urgency to get Addy to safety as she was nearing puberty and would be in increasing danger of being raped and being sold. The board and author also discussed whether the conductor on a streetcar would have physically assaulted Addy or not.[17] In the end, they decided that it was more likely that the conductor would have pushed a grown man than a child.[18] This team of writers, historians, and corporate managers also debated the doll's face mold, skin tone, accessories, and hair texture. According to board member Cheryl Chisolm, the inclusion of the doll's cowrie shell, which represented West African heritage, was crucial to demonstrating Addy's resilience. Further, hair texture was a significant element because it embodied a discrepancy between the desire for historical accuracy and for profit; authenticity demanded textured, natural hair, while the company's market mandate sought silky hair that was easily brushed, easily styled, and easily maintained. The team ultimately settled on a "hair type that was neither superkinky nor bone straight."[19]

Addy's storyline, accessories, and hair were carefully considered, but her illustrations were steeped in conflict. At least four people were hired to illustrate her initial set of books although only three were ever published by American Girl. Charles Lilly, who in 1991 illustrated *Escape from Slavery*, was the first illustrator hired to create Addy's print image.[20] After he withdrew from the project due to ideological differences, Melodye Rosales illustrated the first three books in Addy's series. She has told journalists that her association with Pleasant Company was fraught from her first meeting. Having been referred to the company by a friend who worked there, Rosales arrived at their Middleton, Wisconsin, headquarters to discover the company's workforce was almost entirely white, reflective of the local population, but not reflective of the diverse girlhood the company was seeking to represent.[21] Things only got worse when differences arose over the composition of the illustrations; they might be called creative differences, but they were very much political differences. Rosales claimed that Rowland "wanted smiling slaves" but that her own vision was to reflect the experiences of newly freed slaves who were "hungry and half-starved."[22] The dispute escalated over an illustration that depicted Addy's experience meeting newly freed families at a Philadelphia pier. The text reads that "Addy saw a thin woman who held a bundle in her arms. [She] heard a sharp cry....Quickly Addy pulled her shawl from around her shoulders and handed it to the woman who thanked her and wrapped the shawl around her baby." When Addy offers to carry the baby, the woman smiles "weakly" and when the baby grabs at Addy's cowrie shell the "baby's mother smiled."[23] Rosales says that she was instructed to make her illustration of the woman's smile bigger but she wanted to depict the painful moment the woman would have been experiencing after her harrowing journey.

In another instance, there was a debate over characters' skin tones because Rosales wanted to illustrate Addy's teacher and her wealthy, free born classmate, Harriet, with lighter skin in order to depict colorism within the African American community.[24] The author and editor, however, wanted to make the differences among the characters be based on social class rather than based on color because racism within the black community is so divisive and they did not want to exploit these tensions, nor address issues that might be too complex for young readers.[25] In the end, Rosales' contract was terminated and a new illustrator, Bradford Brown, was hired to finish the collection. Later the entire series was re-illustrated by Dahl Taylor.

This story serves as a point of entry into the discussion of the tensions, conflicts, and challenges of representing diverse American experiences: Which stories are told? By whom are they told? And with what intention? How are racial and ethnic identities represented by American Girl in narrative and material form? At what point do the market interests of American Girl—to make sure their dolls are purchased and loved by children and their parents—override the drive for historical accuracy and diversity? How does the representation of race become complicated by authorial vision that misaligns with corporate vision? This chapter and the next address these questions; the current chapter focuses on the company's material representation of race and ethnicity in the body of the dolls as well as the specific narrative representations of African American experiences in American Girl's history. Chapter 6 explores the narrative representation of race, ethnicity, immigration, and American experience in the stories of Native American, Latino, and immigrant girls.

REPRESENTING RACE

Situating analysis of the American Girl doll body and narratives within research on racial logics, racist ideologies, and representation leads to a more robust understanding of the ideological significance of the brand. American Girl obviously does not construct these ideologies in isolation; still, the brand's narrative and material articulations contribute to girl consumers' understandings of a particular racial hierarchy and view of ethnic and racial identities.

Ideology must be understood as a means through which we come to construct our social world and relations of power within the world. Dominant ideologies work best when they appear to be common sense and not the construction of a world view. Media, like the American Girl series books and dolls, add to the construction of that common sense; they "construct for us a definition of what *race* is, what meaning the imagery of race carries, and what the 'problem of race' is understood to be."[26] In other words, the American Girl stories participate in shaping readers' perceptions of race, racism, and the experiences of people of color in the United States. Indeed, American Girl as a company is aware of this role it plays in shaping girls' understanding of race in the United States; in discussing the importance of depicting institutionalized racism in the story of the brand's first African American doll, Jevens explains, "We viewed that as our responsibility in helping young readers understand not only that era of history but many aspects of our country today."

Hegemonic ideologies about racial identities are not static; rather they are historically situated, impacted by oppositional discourse, both complex and "messy."[27] During the two and a half decades in which American Girl has been producing stories about girls of color, the most prominent contemporary racial discourses have been multiculturalism and colorblindness, both of which emphasize recognition of difference without the support of a social change project to end injustice.[28] In the 1980s and 1990s, multiculturalism was an amorphous term that suggested society was a better place when it embraced and celebrated its many cultures. Resisting the conservative suggestion that race was no longer relevant because we were living in a post-racist era, multiculturalism suggested that race was everywhere and that race mattered. Multiculturalism resisted whiteness as a universal norm and called for a broad understanding of cultural specificity and social impact. At the same time, the concept was filled with contradiction; multiculturalism highlighted culture (and sometimes race) while downplaying "the inheritance and ongoing presence of histories of oppression" and racism.[29] In this way, American Girl could be praised for embracing a multicultural girlhood as it sold the red "Chinese-style dress in medallion brocade and gold piping with mandarin collar," the Chinese New Year Celebration gong, mallet, and firecrackers, the African Dance Outfit of Today with a red, black, and green Kente cloth skirt, the green Irish Dance Costume with Celtic designs and accompanying strawberry-blonde wig, and the Hanukkah accoutrements including a menorah, Star of David necklace, and a blue-and-white holiday outfit. At the same time, this embrace of aesthetic difference had the potential to stereotype cultural groups, each of which were given one or two token outfits or accessories. Furthermore, this attention to stylistic culture was generally not accompanied by a narrative that addressed the institutionalized power relations that played out in economic, political, policy, and social relations that were also defining for girls in these cultures. As will be reviewed below, the historical collection has been inconsistent in this manner; in the stories about African American girlhood, institutionalized oppression has been central to the narrative but in the stories about Native American, Latino, and Jewish girls, there is little to no storyline surrounding discrimination or inequality. When the emphasis on multiculturalism began to wane in the early 2000s, and Mattel took over the business, the production of most of these stylistic outfits and accessories was discontinued.

As the new millennium approached, multiculturalism as the framework for discourse about race was replaced by the ideology of colorblindness. Fueled by the fiction that we are living in a society that is post-racist, colorblindness proposes individuals should also be post-racial or think-ing beyond race. Post-racial discourse argues that racial equality is now institutionalized, possible, and waiting for self-directed, go-getting indi-viduals to embrace the opportunities available to them. Catherine Squires suggests that these "neoliberal ideologies of market individualism" brush institutional racism under the rug and perpetuate the notion that the only thing standing between people of color and the end of social and eco-nomic inequality is hard work and healthy decision making by individu-als.[30] Colorblindness attributes the blame for continued racial inequality to African Americans and other people of color claiming that they are stuck in the past, filled with complaints, and not working hard enough to take advantage of all the opportunities they have now been given.[31] Using language that criticizes the "morality, values, and work ethic" of people of color, this discourse supports and perpetuates racial injustice.[32] Power and privilege become insignificant to understanding racism when the discourse argues that merit and industriousness are rewarded equally for all people.

In addition, colorblindness can make race appear malleable so that it is imagined as an accessory that can, at any time, be added or sub-tracted from one's identity depending on its immediate use value. This post-racial colorblind logic suggests a choice; one can embrace a racial or ethnic image that is market-appealing or tuck it away when it is no longer advantageous, identify or not with his/her race when and if s/he wants, and consume "cultural products that reflect the customs or tastes of racial Others" when and if s/he finds them appealing.[33] In colorblind discourse, focus on race appears to be an option for people of color rather than being an identity that due to historical, social, political, and economic structures shapes their experiences.

This chapter and the next explore how these racial discourses are always at play when girls are at play. These discourses shape the ways in which doll stories and doll bodies are encoded and decoded and help us to situate the complicated analyses of race, narrative, and doll play in the American Girl universe. Representing race in a mass-produced series book and doll is not simple and the aim of this book is not to condemn American Girl but to explore how it has approached this bumpy terrain. Some have argued that the brand is capitalizing on multiculturalism, exploiting "the racial and ethnic identity crisis" of a society that is coming to terms with de-centering whiteness.[34] Others have claimed that to suit its business interests, American Girl "produces and reinforces perceptions that US American history is devoid of race, class, and gender hierarchies [and]... devoid of conflict and inequality."[35] My own analysis demonstrates that these thoughtful critics are simplifying the complex and inconsistent racial logic produced by American Girl. Indeed, American Girl has a capitalist imperative, and when juggling the various interests of the company and various discourses about race, the financial bottom-line is always the ball that will be caught before it falls. But American Girl is not *just* capitalizing on difference. It is dealing with some difficult questions: How does a company represent race or ethnicity without reducing it to semiotic markers? Must stories that feature girls of color address racial oppression? How does a company represent race at a time when it is now common for "proponents of colorblindness" to consider racial categories, race awareness, and the suggestion "that race matters in human interaction" to be distasteful and itself racist?[36]

The moniker American Girl for these dolls with varied stories, ethnic origins, races, and subject positions suggests both an essential American identity and also an expansive, inclusive one. American Girl constructs an "imagined community" in which girls from many different time periods and backgrounds share an identity and values but in which difference, power, and privilege also exist and shape experience.[37] In certain instances, the material representations of race and ethnicity are presented as fluid and flexibly ambiguous, while in other cases they are embraced as culturally and historically specific; race and ethnicity are imagined, at times, as an aesthetic marker and at other times as a location around which structural inequality and cultural identity is built. African American experience is portrayed as located within a society that has institutionalized racism, while Native American and Latino experiences are depicted as existing outside of racial conflict and Asian American experience is almost completely non-existent.

RACIALIZED DOLLS

Analyses of the BeForever and Truly Me collections yield very different definitions and imageries of race. In the contemporary collection, void of narratives as well as clothing and other material objects that can be used to historically, culturally, and racially situate characters, the doll body becomes the sole marker of racial identity. American Girl dolls are not dye dipped. In other words, the dolls of color are not simply white dolls with European features that have been dyed with different skin colors. Instead, they are produced with varied skin tones, face molds, eye colors, and hair textures. In an attempt to create a wider market for dolls by featuring racial ambiguity, the company uses skin tone rather than racial categories to identify its contemporary dolls.[38] Rather than labels such as Asian American, Latino American, African American, or European American, consumers are guided to use skin tone—dark, medium, or "fair"—to identify their doll choice.[39] Given the decision to avoid racial nomenclature for dolls without accompanying narratives, race gets reduced to skin color, eye color, hair texture, and face mold.[40]

All of the doll body shapes are identical, but there are five different face molds currently in circulation and two that are out of production. Fans usually name these molds after the first character to use them, even when they are used in the design of several others.[41] The most commonly used is the Classic mold, first used in Kirsten, Molly, and Samantha. As Rebecca West has pointed out, use of the term "classic," (and I will add the term "fair") suggests that whiteness and European American features are positioned, by fans, not only as original but also as the standard against which all others are measured.[42] Here I offer detail to demonstrate that American Girl is producing a variety of face shapes in part to make attempts at racial and ethnic representation that extends beyond skin color. In the order that they were created, the molds include the following:

1. The Classic mold, created in 1986, was the first face mold and has been used on over sixty dolls in the last thirty years. Its European American features include a thin upturned nose, thin lips, and a rounded chin.
2. The Addy or African American face mold has a slightly wider nose, larger mouth, and chubbier cheeks than the Classic mold. Finally, she has a slight gap between her teeth, which was recommended by an Addy advisory board member who called the gap "a fairly common

physical trait among black people."[43] This mold has been used only nine times and has never been paired with a light skin tone.

3. The Asian mold with eye sockets that tilt slightly upward at the outer edge, and a wider nose than the Classic mold, was first released in 1995 for a Just Like You Doll, and used only once and then taken out of production in 2011.

4. The Josefina mold has an upturned nose that is longer and slightly wider, lips that are fuller, eyes that are more oval, and a chin that is longer and sharper than the Classic mold. This mold has been used for thirteen dolls including Latina and European American dolls.

5. The Kaya mold was designed specifically for Kaya and until 2017 was only used for her. Kaya was the only doll made with no teeth showing because, for the Nez Perce tribe, of which she is a member, bared teeth are a sign of aggression. This face mold is similar to Josefina's mold but with a slightly rounder face, broader nose and a small dimple in her chin. In 2017, American Girl used the Kaya mold for their first male doll, Logan.

6. The Jess mold, used for seven dolls including two biracial dolls, each with one Asian American parent, has a less pointy and less upturned nose and a shorter, slightly rounder face than the Classic mold. For Ivy, and again in 2015 for a Truly Me doll, this mold was altered slightly with a small detail on the outer edge of the eyelid to suggest an epicanthic fold.

7. The Sonali mold has been used for seven dolls in total, including her namesake, South Asian American Sonali, as well as African Americans Cécile, Melody, and 2017 Girl of the Year, Gabriela. This mold has a nose width between that of the Classic and that of the Addy mold, as well as a slightly wider smile than the Classic.

8. The Marie-Grace mold is similar to the Josefina mold but has a more narrow, rounded jaw line and slightly thinner lips. Her eyes are somewhat narrower than the Classic mold. This mold has only been used for the Marie-Grace doll.[44]

American Girl prides itself on what it identifies as "one of the most inclusive and diverse selections of dolls today."[45] In 2017, of all the dolls with a story (the historical dolls and the Girl of Today dolls), five dolls of color and six white dolls with stories are in production. Since the start of the brand, however, there have been four African American characters (Addy, Cécile, Melody, and Gabriela), two Latino characters

(Josefina and Marisol), one Native American character (Kaya), one South Asian character (Chrissa's friend, Sonali), one Chinese American character (Julie's friend, Ivy), two biracial Girl of the Year dolls including one Asian-Scottish-Irish-American character (Jess) and one Japanese-Hawaiian-French-German character (Kanani), and twenty-five dolls of specified or unspecified European American descent.

To an extent, these five variations in hair texture, three skin colors, twelve eye colors, and eight differing shapes of features lead to a non-essentialist and diverse production of racial identity markers. Skin tone and face mold combinations yield variations in racial imagery and somewhat in ethnic imagery. For example, the Addy mold has been used with dark and medium skin tones as well as with straight, curly, and textured hair types and three different eye colors, which suggests a rejection of universal blackness and an embrace of intra-racial diversity. Rebecca, a Jewish doll, shares a face mold with Josefina, a Mexican American doll but not with 2001 Girl of the Year doll, Lindsey, who also had Jewish ancestry. When this mold is used for Josefina, it is paired with medium skin, dark brown hair with auburn highlights, and dark brown eyes. For Rebecca, the mold is matched with light skin, hazel eyes and curly honey-brown hair. This same face mold has also been used to represent Nellie O'Malley, whose name suggests she is Irish. In Nellie's case the mold is produced with light skin, strawberry blonde hair, and blue eyes. There certainly may be economic motivations to using the face molds for more than one ethnicity but this practice also has a cultural implication. Using the same face mold for all three of the characters allows American Girl to avoid using stereotypical facial markers that would essentialize or potentially create caricatures of the token Eastern European Jewish, Mexican American, and Irish American characters.

At the same time, balancing its interest in non-essentialism, inclusivity, and profitability, American Girl undergirds the dolls' imagery with a colorblind discourse. In the current Truly Me collection, no clothes or accessories are culturally or racially specific. This erasure of culture creates a silence around race, ethnicity, and racism. Considering the representation of Asian Americans in the American Girl collection offers an example of how the company uses non-specific racial and ethnic markers to create the sense of race and ethnicity as a commodity that can be called upon when and how it serves the financial interests of the company. In 1995, American Girl released Just Like You #4 with what is known as the Asian face mold and a golden skin tone. At that time, she was the only identifiable Asian American doll. By the time Julie's friend, Chinese American Ivy Ling, was added to the collection in 2007, the Just Like You doll was no longer identified as Asian and her skin tone had been changed to fair.[46] The Just Like You doll was ultimately discontinued in 2011 and Ivy was discontinued in 2014 with all of the other best friends of the historical dolls. Ivy's retirement was met by fans and customers with sadness and anger. Olivia Oguma, co-founder of the Broadway Diversity Project, tweeted about Ivy's retirement, "We should not underestimate the power of seeing ourselves represented." Developing this, she added, "It was bad enough that she was just a 'friend' doll, a la Asian sidekick which is a role we have been boxed into in mainstream media time and time again. But, now to discontinue her, it sends the completely wrong message and is a slap in the face to our community."[47] Also disappointed in the decision to drop Ivy was *Forbes* contributor, Diane Clehane, and her daughter who she had adopted from China. When Ivy Ling was retired, an American Girl spokesperson told Clehane that the Truly Me dolls currently included "three different Asian American choices," but when the mother and daughter visited a retail store an employee told them, "We don't think of these dolls as having any particular race." The duo perused the Truly Me dolls and although they saw dolls with varied skin tones, hair styles, and face molds, they saw no dolls which could be definitively identified as Asian.[48] No dolls were labeled Asian, sold with clothing or accessories that had relevancy to any Asian culture, and all light skinned dolls had non-specific racial features that could or could not be understood by consumers as Asian. This ambiguity allows the company to sell the dolls as any number of (multi-) racial varieties, claiming inclusion and diversity, although clearly customers often reject this positioning. In my interviews, Karen, the adoptive mother of a Chinese daughter, Nora, who loves American Girl, elaborated on the absence of Asians in the collection; "There was no Just Like You [for Nora]. And there was No Girl of The Year like you. And they were all white and the biracial ones don't count. It doesn't count. So, again, you're left being the leftover. You're the outsider [in society] anyway and now you're still the outsider in this place that you love passionately."

The Truly Me collection may appear inclusive when one looks at the website or catalog due to the integration of all the dolls into one pictorial spread which incorporates dolls with varied skin tones, face molds, and hair styles. During our interview Jessica first remarked, "I wish that they had more diversity" but then looking through the catalog during our interview she adds, "I guess looking at them, altogether, it is a lot." But Jessica's first inclination was right; the Truly Me collection currently has only three dolls with dark skin tone, eight dolls with medium skin tone, and twenty-eight dolls labeled fair. In this way, membership in the American Girl community is not guaranteed.

Additionally, although the racial identities of these dolls may be non-essentialist, they are not completely flexible. Despite popular belief, American Girl dolls are not customizable.[49] If the hair, skin, and eye combination that you desire does not exist, American Girl will not create it for you. Therefore, due to the limited diversity in the production of dolls that represent girls of color, this can ultimately produce an essentializing racial identity and tokenization or the absence of identities all together. When one blogger, writing in 2014 for the *Cocoa Mama* blog, shared her frustration and sadness over the fact that the Truly Me doll she ordered online did not have hair like her daughter's, she explained, "I expected dark skin, dark brown eyes, and 'textured' hair. This doll was supposed to be one that looked like my daughter, an 'American girl.' I thought I was getting a somewhat close approximation."[50] When the mother took the doll to the store to see if she could be replaced for a doll with textured hair she discovered that she would either have to settle for a doll with "bone straight…silky curly, or textured curly hair" or she would have to select Addy who was the only doll with textured hair that matched her daughter's. She concluded, with frustration, "If you want kinky hair, you have to buy the slave."[51] Jessica, who identifies as Afro-Latina describes her own experience with her eight-year-old daughter, Riley, who wanted a doll with straight hair.

> For $100 and the fact that it's American Girl, I think initially she should at least have the ones that represent and look more like her, because so many of the images that we see in media and for girls are about this ideal look that isn't what she looks like. So, I just wanted her to get a doll that embraces that. She was happy with the doll she got, but she said it didn't look like her. It really didn't. That's another thing because there wasn't really a doll her shade of brown with straight hair. So, it was either a much fairer doll that would probably not be considered a black doll at all or the darker one that had the straight hair or the one that had the curly hair. So it wasn't truly her but it was closer than the blonde hair and blue eyes.

When the brand attributes the name "Just Like You" or "Truly Me" to a collection parents expect to find something that resembles their child. For mothers of color, this is often difficult given the limited offerings of dolls of color.

Those whose stories are not told in the American Girl series, or whose faces are not represented on the American Girl dolls, either do not participate or, like Nora, Octavia, and Alexie, have to find another route in. Though Nora continues to hold out hope for a Chinese American Girl of the Year doll, she was drawn to her Kit and Molly dolls due to their historical time periods. She had been given a second hand "Asian mold" doll that she took because "it was close" to how she looked, but that doll without a story had less meaning to Nora who is an avid reader and budding historian. When she was a little older, she says, she looked at her collection and "realized all my dolls were white." She wanted her dolls to be more reflective of her own community and friendship group that was multiracial. Her mother elaborates, "She knew that this combo was wrong. I mean, that was an honest answer. She knew that this was not how we live." Nora opted to buy an Addy doll at her next birthday to create a collection that better reflected her circle of friends even though she still was unable to find one that she felt was self-representative. Twins Octavia and Alexie, who identify as multiracial black, Asian, and Irish, were also initially interested in buying a Truly Me doll that represented them, but their mother, Kimberly, directed them toward the dolls with stories. Kimberly says, "When we looked at the catalog, and looked at the skin tone and the hair, there was not one that was going to look like them and I didn't want them thinking that, 'I'm not good enough to have a doll' so it was either, 'It is going to look like you,' or, 'You're just going to get some things totally separate.' I was sort of mad that they didn't have one that was closer to them." And while her daughters were also initially upset that they could not have a doll that matched their image, Alexie rationalized, "I already have me. I want to buy someone different but sort of like me. It's like me in a different person or with different personalities a bit." They found dolls, she says, that were more like them in other ways. Octavia chose Saige because she loves red hair and was attracted to Saige's interest in horses and art and the way she stood up for herself and her friends. Alexie said that she was drawn to Molly because, like the American Girl, she is shy and takes time to warm up to new people. Girls of color who choose to participate in American Girl culture but are unable to find a close approximation to their own image either get as close as possible or find a doll that shares other aspects of their identity.

COLORBLIND ACCESSORIES

Like the doll faces that have ambiguous racial markers, the current accessories collections for both the Truly Me and BeForever dolls perpetuate a racial logic of colorblindness. While earlier collections referenced cultural specificity, historical relevance and sometimes resilience against racial injustice, today's accessories veer, as discussed in Chapter 4, toward beauty, bedroom, and food play. Exploring Addy's original collection of accessories, released in 1993 and discontinued in the early 2000s, illustrates how American Girl previously included a range of accessories that alluded to Addy's history of oppression and struggle for freedom as well as her African American cultural heritage. Currently truncated collections are lacking in historical reference and mark Addy's experience as generically situated within a universalized imagined community of American Girl.

Contemporary doll customers are still able to buy Addy's bedroom set which includes the *Family Album Quilt,* designed in 1993 and based on an authentic 1854 quilt, that tells the tale of one African American family through quilt squares. So, too, can they still buy Addy's lunch pail and pretend that they are eating lunch with Addy and her mother by using the L-O-V-E cookies her mother made to show Addy that she was learning to spell.

However, gone from Addy's collection are many meaningful semiotic markers of her story. Addy's *Winter Fun Set,* which included a working mancala game, a working sansa, and a myriorama is no longer in production. Each of these was contemporary to Addy's world as an escaped slave in 1864. Mancala, for example, is a game that originated on the continent of Africa, was brought to North America during the slave trade, and is often identified as a tool for teaching children about the ancient African contributions to mathematical applications.[52] In *Changes for Addy,* mancala is featured as an activity that represents the partial reuniting of her family after her father and her brother, who had both been sold off of the plantation, are both finally at their new home in Philadelphia while her baby sister, aunt, and uncle have yet to be found. Lying in bed, Addy looks over to "where Poppa and Sam were playing mancala" and Momma was sewing; she thought about how the "lantern light surrounded them with a warm glow" and wished that her entire family could be "whole and safe."[53] A sansa, also known as an mbira, is an African thumb piano that while not featured in Addy's story, was a musical instrument also believed to have been created in Africa and migrated to the United States by African slaves, and myriorama were illustrated playing cards that children in the nineteenth century would shift into various positions to create landscape pictures. These discontinued accessories all held cultural and historical significance related to Addy's narrative.

Also discontinued were Addy's *Sweet Potato Pudding Kit*, her school supplies and school desk, gardening supplies, sled, thread spool puppet show kit, table and chairs, and bird and birdcage. Each of these has significance in her story and is relevant to her social location within her historic time period. The pudding kit, which included a recipe as well as a functional ceramic bowl, cast iron skillet, and wooden spoon, was featured in *Addy's Surprise* on Christmas day. Most items written into American Girl stories were included at the request of the brand which had worked with the advisory board, researchers, and marketing managers on the development of accessories but the sweet potato pudding was added to the collection after Connie Porter, remembering her own grandmother's pudding, added this detail into her writing.[54] In the story, the pudding was symbolic of a bittersweet day for Addy who was experiencing her first free holiday in the fellowship of the church that had welcomed her and Momma into their community, but who still longed to be reconnected with the rest of her family. As Addy "savored each smooth sweet bite" she dreamed that next year she and her family would all be eating Momma's sweet potato pudding. The other dicontinued items also had cultural significance: the school supplies represented the importance of education in the lives of those who had long been denied the right to learn; the gardening supplies, used for laboring in her family's own plot of land, represented freedom from toiling in the fields of the slave owner's planation; the puppet show referred to the day Addy creatively raised funds for newly freed African Americans; and the sled represented a free, physically active child who was no longer enslaved.

Cut from the collection in 2009, the songbird and cage referred to one of the most significant storylines within Addy's series. Porter used the songbird, drawing on Maya Angelou's metaphor of the captive bird, to represent the lack of freedom African Americans experience in a racist society. When Addy meets her elderly neighbor, M'Dear, she also meets the woman's bird, Sunny. When Addy asks why Sunny is locked up in a cage and expresses concern that Sunny is sad and lonely in his confinement, M'Dear promises, "That cage can't contain Sunny's spirit. It soars right out from behind those bars. That's what's important for all of us. To let our souls sing out." After Addy is discriminated against at the pharmacy and on a streetcar for her skin color, the old neighbor reminds her,

"Don't let prejudice make you a prisoner. Remember Sunny. His spirit goes beyond his cage with every note he sings...You have to keep right on living, right on singing your song."[55]

The original collections of all the historical dolls encouraged a certain scripted play that valued historical and cultural specificity. Changes in the doll accessories and clothing have minimized the material representation of cultural, ethnic, and racial specificity. For girls who do not read the accompanying books, these changes serve to construct a colorblind discourse of universal American girlhood.

LOVE, PAIN, AND AFRICAN AMERICAN DOLL PLAY IN AMERICAN GIRL

In her analysis of African American dolls during the era between slavery and the Civil Rights Movement, Robin Bernstein asks, "What historically located behaviors did this artifact invite? And what practices did it discourage?"[56] She finds that during the nineteenth century many white children were given black dolls on which they were intended to inflict atrocities such as burning, beating, and hanging. She argues that the literature that accompanied black dolls, as well as the nature of their doll bodies, served as scripts which invited violent racist play by doll owners. Importantly, because the dolls "endured these acts without complaint," children's play constructed and perpetuated the lie that black people did not feel pain. This violent play—in which a doll was neither fully object nor person—referenced rationalizations for slavery and continued to serve as justification for abuses against African Americans.[57]

If we apply Bernstein's line of questioning to American Girl, one might ask what scripted doll play looks like after reading Addy, Cécile, and Melody's stories. For eighteen years until Cécile, a free born girl living in New Orleans in 1853, was released in 2011, Addy, born a slave, was the only African American doll with a story. When Cécile was retired in 2014, Addy again served as the only historical doll of African ancestry until Melody, an African American girl coming of age during the Civil Rights movement, was released in 2016. While Pleasant Rowland celebrated in 1993 that part of her legacy would be the creation of a black doll that would be loved by white children, Bernstein discussed the complexity of love that is also accompanied by violence; "Love and violence were not mutually exclusive but were instead interdependent."[58] She writes, "even as historical white children loved their black dolls, they whipped, beat, and hanged black dolls with regularity and with ritualistic and sometimes sexually sadistic ferocity."[59] In this vein, girls playing with Addy could act out the horrific scene in *Meet Addy*, in which we first encounter the girl protagonist surrounded by racial hatred on the North Carolina plantation in which she is enslaved. Girls might reenact the passage in which Addy's father is sold off the plantation or the moment in which the overseer shoves worms into Addy's mouth. Girls reading *No Ordinary Sound* might imagine that they are Melody and her brother followed around a department store like criminals simply because they are black or that they are the four little black girls who died in their Alabama church after a racist bombed it.

None of the girls I interviewed admitted to this kind of play but if they do engage in play that reenacts violence against their black dolls, there are two distinctions between American Girl's African American dolls and the dolls Bernstein discusses that will ultimately likely lead girls to a very different kind of engagement: (1) Addy, Cécile, and Melody's narratives are all filled with pain. Readers learn that their pain is in many ways brought on by the institutionalization of racism and everyday acts of racist aggression. The dolls do not receive violence painlessly nor does their pain dissipate quickly; (2) The narrative around the preciousness and innocence of the American Girl doll body extends to include all of the collection's dolls of color.

Throughout her tale, Addy experiences pain, discusses her pain, and to the extent that she can, uses her agency to relieve herself of pain. Addy's physical pain—and that of her family members—is only witnessed on the plantation but her emotional pain is evident throughout. Addy experiences racism in many ways and readers are well aware of the emotional harm these experiences inflict on her; she feels hated and hatred, she is separated from her family, and she is discriminated against in a Northern state she hoped would be free from prejudice. As Bennett writes, "Addy humanizes slavery for children, which is crucial since slavery, by definition, strips humanity away."[60] Throughout the series Addy questions the adults in her life about why racist practices exist and how she is supposed to process what she considers "unfair." In *Addy Learns a Lesson* she sees a Philadelphia streetcar for the first time. When her friend Sarah tells her they cannot ride it because they "don't let colored people ride that streetcar," Addy questions the practice. "That ain't right," she says and Sarah replies, "It ain't but it's the way things is."[61] That night, unsatisfied with Sarah's answer, Addy expresses frustration to her mother, arguing "This where freedom supposed to be at...There ain't supposed to be things colored folks can't do."[62] In this, and other sub-plots, Addy's story makes clear that just because she has escaped the institution of slavery does not mean she has escaped institutionalized racism.

Throughout the series Addy repeatedly expresses the lack of "fairness" in racism and she is told "That's the way it is."[63] This language might be seen in a number of different ways. It might be read as a placating message to accept racism as unchangeable, denying consumers the space in which to resist injustice or understand the importance of how systems of power and hierarchy work. Alternatively, Porter's inclusion of the streetcar incident and her repeated demonstration of Addy questioning the disparity she witnesses, challenges the notion that African Americans accepted their oppressed position in society. This continued questioning demonstrates Addy's emotional pain while capturing bell hooks' sentiment that "whiteness in the black imagination is often a representation of terror" and that black children often learned "that to be 'safe' it was important to recognize the power of whiteness, even to fear it."[64] To the extent that she can, as an African American nine-year-old living in the 1860s, Addy resists the institutionalization of racism; she works hard to learn to read, to teach her mother to read, and to unite her own and other families torn apart by slavery.

In another act of resistance, Addy formalizes and celebrates her very existence in the world by naming her own birthday in a country that did not make birth certificates for slaves. Porter writes, "Addy felt ashamed that she didn't know her birthday" but her older neighbor tells her,

> Slavery has taken a lot away from colored people...If we want to get some of it back, we're going to have to take it. It's going to be some time before your family gets back together. But one thing I know you can take for yourself right now, Addy. Whenever you want, you can choose a special day and claim it for your birthday.[65]

After much contemplation, Addy finally picks April 9, the day that the Civil War ended, as her birthday. She thinks, "This was the day she had been waiting for. It was not perfect. If it were, her brother and sister would be right there with her, but this was the best day she could imagine without them."[66]

In my interviews with mothers, many white mothers said that they had not yet read Addy's story with their girls because they worried about exposing their daughters to such pain being inflicted on a girl their age. While their daughters know about the history of slavery in the United States, these mothers were particularly concerned about the imagery of a young girl experiencing physical violence and the loss of her family. Other parents, white, African American, and Afro-Latino, have read Addy's books with their daughters. Violet, who identifies as African American, told the focus group, "One of the things I liked about the Addy books was the ability for me to bring up the subject with [my daughter] about how somebody's always going to look at you based on the color of your skin or based on the fact that you're a girl. But you don't have to worry about this type of situation [slavery] anymore." Sharon, who identifies as white, added,

> It was a very good way for me to talk to my daughter about slavery. Addy is a girl just like her. It is horrifying when the overseer stuffs worms in her mouth. It is horrifying when her father and brother get sold and when Addy gets whipped. It is terrifying when she is almost caught during the escape. It is terrible when she gets to Philadelphia and she is still facing racism. But Addy is strong, her mother is always there for her, and her family is reunited at the end.

One mother in an online forum wrote,

> I was looking for some age-appropriate way to discuss racism with my not quite eight-year-old. I had very low expectations for this sort of brand considering the dolls are so overpriced. [But] it had just enough detail to explain the hardships of slavery, but not enough to traumatize a young child. The story is beautiful, touching and a great introduction to conversations about empathy, being grateful for what you have, empathy for others, racism and many other big topics.

Another wrote, "I cried and it brought up some really interesting conversations with my eight-year-old. Not just about slavery, but about war and how we treat other human beings that are different from ourselves." Tied to Addy's narrative that highlights the physical and emotional pain in her life, as well as her attempts to resist the institutions that cause her pain, consumers would have a difficult time imagining the doll—or the girl—experiencing pain without complaint. In Porter's hands, Addy is made real, pained but resilient and lovable.

An economically privileged girl living in New Orleans in 1853, Cécile is a free-born Creole girl who experiences much less pain than Addy (Fig. 5.2). During the 1820s when Cécile's story, written by Denise Lewis Patrick, took place, racism certainly was present in New Orleans, but it was different from the rest of the country because those of French, Spanish, and African descent were somewhat more integrated into one another's lives.

Fig. 5.2   Cécile Rey doll

In New Orleans, free people of color were business and property owners, involved in the city's culture, and often amassed great wealth.[67] Jevens says that the selection of this time period and social location was intentionally driven by the brand's response to consumer requests for a doll that told a story of "the success many black families achieved *despite* the prejudice they faced." Cécile's story, in which her father owns a thriving business, her mother owns and manages real estate properties, her brother is working toward becoming a painter, and she studies poetry and opera, allowed the brand to focus on African American businesses and arts.

However, racism was not absent from Cécile's life. Living in a society in which black people were both enslaved and free, Cécile and her family are sometimes misidentified by people who are not familiar with the local culture. In *Meet Cécile*, the protagonist and her grandfather are in Madame Zumile's candy shop buying pralines when two "Américains" walk into the store. When one of the men and her grandfather accidentally bump into one another, grand-père says, "*Excusez-moi*" and the white stranger retorts, "Watch where you're goin' boy!" He then turns to his friend and complains, "These French don't teach their slaves enough respect." Cécile's emotions quickly begin to impact her physically. Her "heart began to beat very fast" and "she could feel her face flush rosy red." Her grandfather tries to ignore the whole situation but Cécile can't. With a shaking voice, she responds, "How dare you, sir!" and explains their status to the men. Author Denise Lewis Patrick wrote this scene based on her own experiences seeing "how someone that you admire and adore is subjected to something like this and how they respond." She said, "I wanted kids to see that these things have an effect on people, and people handle them differently."

Most of Cécile's encounters with white characters, though, focus on racial understanding in her friendship with her white friend, Marie-Grace, with whom she discovers she has much in common. The story has been critiqued by one scholar for its celebration of this seemingly colorblind friendship.[68] Indeed, sameness is often highlighted, as when the girls dress in the same costume and sneak into each other's segregated Mardi Gras balls, or in their mutual love of singing and volunteer work at the orphanage. The pain of racism, however, is not absent from their friendship story. When a racially ambiguous baby is left on Marie-Grace's doorstep her father surmises, "If the baby's mother was a slave, she may have taken this desperate measure to keep her child from growing up in slavery."[69] When a slave owner comes to claim the baby as his property Marie-Grace's father tricks the man into leaving by claiming that the baby has a very large outstanding medical bill. He tells his daughter that the only way to protect the baby now is to get him into the orphanage for white children where the slave owner will not look for him. Remembering how she and Cécile traded costumes at the ball, Marie-Grace asks her friend to help find fancy clothes to dress the baby in so he will look wealthy and white. Readers are taught that they, like Marie-Grace and Cécile, should protect people of color from racism, racist violence, and pain.

Melody, whose story is also written by Denise Lewis Patrick, is growing up in Detroit during the Civil Rights movement (Fig. 5.3). Her story, which features a middle-class family with parents and adult relatives who work as teachers, business owners, autoworkers, and aspiring Motown singers, was also developed with the aid of a six-member advisory board. This advisory board included Julian Bond, founding member of the Student Nonviolent Coordinating Committee (SNCC) and former chairman of the NAACP, as well as professors of African American Studies and Detroit-based historians and activists. Melody, whose release came shortly after the peak of the Black Lives Matter movement, feels real emotional pain when she identifies that racial discrimination is responsible for her sister

Fig. 5.3   Melody Ellison doll

being refused a job at a bank and for her cousin's family being denied the ability to buy a house in the neighborhood in which they seek to live. When Melody goes house-hunting with her aunt, uncle, and cousin, Val, they come upon a perfect house for sale. As the family looks through the house's picture window they see a fireplace and a backyard that Val hopes is big enough for a swing set. But they also see a white neighbor who peers out of a nearby window and quickly closes her curtains when the girls wave up at her and they later learn that the neighborhood has been in the news recently because real estate agents have been closing open houses when black families arrive.

Most significantly, Melody's pain is represented by the loss of her voice when she learns about the four girls in Birmingham who were killed by a bomb in their church when they were attending Sunday school. Not only does Melody fear that entering her own church, where she is practicing her choir solo, will be dangerous, she can't get the image of the victims out of her head. On the night of the bombing she ponders, "What were those little girls doing when the explosion happened? Laughing? Praying? Singing? What were their names?"[70] and then again a few nights later, "What did the four little girls look like? Were they dark brown, with skinny legs, like Sharon, and did they run so fast that their hair came undone? Were they tall and golden like Val, with ponytails that bounced and swung from side to side when they talked and waved their hands? Did they have sisters and brothers?"[71] Melody's fear and pain grow so intense that she develops a post-traumatic mutism; she feels as if "her voice died" with the four girls. Working through her anxiety, with the support of her family and friends, Melody decides that she will not give up this chance and that she will sing in honor of the little girls. Finally, her two friends and her cousin step forward to support Melody as she sings, to help her to know that she "would never stop speaking out for what was right."[72] Symbolically, the four girls claim their places and their voices in the church, in the world, and in resistance against racist violence. Like Addy, Melody is a human face of racial injustice and while Addy's is a personal struggle to save her life and her family, Melody's story is of the social struggle to end racial oppression. It is clear, by the end of the two books, that Melody does not live in a post-racist society and that fighting for equal rights is an unfinished struggle for her. Her pain is palpable and her resistance ongoing.

Because Melody is the newest historical doll, most of the interview participants had not read her books, but several of them had seen the movie that was loosely based on her story and streaming on television. Eight-year-old Charlotte, who is white, owns the Melody doll and has seen the movie. She chose Melody as her newest doll because of the character's love for music, a passion that Charlotte shares. Melody's brother is in a Motown singing group and for one of his songs he invites Melody to sing backup. Although Charlotte has some facts wrong about Motown and about the Melody story, she captures the complexity of Melody representing a universal girl experience but also the pain of segregation:

Well, Melody's story is about segregation. I feel that she's fighting for what's right. And I feel like I should do that, too. I try every day to play with her and make more memories in my mind to see what's going to happen next about her. I have [Melody's toy] recording studio and I love to play with it. But then after a while, I think about segregation and about her because she's African American and she's one of the first Motown stars to be black. I was really shocked right there when I heard about that, and I just didn't know what to do. And I was really confused about maybe I should just let her be a singer without thinking about segregation. But it always comes back to my head.

Like Addy, Melody feels pain from institutionalized racism and is resilient, but she is also just a girl who likes to sing.

In many ways, the stories of the African American dolls in the collection position the girl owner/reader as a friend to Addy, Cécile, or Melody. As they directly address institutional racism that is unfinished and visible in different forms throughout the years, they also deny the reader innocence or apathy. Denise Patrick Lewis explained of her writing, "I'm trying to write something that encourages children [to know] that they can make a change, that they are free" and that they "still have to work for change." The scripts of play for African American dolls, then, encourage kindness, political awareness, and love.

The humanity in their stories alone may not distinguish Addy, Cécile, and/or Melody as dolls that are intended to be loved and not abused, but their price tag and their accessories certainly do. The cost of the dolls, now $115 just for the doll and her first book, prescribes a kind of play that requires gentle care. The exclusivity of the doll—at its price point, available only through the company and not toy stores, and in its signature red packaging—creates what some parents describe as a "magical" quality to the dolls.[73] For this reason, parents often require their children to be careful with the dolls and girls express that their American Girl dolls are more precious than other dolls with which they play. They often repeat that these dolls are like friends or sisters as well as that these dolls are more expensive and therefore owned in fewer quantity than fashion dolls. This limited ownership, and knowledge of the doll's luxury status helps create an attachment and love for the dolls as well as a higher level of care for these dolls than for others.

So, too, do the American Girl accessories—many of which focus on food, hair care, grooming, and bedroom culture—encourage tenderness for the doll.[74] Ironically, these same accoutrements that normalize a stereotypical femininity, as discussed in the previous chapter, also script play that revolves around tenderness and care, including tenderness and care for dolls of color. Girls who play with these American Girl dolls *do* often tuck their dolls in at night, spend time during the day washing, brushing, and styling hair, dressing their dolls, and nourish their dolls with food. The dolls' price, exclusiveness, and accessories script a play of love and kindness.

CONSTRUCTING RACIAL IDENTITY IN THE AMERICAN GIRL BEFOREVER COLLECTION

Studying the African American Barbies of the early 1990s, Ann duCille argues,

> The toy industry is only one of many venues where multiculturalism, posed as an answer to critical questions about inclusion, diversity, and equality, has collapsed into an additive campaign that augments but does not necessarily alter the Eurocentric *status quo*. Barbie "gone ethnic" by way of dye jobs and costume changes seems to me but a metaphor for the way multiculturalism has been used as a kind of quick fix by both liberal humanism and late capitalism. Made from essentially the same mold as what Mattel considers its signature doll—the traditional, blonde, blue-eyed Barbie— tawny-tinted ethnic reproductions are both signs and symptoms of an easy pluralism that simply melts down and adds on a reconstituted other without transforming the established social order, without changing the mold.[75]

To an extent, American Girl still carries on where Barbie left off, but in other ways the brand *does* challenge the status quo. The Truly Me collection has a limited number of dolls of color with slightly different face molds that suggest ethnic and racial difference. Woven into the brands' full advertising displays, dolls with multiple face molds, hair textures, and skin tones imply an American identity that is both specific and universal. The contemporary collection has even dispensed with culturally suggestive outfits and linguistic racial categorization so that both sameness and flexibly ambiguous race and ethnicity prevail. At the same time, the American Girl historical collection is deeply invested in carefully considering the ways in which difference, power, and privilege are constructed through the collection. In particular, for the African American dolls in the collection, the company has worked closely with advisory groups and writers to create stories of African American identity that is located within institutionalized racism. These dolls are meant to be loved and cared for, they are meant to be protected as one would protect a friend or sibling, and they are meant to represent both the pain and resilience that are part of the core of African American experience.[76]

Notes

1. "Rejecting Barbie, Doll Maker Gains," *New York Times*, September 1, 1993, D1.
2. Beth Francis, "Popular American Girl Dolls Give Children a Chance to Play and Learn," *Gannett News Service*, August 1, 1996.
3. "Rejecting Barbie."
4. Pleasant Company, "Addy Advisory Board," Pleasant Company, press release, received by mail December, 1996.
5. Barbara Brotman, "The Multicultural Playroom: Today's Dolls Have Ethnicity That's More Than Skin Deep," *Chicago Tribune*, October 31, 1993, http://articles.chicagotribune.com/1993-10-31/features/9310310429_1_black-dolls-white-dolls-ethnic-groups/2.
6. Megan Rosenfeld, "Wholesome Babes in Toyland," *Washington Post*, May 24, 1993, https://www.washingtonpost.com/archive/lifestyle/1993/05/24/wholesome-babes-in-toyland/b4ed92ca-1571-4ec9-9290-4dfb4ded0b7b/?utm_term=.b64423f5abf9.
7. Brit Bennett, "Addy Walker, American Girl: the role of black dolls in American culture," *The Paris Review*, May 28, 2015, http://www.theparisreview.org/blog/2015/05/28/addy-walker-american-girl/.
8. Ibid.
9. Ibid.
10. Jennae Petersen, "American Girl, Your Slave Doll is a Big, Fat, Offensive FAIL," *green & gorgeous*, October 26, 2015, http://www.greenandgorgeous.net/2012/10/26/american-girl-your-slave-doll-is-a-big-fat-offensive-fail/.
11. Rosenfeld, "Wholesome Babes in Toyland."
12. Connie Porter, in discussion with the author, November 12, 1996.
13. Ibid.
14. "American Girl, Your Slave Doll is a Big, Fat, Offensive FAIL."
15. Pleasant Company, "Addy Testimonials," Pleasant Company, press release, received by mail December, 1996.
16. Aisha Harris, "The Making of an American Girl," *Slate*, September 21, 2016, http://www.slate.com/articles/arts/culturebox/2016/09/the_making_of_addy_walker_american_girl_s_first_black_doll.html.
17. Porter, in discussion with the author.
18. Connie Porter, *Happy Birthday, Addy* (Middleton, WI: American Girl Publishing, 1994; reprint, Middleton, WI: American Girl Publishing, 1998), 35.
19. Harris, "The Making of an American Girl."
20. Todd Moore, "Unpleasantries at Pleasant Company," *Capital Times*, September 16, 1993, A1.
21. Harris, "The Making of an American Girl."

22. Moore, "Unpleasantries at Pleasant Company."
23. Connie Porter, *Addy's Surprise* (Middleton, WI: American Girl Publishing, 1993; reprint, Middleton, WI: American Girl Publishing, 1998), 29–30.
24. Harris, "The Making of an American Girl."
25. Porter, in discussion with the author.
26. Stuart Hall, "The Whites of their Eyes: Racist Ideology and the Media," in *The Race and Media Reader*, ed. Gilbert Rodman (New York: Routledge, 2014), 41.
27. Michael Omi and Howard Winant, "Racial Formation," in *Race Critical Theories: Text and Context*, eds. Philomena Essed and David Theo Goldberg (Malden, MA: Blackwell, 2002), 139.
28. Ibid., 123–139.
29. Avery Gordon and Christopher Newfield, "Introduction," in *Mapping Multiculturalism,* eds. Avery Gordon and Christopher Newfield (Minneapolis: University of Minnesota Press, 1996), 3.
30. Catherine R. Squires, *The Post-Racial Mystique: Media and Race in the Twenty-First Century* (New York: NYU Press, 2014), 6.
31. Eduardo Bonilla-Silva, *Racism Without Racists: Color-Blind Racism and the Persistence of Racial Inequality in the United States* (Lanham, MD: Rowman & Littlefield, 2003).
32. Ibid., 4.
33. Squires, *The Post-Racial* Mystique, 6.
34. Angharad Valdivia, "Living in a Hybrid Material World: Girls, Ethnicity and Mediated Doll Products," *Girlhood Studies* 2, no. 1 (2009): 74.
35. Veronica Medina, "Celebrating Whiteness American Girl-Style: Representing Race at American Girl's Twentieth Anniversary" (presentation, Department of Women's and Gender Studies Colloquium, University of Missouri, Columbia, MO, March 2009), 16.
36. Ashley Doane, "The Changing Politics of Color-Blind Racism," *Research in Race and Ethnic Relations* 14 (2007): 165.
37. Carolina Acosta-Alzuru and Elizabeth P. Lester Roushanzamir, "'Everything We Do is Celebration of You!' Pleasant Company Constructs American Girlhood," *The Communication Review* 6 (2003): 45–69. Acosta-Alzuru and Roushanzamir draw on Benedict Anderson's concept of imagined community.
38. Susan Jevens (Associate Manager, Public Relations, American Girl,) e-mail message to author, March 10, 2017.
39. Some fans believe that originally African American dolls (including Addy) had darker skin with a blue-black tint, while current dolls with dark skin tone have been lightened to a more golden tone. See "Basic Doll Anatomy," http://americangirl.wikia.com/wiki/Basic_Doll_Anatomy.

40. From 1990 to 1995, Our New Baby dolls were available as Caucasian, African American, or Asian American. When they were re-packaged as Bitty Baby in 1995, the racial nomenclature was removed.
41. "Face Mold," http://americangirl.wikia.com/wiki/Face_Mold.
42. Rebecca Joan West, "Some of My Best Dolls Are Black: Colorblind Rhetoric in Online Collecting Communities" (PhD diss., University of Loyola Chicago, 2014), 117.
43. Harris, "The Making of an American Girl."
44. http://americangirl.wikia.com/wiki/Face_Mold.
45. American Girl, "Product Diversity," https://www.americangirl.com/corporate/product-diversity.
46. "Just Like You 4," http://americangirl.wikia.com/wiki/Just_Like_You_4.
47. As quoted in Feminist Asian Dad, "American Girl Power," September 10, 2016, https://feministasiandad.com/2016/09/10/american-girl-power/.
48. Diane Clehane, "Why Is American Girl Rebranding Their Historical Line Without an Asian Doll?" *Forbes*, July 8, 2014, http://www.forbes.com/sites/dianeclehane/2014/07/08/why-is-american-girl-rebranding-their-historical-line-without-an-asian-doll/#56ea9ad22fa2.
49. This may change in the near future as suggested by a Mattel talk to shareholders.
50. Dr. Mama Esq., "Black Girls and the American Girl Doll Dilemma," January 23, 2014, https://cocoamamas.com/2014/01/23/black-girls-and-the-american-girl-doll-dillemma/.
51. Ibid.
52. Philip M. Peek and Kwesi Yankah, eds., *African Folklore: An Encyclopedia* (New York: Routledge, 2004), 473–476; Claudia Zaslavsky, "'Africa Counts' and Ethnomathematics," *For the Learning of Mathematics* 14, no. 2, 3–8.
53. Connie Porter, *Changes for Addy* (Middleton, WI: American Girl Publishing, 1994; reprint, Middleton, WI: American Girl Publishing, 1998), 14.
54. Porter, in discussion with the author.
55. Connie Porter, *Happy Birthday Addy!* (Middleton, WI: American Girl Publishing, 1994; reprint, Middleton, WI: American Girl Publishing, 1998), 38.
56. Robin Bernstein, *Racial Innocence: Performing American Childhood and Race from Slavery to Civil Rights* (New York: NYU Press, 2011), 8.
57. Ibid., 196.
58. Ibid., 209.
59. Ibid., 209.
60. Bennett, "Addy Walker, American Girl."
61. Connie Porter, *Addy Learns a Lesson* (Middleton, WI: American Girl Publishing, 1993; reprint, Middleton, WI: American Girl Publishing, 1998), 17.

62. Ibid., 17.
63. Ibid., 17, 31; Porter, *Happy Birthday, Addy!*, 7.
64. bell hooks, "Representing Whiteness in the Black Imagination" in *The Race and Media Reader*, ed. Gilbert B. Rodman (New York: Routledge, 2013), 89, 91.
65. Porter, *Happy Birthday, Addy!*, 16–17.
66. Ibid., 50.
67. Willard B. Gatewood, *Aristocrats of Color: The Black Elite, 1880–1920* (Fayetteville, AR: University of Arkansas Press, 2000), 83.
68. Sonja Zepeda Pérez, "Mis(s)Education: Narrative Construction and Closure in American Girl" (PhD diss., University of Arizona, 2015), 82.
69. Sarah Buckey, *Marie-Grace and the Orphans* (Middleton, WI: American Girl Publishing, 2011), 10.
70. Denise Lewis Patrick, *No Ordinary Sound: A Melody Classic Volume 1* (Middleton, WI: American Girl Publishing, 2016), 182.
71. Ibid., 186.
72. Ibid., 215.
73. As of the writing of this book, American Girl had begun to sell a small number of products at Toys R Us and Kohl's department stores as well as change its packaging.
74. Bernstein, *Racial* Innocence, 234.
75. Ann duCille, *Skin Trade* (Cambridge, MA: Harvard University Press, 1996), 38.
76. Debra Walker King, *African Americans and the Culture of Pain* (Charlottesville, VA: University of Virginia Press, 2008).

CHAPTER 6

"This Is My Home": Representing Race, Ethnicity, and the American Experience in American Girl

In *The One and Only*, Maryellen Larkin enters fourth grade in 1954 to find that her class has a new student. When they learn that the student, Angela Terlizzi, is an Italian immigrant, some of her classmates begin to discriminate against her. Giving the new girl a "sideways glance," Karen tells the class that her uncle fought in World War II and was killed in Italy by their Italian enemies. Later, Karen tells Maryellen who has begun to develop a friendship with Angela, "She's so different...She has those long braids, and *pierced ears*.... [and] for Pete's sake, she's *Italian*....I could never be friends with an Italian." Another friend adds, "Italy was friends with Germany and Japan during the war....The Italians were our *enemies*." Reminding them that the war was close to ten years prior, Maryellen, whose story focuses on her own uniqueness, adds, "Anyway, Angela is just Angela."[1] Although the girls part with animosity based on their opposing perspectives on Angela, they all soon learn that the new girl is just like them, only different. Angela's difference is limited to her periodic use of Italian words, the fact that she has extended family living with her (it is her *Nonna* who is home when she arrives from school rather than her parents), and that she eats slightly different food. This difference excites Maryellen who, upon entering Angela's house, is surprised to see *Nonna* making meatballs because in "her house spaghetti and meatballs came straight out of the Chef Boy-Ar-Dee can."[2] Angela studies the English language every day at lunch and soon becomes fluent, joins Girl Scouts, and learns to jitterbug. Angela has a small role in Maryellen's story but her positioning as simultaneously same and different

© The Author(s) 2017
E. Zaslow, *Playing with America's Doll*,
DOI 10.1057/978-1-137-56649-2_6

is characteristic of the way in which ethnicity is explored in American Girl narratives. While the stories of the African American historical dolls, discussed in the previous chapter, portray racism and offer political, economic, and social context for the discrimination the characters' experience, many other American Girl stories of race and ethnicity fail to address that discrimination exists, fail to provide context for such discrimination, or identify discrimination as temporary. In this way, readers are sometimes asked to notice cultural differences like customs, family arrangements, language, and food but to disregard the systematic injustices against those who are not African American.

Also emblematic of the way that race and ethnic origin are treated in the collection is the implication in Angela's story that anyone at a disadvantage in the United States can work hard to be equal. This theme is often secured by the narrative formula of connecting the American identity of ethnic and racial Others to their business savvy and entrepreneurialism, suggesting that difference can be overcome by an industrious American spirit that equalizes us all. Although readers and parents often identify the brand's narrative theme as "standing up for what is right," there is an equally strong message that supports the myth of social mobility, suggesting that American identity is rooted in individual self-determination that is supported by a country that appreciates diversity.

Revisiting Stuart Hall's point that media texts, "construct for us a definition of what *race* is, what meaning the imagery of race carries, and what the 'problem of race' is understood to be," this chapter explores how these divergent approaches to race and ethnicity within the American Girl universe construct conflicting logics.[3] On the one hand, we can respect that authors and advisory boards do not want tales of pain and discrimination to become stand-ins for race and ethnicity. Those who seek to highlight vibrant cultures do so intentionally to augment and challenge grade-school histories about diverse American cultures which often focus on persecution. Yet, if institutional racism and ethnic discrimination are missing from the stories of the Native American, Latino, and immigrant dolls, do readers miss important elements of these characters' identities as well as the source of the race 'problem' in their communities? For example, if Kaya's series doesn't address racist violence against the Native American population or the institutional policies of discrimination that are the foundation of the reservation system, how do girl readers come to understand the high levels of poverty or land rights disputes in contemporary Native American populations? Race and ethnicity presented without a deep examination of the system of power relations in which they operate, as they are in the stories about Kaya, Kirsten, Josefina, and Rebecca, risk becoming symbolic, erasing the shameful truths of racism and prejudice, and problematically implying that Americanness and equality is available to all who work hard for it.

Whose Stories Get Told? Race, Ethnicity, and the American Experience in American Girl

Of course, the very decision of whose American stories get told, by whom, and in what way is political and loaded with meaning. Equally significant are the stories and parts of history that are not included in the collection. Why, for example, do we have Molly's story on the WWII home front but not one of an interned Japanese American girl?[4] Why does Maryellen's friend Angela, the Italian American girl who is discriminated against based on her country's role in the Axis powers in World War II, play a secondary role? Why is Samantha the star and her orphan friend Nellie the understudy? Where is the anti-Native sentiment in Kaya's story? Because the BeForever fictions are written by independent authors over the brand's thirty-year history, the answers vary from case to case.

Over the past thirty years the development of the various American Girl characters has evolved out of the interest in teaching girls about significant historical moments, consumer demand for certain types of characters, and the recognition of changing markets. In my communication with American Girl, Public Relations Manager Susan Jevens writes that in order to determine a new historical character's story, the brand considers many factors, but the primary one is "Which period is the most emblematic or significant in terms of telling not just the story of this particular ethnic group, but the story of America?"[5] The first three dolls were each intended to represent a significant element in American history. The cultural shift in women's lives that resulted from their work during World War II, which defined the era into which Rowland was born, was selected to be the backdrop of Molly's books because it was foundational for a generation of women and girls whose civic and professional participation in American society was altered by the war. The author, Valerie Tripp, says that she "was inspired and influenced by [her] mother's stories about working in an aircraft factory and [her] aunt's stories about being in the Red Cross and going to France shortly after D-Day."[6] For Tripp, Molly's was a "quintessential American story to tell" because it was one of "endurance, courage, and patriotism—and good old ingenuity and industriousness."[7] Likewise, Samantha's story, situated just after the turn of the twentieth century, was chosen to depict an emergent historical moment that saw many social changes including the suffrage movement and the reform movements for better working conditions.[8] Finally, the third original doll, Kirsten, was included because Rowland and Tripp felt that an immigration story that explored the hardships faced by women and children was essential to American history. In the case of Kaya, a Native American doll whose story takes place in 1764 and who the company sometimes calls the "First American Girl," brand representatives have said that it was important "to show [readers] that our country's history did not begin with the American Revolution."[9] Similarly, when it came to crafting the Josefina character, Tripp explains that she wanted to educate girls about the American history that they sometimes did not learn. She explains that in grade school texts we often have "Columbus in 1492, and we've got the Pilgrims in 1620. Growing up in New York State I never learned the history of the Western settlements and how Josefina's family has been in New Mexico for centuries."[10]

For some characters, consumer demand has been evident. When Jewish families made it clear that there would be a market for a Jewish doll, Rebecca Rubin, the Jewish daughter of Russian immigrants living in New York City in 1914, was created.[11] As well, Maryellen, who survived polio and walks with a limp was inspired, in part, by requests from differently abled girls who wrote to Tripp asking her to tell a story about how a "character's physical or developmental challenge is not what defines her."[12] More recently, the two newest historical dolls, released in 2015 and 2016, were done so in the midst of the company's first consistent profit loss.[13] In an attempt to combat this downturn in profit, the brand released two historical dolls whose stories are situated in eras—the 1950s and 1960s—during which the grandmothers of current doll owners would have lived. American Girl hoped that grandmothers would buy their grandchildren dolls that represented the childhood eras in which they came of age.[14] Indeed, this market-driven selection was alluded by the company's public relations team who said of 1970s Julie, "We have high hopes for this character, because it's striking such a connection between girls and their moms" and of 1950s Maryellen, "One of the hopes we have for Maryellen's stories is for girls to want to find out more about their own grandparents' experiences growing up during this time."[15] In the case of Melody, some journalists have suggested that she is a response to the need for more diversity in children's literature and products and especially a response to criticism the company received for discontinuing Ivy and Cécile.[16]

Despite their distinct tales about the various ways in which the historical characters are chosen, company public relations officers have always told a consistent story about the process involved in creating the fictional accounts and the company's commitment to historical authenticity. It takes approximately three to four years from the time a historical doll is imagined to the time she hits the shelves. During this period, her story is developed, sometimes with input from an advisory board, authenticated by staff historians who examine a range of historical documents and often visit her story's location, sartorialized by designers, and written by an independent author.

From its inception, American Girl has presented authentic specificity and universality as the two most significant elements in a story's creation. In 2016, Julia Prohaska, Vice President of Marketing for American Girl, told *CBS News* that "The doll industry has a very heavy responsibility in reflecting what is true about our society."[17] This emphasis on truth-telling is supported by Prohaska's claim that the company is "looking to tell stories in the most authentic and genuine way that we possibly can."[18] Authenticity, American Girl believes, can be supported by historical research and by advisory boards. The company's senior historian, Mark Speltz, says, "My role as a historian is really important because parents and educators look to us for authentic materials, content, and product."[19]

For dolls with accompanying narratives the company consults with a range of historians, educators, cultural leaders, and museum curators and formalizes this consultation into an advisory board in cases where the "character is from a culture that the [internal development] team is not as close to." Advisory boards help "ensure [a doll's] historical accuracy and cultural authenticity."[20] For example, it was Kaya's advisory board that influenced the way that the doll's braids were positioned, the patterns on her pow-wow outfit, and her closed mouth face mold.[21] In making decisions about the color of Josefina's hair, board member Felipe Mirabal was integral; Tripp explains, "When we wanted to know what Josefina's hair should look like, Felipe cut off a chunk of his own hair and that's what we sent to the factory because it was sort of goldish and auburn and brown and black and this beautiful mixture." But the advisory boards did not only shape visual representation. Janet Shaw, who is not a Native American, has described how the board turned her "black and white" historical research, that involved reading books, studying photographs, and visiting museums, "into color ... with stories of all kinds—personal stories, family stories, legends, and tales—as well as all kinds of special knowledge."[22] The advisory board also gave her a tour of Kaya's lands and corrected the author's mistakes. Of the advisory board members, Shaw declares, "The authenticity of Kaya's world is their gift to all of us."[23]

When the author or team is "close to a particular culture, the advisory board is built in, ...[but still] reviewed by at least three outside consultants for historical and cultural accuracy" as in the case of Rebecca whose team included a Jewish author and editor.[24] This focus on authenticity and the claim that the authentic is tied to group membership presumes that historical veracity is possible, that the company is providing stories with undisputed truth, that those who have insider status can guarantee this truth, and that advisory board members are neutral and without agenda. Within the field of children's literature these presumptions are contested and unresolved. Asking "How *is* cultural authenticity in children's literature defined?" illustrator Susan Guevara considers, "If an author/artist creates from his/her experience, intuition, and research, is that artist/author's creation truly authentic to a specific culture?"[25] Recognizing these challenges, American Girl attempts to find authenticity in insider status. Yet, this focus on in-group authenticity may become problematic when a racial or ethnic group only has one or two representations of its American history within the American Girl collection and that story becomes *the* authentic story belonging to that group.

While authenticity and historical specificity might be seen as antithetical to representing a universal, relatable experience, the twining of these concepts is the cornerstone of American Girl's neo-historical approach to storytelling.[26] Tripp called it the play between "intimate and infinite, unique and universal."[27] It is an approach that allows American Girl to situate its stories in the past, create nostalgia for an older aesthetic, and attend to some historical specificities while marketing to contemporary girls who are consumed with the present and desirous for a story to which they can relate. Valerie Tripp explains, "Every story I write makes a connection between girls of today and the characters I write about from the past. Some issues have changed, but some issues about growing up are the same no matter when a girl lives."[28] For example, Kit's story is based in Cincinnati during the Great Depression but explores the universal experience of loss and financial hardship.[29] Similarly, when Jaqueline Dunbar Greene included a story about Rebecca's class at school being required to make a Christmas decoration and Rebecca not being sure how to react and what to do, American Girl "felt there was something universal [in her story] of the tension in being a minority culture in America."[30] Tripp explains her perspective that all children, no matter the era in which they grow up, experience the "push me/pull me of 'do I conform to what I see around me or do I assert myself as an individual?'...The push me/pull me between your family and yourself [where] you may even start to challenge some of the traditions or some of the beliefs that your own family has." No matter what time period one is reading about she hopes to communicate that, "Every decision that you make, every action that you take is forming your character and every woman who has preceded you is actually helping you as you make that decision [about] how you, specifically, are going to use your quirky combination of talents and abilities and energy." There are, these writers argue, some universal experiences of girlhood.

These balancing acts, along with the limited diversity in dolls, have led some critics to argue that outside of the doll's stylized attire, "sameness prevails" and difference, while acknowledged, is erased.[31] Carolina Acosta-Alzuru and Elizabeth Roushanzamir maintain that the focus on same/difference and historical/enduring leads to a particular "imagined community" of American Girls (both characters and consumers) that is racially and ethnically diverse but homogenously wealthy and privileged.[32] In addition to balancing the present and the past, the company has to balance its desire to share American histories of brave girls who, as many children identify, "stand up for what is right," with its fiscal imperative to create profit from the dolls. As Tripp explains, "Pleasant used to say, the best book in the world is useless if it is sitting on a shelf gathering dust."[33] The financial bottom line does not diminish the writers' interests in particular time periods and plot lines, but it does shape the stories it tells so that American history and its adorable pint-sized tour guides can be consumed without eliciting the shame that girls might feel if they were reading, for example, an American Girl version of *A People's History of the United States* by historian and activist Howard Zinn. Susan Jevens explains, "We seek to show the reality of the times, while at the same time, offer our readers an optimistic perspective. We want girls to see how struggles and challenges pay off...and we want to leave our readers feeling hopeful and strong about themselves and their possibilities for the future at the end of every American Girl story."[34] This tension between the capitalist imperative to manufacture a toy or write a book for enjoyable consumption and the brand's mission to tell stories that are historically accurate and authentic leads to a particular view of who is American and what it means to be an American girl. Many painful stories—particularly those that revolve around social class, race, and ethnic difference—are absent or easily resolved.

Although this chapter focuses on race and ethnicity, the act of maintaining the brand's optimistic message through stories that gloss over challenging times throughout history extends in many directions. In Julie's story for instance, author Megan McDonald introduces readers to Hank, a Vietnam Veteran. Their mother tells the girls that they should be nice to Hank because he has "seen so many terrible, horrible things."[35] Julie learns that Hank is gathering signatures for a petition to re-fund the Veterans' social center where homeless veterans had gone for meals, showers, and shelter from the elements. However, there is no further discussion of the Vietnam War, which was so central to the 1970s, nor do readers learn about the gay rights movement, the fight for affirmative action, or Roe v. Wade.[36] Instead, McDonald interprets the 1970s as "trying to return to optimism after the Vietnam War and Watergate" and focuses on the bicentennial which she believes "was a good way to show that the country was trying to heal and celebrate."[37]

In Felicity's story there is a study of race and social class issues that asks girls to engage in questioning rights, ownership, and freedom as the country gains its independence but it does so softly and with an easily digestible ending. Felicity's bravery, integrity, and non-normative female role positioning are bolstered by her whiteness and the privilege, innocence, and power over others it provides her. Felicity lives in a household that employs slaves—Marcus in the store and Rose in the house—but neither character is afforded a last name or any dialogue in the series. Both characters remain spoken about but never utter a word. When Felicity visits her grandfather's plantation she describes it as a wide-open blissful space with dazzling light and a blue river, never imagining the closed-in darkness experienced by the slaves who worked the land. Tripp writes that "It seemed to [Felicity] that life on the plantation was busy and lazy all at the same time."[38] Lazy for some, perhaps, but not for others. Neither Felicity, nor the reader, engages with any slaves on the plantation; they remain nameless, faceless, and voiceless. In *Happy Birthday, Felicity*, we learn that Felicity is not only clueless about racial issues, she is fierce in her privileged role as a white girl in the owning class. When she hears about the British governor's plan to steal the patriot's gun powder, Felicity asks Isaac Wallace, a free black teenager who serves as the militia's drummer, to sound the alarm signals. Isaac tells Felicity, "It is very dangerous for a black person like me to be seen at night...If I were found...it would not go well for me." She responds, "I know...But you must trust me, Isaac. We've got to stop them...please. You must help."[39] Here, Felicity has to decide what is more important, the life of an older African American teen or the freedom of her country. As a mass market children's book that veers away from frightful conclusions, Isaac and Felicity do protect the patriot's stockpile and save Williamsburg.

This balancing act of addressing deep social issues with ameliorative endings extends to social class in Felicity's tale. She initially treats Ben, her father's apprentice, like a brother and develops a friendship with him based on a shared feeling of oppression, the way her life is regulated by gendered prescriptions and his by social class limitations. When Ben decides to run away and join the patriot army, Felicity initially helps him. When she discovers that two "rough" men are seeking a reward for returning him and might hurt Ben, she persuades him to return for his own safety. Although her intent is to protect Ben, she does so by convincing him that it is shameful for him to run from his obligation to her father rather than by helping him find an alternate route where he would be safe. Felicity says, "It's cowardly to run away, to break promises, and to hurt those who need and trust you."[40] Tripp explains that this was her way of demonstrating that just like for the country, independence for Ben and for Felicity "is not self-indulgence [but] self-governance.... It's learning how you can function within your society, but still be you."[41] Despite the fact that Felicity does a good deed by talking to her father about considering an early release for Ben from his apprenticeship, she ultimately maintains the status quo in the social hierarchy. Felicity, who has been a rebel in her own right and a fighter for causes she believes in, speaks from her position as a member of the owning class when it comes to her father's property.

Scholars have routinely critiqued the brand for sanitizing America's history in order to sell dolls. Arguing that the brand presents a mythical America that romanticizes and cleanses disgraceful moments in American history and inequitable hierarchies in American society, these scholars explore the ways that the collection, as a whole, depicts America as a safe, innocent country that is supported by the promise of equal opportunity.[42] On the other hand, many mothers I interviewed were drawn to this soft approach to difficult topics such as poverty, gender inequality, racial discrimination, and worker's rights. This small multi-racial group of mothers does not shy away from discussing or reading about social issues with their daughters (one even maintains a blog focused on books about social justice and equality) but they do seek what they believe to be age appropriate material for their children. Furthermore, while children are certainly absorbing ideologies that they are not yet able to articulate, it is worth mentioning that the children I interviewed identify characters' efforts to participate in positive social change, rather than their generic aesthetic or their American industriousness, as the characters' common unifying traits. From Cameron, a white five-year-old, who noted that all the characters "are trying do something that helps others," to Jewish nine-year-old, Hannah, who says the stories tell girls to "fight for rights during history and now, too, because some rights we still don't have," to Alexie, a mixed race eleven-year-old who understands the American Girls to teach readers to "be brave and stand up for what is right," and thirteen-year-old Chinese American, Nora, who says that American Girls "make a differ-ence in their communities by standing up for what is right" like "welcom-ing those who suffered" and "speaking up for equality," girls consistently identified the role of characters in activist positions that vocalize justice or in the interpersonal position of championing equality and fairness as the fundamental sameness of their American identity. Similarly, in her analysis of girls' writing about the brand, Veronica Medina found that many of her respondents "drew inspiration from the characters' good deeds and became involved in community service activities or philanthropic causes. This sense of stewardship and commitment to help others is a fundamental component to what it means to be an American Girl."[43]

Taking both a critical stance, and acknowledging girls' meaning making of the texts, this chapter builds upon the previous one, exploring ways in which girls are guided to understand race and ethnicity within the American Girl universe. The stories analyzed in Chapters 4 and 5 that depict injustice against workers, African Americans, the impoverished, girls, and people with disabilities often provide more than a cursory glance at structural inequities that hierarchize difference and the institutions that maintain hegemonic power. Yet in the stories about the Native American experience, and the experience of ethnic Others (a Swedish immigrant, the daughter of Russian Jewish immigrants, and a Mexican American girl) there is a silence around both individually enacted and structurally supported prejudice.

While the African American authors who wrote for Addy, Cécile, and Melody were intentional in their focus on institutionalized oppression, those who wrote for Kaya, Kirsten, Rebecca, and Josefina may have had other equally political intentions. Like Porter and Patrick, who wrote books for the African American characters, Tripp who outlined the Kirsten book prior to Shaw writing the series, and who authored the Josefina series, is explicitly political in her intention. She maintains that her goal is to educate children to "challenge assumptions" and also to "teach children to celebrate the values of tolerance and compassion as well as the value of drive, hope, creativity, individuality, change, and work."[44] Yet, she maintains a clear philosophy about literature for children that informs all of her characters. Her goal is to transform and educate children through optimism and "cheerful skepticism" rather than through "anger, resentment, bitterness, and jealousy."[45] In this way, difference is indeed highlighted and valued; the author can celebrate and teach "the integrity and strength of...a unique culture," rather than conflate that culture with pain and oppression.[46] Pairing the importance of this philosophy to brand strategy, Susan Jevens notes that Josefina's story is told in 1824 because it allowed American Girl to represent "Hispanic culture at its peak," showcasing the ranching tradition and Pueblo culture that has appreciably shaped not just Latino culture but the American Southwest more broadly. She also identified that the choice to depict Kaya before "white contact" gave the brand the opportunity to "depict the remarkable skills and strengths of the Nez Perce tribal community" rather than "a Native people diminished by decades of oppression, war, and disease."

In explaining the decision-making processes surrounding the stories that would be told about the first historical Latina and Native American dolls, and how those differ from the stories of the African American dolls, Susan Jevens contends that American Girl could not tell the story of an African American girl without addressing systemic racism and discrimination. "In short," she explains, "there was no 'pre-contact-with-whites' story to tell [with Addy, Cécile, or Melody] as there was with Kaya and Josefina....because racism and a struggle for justice, freedom and equality.... [have] been omnipresent ever since the first Africans were brought to America as slaves." This dichotomy, while not false, is not necessarily productive in considering a path to social justice; it inextricably and exclusively links black identity with oppression and disconnects other ethnic and racial identities from the legacies of racist oppression against which they have struggled since their first identification as Americans.

In the case of dolls of color who are not African American, the authorial or capitalist desire to narrate optimism, universality, and relatability leads the brand to produce narratives about difference but not about the oppressive conditions through which difference may be experienced. The lack of recognition of injustice leads to a discourse of colorblindness that suggests that all Americans (excepting perhaps African Americans) share the privilege of feeling safe in their communities, having equal opportunities in society, and living in a country that supports their culture and cultural expression. Girl consumers who enter into this imagined community, through books and movies, are positioned to engage in an act of noticing *and* not-noticing race, ethnicity, and social class.[47] While girls are asked to be attentive to differences in racial, ethnic, religious, and/or social class identities, the absence of discussion about violent histories and ongoing structural oppression of these ethnic and racial groups may lead girls to remain ignorant of these factors and potentially to place blame upon oppressed groups for their own oppression.

Noticing/Not-Noticing Native American Experiences

When Kaya, full name Kaya'aton'my, a translation of "she who arranges rocks," was released in 2002 she was not the first Native American character featured in the American Girl collection. Though she was the first Native American doll, and the first Native American girl to have her own story, a Native American girl had appeared in one of the very first series books. Singing Bird, who becomes an acquaintance of Swedish immigrant Kirsten Larson in the story that takes place in Minnesota in 1854, is featured as a fleeting figure in her story and serves to confirm Kirsten's Americanness. From the beginning of her new life on land that would eventually become the American Midwest, Kirsten learns about Native Americans.[48] Her teacher reprimands students who speak out of turn or engage in other minor misbehaviors telling them not to act "savage like the Indians."[49] Her cousin Anna remarks that an Indian who once came to their door asking for a piece of meat was trouser-less, "had red paint on his cheeks and eagle feathers in his hair" and wore soft shoes that made it seem like he was "suddenly in the doorway."[50] Anna attributes this sudden appearance to "Indian magic" but is corrected by her older sister who is more culturally astute and understands that the Native Americans are not magic but wear "soft shoes" that obscure their approaching footsteps.[51] Moreover, her cousin Lisbeth tells Kirsten that the Indians are a source of fear for the new settlers: "Papa worries about the Indians...He says that if we plant crops on their hunting land, the wild animals will go away. He says the Indians won't have enough to eat then, and they'll surely be angry. I don't know...Papa says we need the land, too."[52]

Readers are meant to disagree with Miss Winston for her use of the word savage to describe indigenous cultures and with Anna who says that the Native American man at their door "*looked* savage" and used "Indian magic." In fact, readers are guided to directly challenge the notion of Natives as savages when Kirsten meets Singing Bird. The protagonist finds interest in the girl's "soft deerskin dress," and using the colonializing language that animalizes Native cultures, the way "the Indian girl slipped silently through the cattails."[53] Kirsten bonds with Singing Bird, celebrating their triumph over the language barrier. Feeling isolated, as a recent immigrant who is forced to learn English, she finds comfort in a girl who is friendly and also struggling to learn the language. Readers are asked to notice and not-notice difference and are guided to look down on acts of prejudice against those whose ethnicity is different from their own.[54] Yet they are also asked, as Lisbeth asks Kirsten, who keeps asking questions about the Native population, to not to be "too curious" and to "just play."[55]

Demonstrating the competing needs and interests of immigrants and Natives, Kirsten's uncle's fear is validated, in part. The settlers' crops *do* destroy the Native Americans' hunting grounds. Instead of getting angry, however, the tribe packs up to migrate. When Singing Bird tells Kirsten that her family must leave because they no longer have any food to eat, Kirsten remembers her uncle's prediction, but evokes no emotional reaction to her family's culpability. The protagonist worries about Singing Bird being hungry but also imagines her friend's move to be freeing. When she visualizes joining Singing Bird and her family, as Singing Bird has suggested, "She imagined herself sleeping...under the buffalo hides. If she lived with Singing Bird she would be free to roam the woods all day."[56] She never imagines here, nor do we find out later in the series, that Singing Bird's family may be ravaged by smallpox or by feuds with whites over displacement from their tribal lands.

Kirsten's sense of herself as an American is directly tied to Singing Bird. When she tells her friend that she cannot migrate with the tribe, Kirsten declares, "I want to come, but this is my home. I can't leave my home."[57] Later, when Kirsten returns to school after saying goodbye to Singing Bird she discovers that she suddenly feels that "she belonged here now."[58] While Kirsten can stay and build on the land, Singing Bird is displaced; Kirsten's American dream can come true but Singing Bird's cannot. As Sonja Pérez has argued, rather than dealing with the violence and racial persecution at the core of these differing experiences, Kirsten's story paints a false picture of American history by creating a dichotomy between Kirsten's family as a hard-working immigrant family that is working the land and Singing Bird's as a romanticized indigenous free-roaming one.[59]

Kirsten's role in enacting Manifest Destiny, in taking over the land from the Native American population and driving Singing Bird's family off of their territory, is never fully noticed. Kirsten's family's innocence—the innocence of white America—is validated by their own (immigrant) need to settle their new land and make a home, as well as by the romantic description of Signing Bird's displacement. Kirsten's American identity, then, is cemented in her performance of noticing/not-noticing. She is invested in her friendship with Singing Bird and rejects the stereotyping she hears from Miss Winston and cousin Anna, but she is also invested in a racist national identity undergirded by her ability to overlook the role that she and her family play in endorsing imperialism.

Just a little over fifteen years after Singing Bird appeared in Kirsten's story, two other stories about Native Americans, one popular and one obscure, were released by American Girl. Before further exploring Kaya's tale, released in 2002, which is a part of the BeForever series, it is worth touching upon Minuk's story. Published in the same year as Kaya's story, Minuk's narrative was a part of the short-lived eight character Girls of Many Lands collection.[60] While the seven other dolls hailed from Europe, Africa, and Asia, and could easily be considered girls of "many lands," Minuk who lived in Alaska in 1892, twenty-five years after the Alaska purchase by the United States from Russia, would according to standard brand practice be considered an "American Girl." While it is true that Alaska did not receive statehood until 1959, other historical characters were identified as American despite the fact that their lands were not yet states during the time in which their stories occur.[61] It is unclear why two Native American stories were released in the two different collections during the same year but their different approach to internal colonialism is significant. Most notable, Minuk's story takes place *after* her Yup'ik culture has encountered white settlers and her story includes some of the pain of the diseases and assimilationist practices they brought. Minuk accepts acculturation and is enamored with the white Christian missionaries, who are generally kind, but she also questions the supposed superiority of the proselytizer's belief systems and practices. For instance, when the missionary, Mrs. Hoff, tells all the children that once they are baptized they will be given English names Minuk thinks about the impact that would have on the Yup'ik culture in which children are named for the most recently deceased villager. She remarks, "It would make people very unhappy to have to believe in Mrs. Hoff's way—that their relatives were gone forever and could not come back"[62] Minuk also questions the basic tenants of the proselytizers' Christianity. She asks why God is suddenly speaking to and protecting the Yup'ik and how that impacts their ancestors who have already died without having been baptized as well as why the missionaries did not talk about protecting animals, trees, and plants when these were important living things in her culture. At the end of her story, her mother and several members of her family die from diseases that the missionaries brought with them to Alaska. Minuk's story and her doll have been out of production since 2005.

Kaya's story, which takes place more than 120 years before Minuk's, is written about the Nimíipuu, which is now commonly known as the Nez Perce tribe, *before* their encounter with white settlers (Fig. 6.1). Given the time period in which Kaya's story occurs, not only does author Janet Shaw not need to address the encounters with missionaries, it also allows her to avoid engaging with the shameful history of the tribe's expulsion from its lands as well as the starvation and disease its members faced when they were driven into prisoner of war camps and onto reservations after the United States declared war against them in 1877.[63] Well aware of the cultural and political implications of this narrative decision, as it was when its then-only African American doll told the story of slavery, American Girl declared that the desire to tell the story at the height of Nez Perce culture came from the advisory board members who supported the production of the character.[64] Journalist Michelle Healy reports that it was the advisory board members who requested that Kaya's experience address themes of community and culture rather than cultural decimation and loss. The goal, according to author Janet Shaw, was to give readers an

Fig. 6.1   Kaya doll

opportunity to "understand, appreciate, and respect a rich and intriguing way of life so different from their own."[65] The advisory board issued a statement explaining,

> We chose this time period because our children—and children yet to come—need to know where they have come from. And, because we chose to interpret a time before conflict and tragedy, they will be able to visualize our people at the height of our culture. As grandparents, we want the children to know of a life before contact with the Euro-Americans—a time when our institutions of education, law, health, and beliefs were still intact. We want them to know of the peace that was in our lives, our families, and our villages. It also validates that we were here since time immemorial. Most important, however, is believing that someday things will come full circle and we will live like we once did—not as subjects of an inner colonial system or as a minority group of America, but as the true, real people that we were created to be—a people with strong beliefs who will once again be the stewards of this land from which we all came.[66]

For its part, American Girl says that it sought to find a tribe that was still active and that it "needed to figure out which tribes would be willing to work" with them.[67] In recent communication with the brand's representative, Susan Jevens reported that the company did consider setting the story during the second half of the nineteenth century, when the tribe was forced off its lands by the US government and by white miners who had discovered gold within the tribal territory. She says that the advisory board "affirmed" that Kaya's was the "more valuable story to tell for young readers (of either culture)." It is unclear, then, whether American Girl selected the Nez Perce tribe in particular because they were willing to work with the company to support this sanitized narrative or if the choice to write about the culture's peak was determined after the selection of the advisory board members.

Whether American Girl sought out a tribe that would tell the story it wanted, or decided to work with a tribe and used the story the tribe's advisory board recommended, it is significant that it chose to work with a specific tribe and to portray the community with tribal specificity. Scholars have noted that most children's literature does not include tribal differentiation despite the existence of over 500 different tribes in the United States.[68] The choice to work with a tribe that continues to thrive culturally is laudable since it is common for children's books to portray Native cultures as being from the past and having little to no present community.[69] As historical fiction, American Girl can do little to combat the trope of Native Americas as people of the past, though there is some attempt to overcome this by specifically selecting a tribe that was still intact and through the "Looking Back" supplements in each book that also looked forward and pictured contemporary Nez Perce children. Still, American Girl knew that unlike their other dolls of color the Kaya doll was not being manufactured to "capitalize on ethnic spending power" since Native Americans as a market are too small, too scattered and too low on the socioeconomic ladder to create a viable market.[70] Rather, Kaya, the "First American Girl," was going to be sold, in part, to satisfy the brand's desire for historical authenticity but also to capitalize on the longstanding white American desire to dress up and play Indian.[71]

Whatever means was used to determine the story's timeline, there are political implications of the brand's only Native American doll narrative as one that is absent of conflict with European American settlers. The early time period of the story sets the stage for a typical portrayal of Native Americans who are frequently imagined in children's books as uncorrupted by European American civilization and as having a romantic spiritual connection with nature.[72] Throughout her collection, Kaya's community is depicted as having a primitive civilization; the children receive corporal punishment from Whipwoman when they misbehave, women and girls who are sad are told to refrain from participating in the root harvest as their emotions might seep into the food, and Snow Paws, the dog who heads up the pack that travels with their tribe, is portrayed as having leadership skills. In addition, a harmonious relationship to land and all living things is woven into Kaya's story. In *Kaya and the Lone Dog* the two title characters seem to have a spiritual communication. Kaya tells her grandmother, "Sometimes Lone Dog seems to be talking to me with her eyes." When she asks her grandmother if the older woman believes her, the response is, "I believe you. Animals talk to us in many, many ways." Kaya presses on, "But I mean she really *speaks* to me, too." The grandmother responds by telling Kaya a story about her own mother who was visited by a wolf spirit that allowed her to talk to a wolf and then about one wolf who gave her mother "the gift of her wolf power."[73] Doris Seale and Beverly Slapin also note that Kaya's thoughts are often compared to nature as in "her thoughts whirled like smoke in the wind," "she glides over the ground like the shadow of an eagle," and "her feelings were all tangled up like a nest of snakes."[74] The implication is that Kaya's connection to nature is otherworldly and uniquely Native American.

Kaya's story, then, asks readers to participate in an act of noticing/not-noticing her ethnic and racial difference. Readers, most of whom will not be Native, are asked to see difference as a positive; Kaya's Nez Perce rituals are depicted as distinctly cultural and special. Indeed, reflecting on her memories of Kaya, thirteen-year-old Ruby thinks about how it was special for her to be reading about an "original" American "before the settlers came because at school we usually learn about white American culture." She also finds it significant that Kaya "had more freedom and independence" than Felicity because she was from a different cultural background, "from a tribe that allowed girls to be strong." However, the absence of institutionalized violence and racial extermination against the Native populations in Kaya's story, as well as in those that represent Singing Bird, also asks readers to participate in not-noticing. They are asked to notice difference but not oppressive conditions that result from policies, institutions, and practices that discriminate and enact violence against different Others. This preferred reading position ultimately romanticizes difference and avoids an engagement with real relations of power that organize racial logics.

NOTICING/NOT-NOTICING ETHNIC OTHERS

Kirsten, Josefina, and Rebecca all have very different stories and experiences, but each of them is represented as an ethnic Other who is also American. Kirsten, as discussed above, is a Swedish immigrant to the Minnesota farmland in 1854, Josefina is a Mexican national in 1824 on land that will eventually become New Mexico, and Rebecca is the daughter of Russian Jewish immigrants to New York City in 1914. Comparing Kirsten's story to that of Josefina, Communication Studies scholars Carolina Acosta-Alzuru and Peggy Kreshel write that Kirsten represents the positives and negatives of the assimilation process because she "successfully adapts to her new country; she learns English and her family buys a new house....[her] outfits and accessories artfully mix her Swedish roots with the American Style, rendering a visual representation of the American melting pot."[75] In contrast, they argue, "Josefina's 1824 world...is purely Mexican....[her] outfits and accessories never mix and blend her Mexican heritage with American style and objects."[76] In portraying the history of a girl who is fully Mexican, rather than an ingredient in the American melting pot, they argue, Josefina remains an outsider.[77] From their perspective Josefina has neither legal citizenship nor cultural citizenship in the United States. In other words, she has no sense of belonging to or in the nation. On the other hand, Rebecca's story has been criticized for making assimilation look *too* easy and not reflecting the anti-Semitism that Jewish immigrants, at the turn of the century, experienced in the United States. Lisa Marcus argues that Rebecca's environment presents "an idealized America" that is welcoming, tolerant, and into which a Jewish identity "fits comfortably."[78] Because individuals and communities from various cultures experience their relationship to American identity in a variety of ways and are both forced or chose to make various decisions about the level of assimilation in which they participate, there is no one accurate or authentic depiction of an ethnic experience.[79] In the American Girl collection, authors have sometimes chosen to create assimilation stories in which native ethnic cultures are woven into the fabric of a new American culture. In other cases, the brand's authors have chosen to create stories that present an ethnic culture that has yet to be tarnished by intercultural relations of power. These two narrative techniques encourage readers to continue the performance of noticing/not-noticing discussed above. Girl readers are intended to celebrate difference in language, food, and rituals but are generally left blind to a critique of the ideologies and practices of Othering that leads to the systematic oppression of ethnic Others in the United States.

If the American identity of these ethnic Others is not determined by their experience of oppression and its resulting pain, it is their embrace of an entrepreneurial spirit and business savvy that casts each of them as part of the imagined community of American Girl. Framed in a neoliberal, color-blind discourse of individual responsibility and the myth of social mobility, the girl within her family unit "serves the nation through...support of the free market" and becomes imbricated in the nation through her success in this market.[80] Although located in the past, these girls become the contemporary powerful "can-do girls" of girl power who are self-driven and self-made.[81] Jevens explains, "As a company, we want to encourage girls to have big dreams and to give them the tools and confidence to go after them wholeheartedly. Our historical and contemporary characters serve as role models in helping shape girls and their ideas of what's possible, and entrepreneurialism, and the values inherent in its pursuit, is one of the lenses by which we can convey for girls how they can achieve their goals...." Tethering entrepreneurialism to the dolls' American identity, she elaborates,

America was founded on the freedom to pursue happiness and the idea that hard work was the path to success. Success is not necessarily financial, especially when you're a girl. In our stories, success just as often could be artistic, athletic, social, or even gaining your freedom and reuniting your family; but it can be financial or professional as well. To the extent that our stories support and reinforce this founding principle, they perpetuate this idea of the American identity.

While possibly inspiring to girl readers, who say that American Girl celebrates "being yourself" and pursuing your own dreams, these representations of self-determination leading to success may also fail to offer girls a broad systemic analysis of race and ethnicity in the United States.

Kirsten enters the country feeling scared and overwhelmed. She speaks very little English, has lost her friend, Marta, who fell ill with cholera and died during the passage from Sweden, and has just learned that all of her belongings will have to stay in a trunk in Riverton while the family settles on Uncle Olav's farm miles away. Kirsten longs for the material objects that will make her feel connected to her Swedish culture. She thinks fondly of her doll, the Christmas clothes that her mother and her grandmother knit, and especially longs for the family's candlesticks that she would need to celebrate the Swedish custom of Saint Lucia's Day.

While she desires her ethnic cultural objects, she seems to have a relatively easy time assimilating to life in the United States. As discussed above, Singing Bird is used as a narrative device, in part, to secure Kirsten's American identity; the language Kirsten teaches Singing Bird is English rather than Swedish, and when Singing Bird's family is displaced from their hunting grounds, Kirsten confirms her own feeling about the new land being home. Our protagonist's national identity is further firmed up by her embrace of the myth of American industriousness.[82] Not only does Kirsten learn to value work over play, believing that this is crucial to her family's success, but she also helps to launch a family business during her town's Fourth of July day celebration. Life on the farm is difficult and her mother often reminds her that her participation in the domestic work of the household takes priority over other interests. Kirsten soon finds that:

> Every night when her chores were done, [she] went straight to bed and fell asleep. And as soon as she woke in the morning, she started on that day's tasks.[83]

She may not always love it but Kirsten becomes the self-directed, hardworking, pioneering American girl that will lead to her family's success and stability in the new country. In *Happy Birthday, Kirsten!* the protagonist discovers a beehive filled with honeycombs. Her brother and father gather the honey and she and her mother turn it into a product to sell. She is not able to harvest the honey on her own and has to rely on her male family members to complete the task, yet she is the brains of the operation declaring that Independence Day would be "the perfect time" to sell honey in town.[84] This symbiosis of entrepreneurialism and the celebration of the nation confirms that Kirsten is no longer noticed as different.[85] Marked with her blonde braids and blue eyes, her family's ownership of the Minnesota plains, her mastery of the English language, and her connection to American independence, there is no longer anything to notice about Kirsten's difference; she has become a fully assimilated American.

Like Kirsten, Rebecca's American identity is also fortified by economic success and assimilation. Rebecca's ethnic Otherness is made clear throughout the series. When we first meet Rebecca, she is playing with the nesting dolls that "belonged to Mama when she was growing up in Russia."[86] We quickly learn that her family's conversations are sprinkled with Yiddish, their day of rest is Saturday rather than Sunday and that they share folktales about the Russian tsar during family dinners. The series does deal with many of the challenges of immigration including a teacher who does not allow any Yiddish to be spoken in her classroom and the dangerous working conditions of the sweatshops in which many immigrants worked. Rebecca's grandfather expresses the tensions of assimilation when he says, "Immigrants have to learn new ways to live here in America...but we can't forget who we are, even if that means being a little different," yet the story often portrays those who are willing to hide their differences more favorably than those who struggle to maintain their ethnic identity.[87]

Rebecca's cousin Ana, who initially has trouble conforming to the English-only rules at school, does not know what patriotic means, and says that she still loves her Russian homeland, quickly learns to fit in. At first Ana is not sure that she wants to pledge her allegiance to a country that has temporarily detained her brother on Ellis Island simply because of his injured leg. After just one week in her first American school, however, Ana joins her cousin in a rendition of "You're a Grand Old Flag" for a school assembly after which she looks into the crowd to see her brother on crutches and exclaims her new feeling of patriotism toward the United States. The siblings proceed to wave small American flags at one another claiming their new identity. Likewise, Rebecca's mother's cousin, Moyshe, who had been in a traveling vaudeville act and sometimes had to borrow money from Rebecca's father, begins an easy assimilation process when he decides to shed his ethnic identity. It is when Moyshe changes his name to Max and is hired by a movie studio that he begins to earn a steady paycheck and meets his fiancé. If Ana and Moyshe assimilate easily, Bubbie, her grandmother, does not. She demands that Rebecca stop singing "Jingle Bells," even when the granddaughter reminds her that than the song is not about Christmas but rather celebrates winter and sleigh rides like the ones Bubbie had taken when she was a child in Russia. And when Rebecca is invited to visit Max on his movie set, Bubbie, failing in her English pronunciation, worries that the "pitcher-making place" is not an appropriate setting for a young girl and that Rebecca will not be able to follow the dietary rules of Passover if she goes to work with Max. Bubbie is juxtaposed not only with Max but also with lead actress Lily Armstrong, also Jewish, who will become Max's fiancé. When Rebecca sees the film star with shortly cropped hair she thinks, "Bubbie had been worried about the actresses not being 'ladies.' She would think it was perfectly scandalous to see a young woman with her hair bobbed."[88] Max and Lily's assimilation has allowed them to thrive in the American economy while Bubbie's stubborn attachment to ethnic Jewish identity and ritual makes her appear out of alignment with American progress.

Rebecca is born in the United States and therefore does not have the same issues as her relatives surrounding assimilation but author Greene still makes the case for her Americanness. When Rebecca reveals to her parents that she has secretly been selling lace doilies in the back of her father's shoe store, her father shares his own secret; he has known all along. He tells Rebecca, "When your daughter is a successful American businesswoman, what can a father do except sit back and watch?"[89] Rebecca's American identity surfaces again when she completes the Christmas table centerpiece project assigned by her teacher. Her friend Rose, who is also Jewish, can hardly stand making the Christmas ornament that violates her sense of self, and she throws it away as soon as she leaves school. Readers learn that while her teacher's ignorant requirement that all students make the holiday decoration may be unfair, Rebecca figures out a way to assimilate, highlighting both her sameness and difference by giving the centerpiece to her building's Italian landlord, Mr. Rossi. In return, Mr. Rossi gives Rebecca two candlesticks; He explains, "I know you don't celebrate Christmas...but you light candles for Hanukkah." Again, readers are asked to notice/not-notice Rebecca's difference. She may not celebrate

Christmas but the difference between the two holidays, is made primarily symbolic.[90] Although Mr. Rossi did not understand the symbolism of the eight menorah candles and instead gave her two candlesticks (which she will use for Shabbat), Rebecca understands that Americans share the universal experience of celebrating winter holidays but with different iconography. Interestingly, when Rebecca stands up for worker's rights, and not for the owning class, her Jewish identity is noticed again. She tells her Aunt Fannie that she must do her part because of her grandfather's message of *tikkun olam*, a Jewish concept meaning doing one's part to help repair the world. Rebecca's organizing is represented as reflective of her Jewish heritage, not her American culture.

It is most difficult to make the case for Josefina's American identity which is why some young people may understand Josefina to be foreign and exotic.[91] As with Addy, Kaya, and Melody, Josefina's story and appearance were created in consultation with an advisory board. The eight-member board met regularly in New Mexico to help develop a story for Josefina as well as a face mold that reflected Josefina's ethnicity.[92] The new mold was based on a local girl model from Santa Fe and had several changes from the original face mold including a nose that was slightly longer and less upturned, lips that were fuller, eyes that were more oval, and a chin that was longer and sharper.[93] In many ways readers are asked specifically to notice Josefina's difference. Josefina is always Mexican and Other; her family lives on a *rancho*, not a farm, she has a *tia*, not an aunt, she goes to *fiestas*, not parties, and her dream career is *curandera* or healer, not doctor. Moreover, Josefina does not identify as *Americano*; instead, this is a term ascribed to Anglo traders who arrive on the Santa Fe Trail. Giving a Mexican identity to the first Latino doll made economic sense given that close to sixty percent of all Latinos in the United States are Mexican Americans.[94] However which Mexican American story would be told was determined by Valerie Tripp along with an advisory board. Tripp says that her inspiration to write about New Mexico primarily before its encounter with Anglos came from her own schooling during which she did not learn about the history of the American Southwest. She says, "I wanted to show this was a culture that had gone on for a long, long time and I wanted to show it in its essence and in its strength" before "the strong influence from the East." Recounting how she came to create Josefina's life and culture, Tripp says that she spent three summers in New Mexico immersing herself in its history and culture and,

> I spoke to the oldest ladies I could find and asked what they remembered of what their mothers had taught them—things that had been passed down.... They told me about daily life and skills such as cooking and weaving. But more than anything else, they told about the importance of love and loyalty to family. Again and again, they took me to rooms filled with old family photographs ... to show me how important the family was and still is.... So it became clear to me that Josefina's family would be very important in the stories. In Josefina's day, your family was your community. Many generations would live on the same rancho, and everyone had a role.[95]

It was important to Tripp that American Girl customers understand Josefina as "an American Girl, too, even though she spoke Spanish." For Tripp, Josefina's story, like Kaya's, does not have to be the story of struggle and sadness; rather it can be the story of a community filled with love and hope.

Alternatively, critics argue that Josefina's status as American is tenuous and suggest that the company's choice to place Josefina in an era before the escalation of conflict in the region sanitizes the American history of racism and colonization.[96] Veronica Medina's analysis finds that Josefina's location on lands that belonged to Mexico and not yet to the United States—and prior to the United States' "imperialistic and militaristic venture" on the southwest border—allows the company "to ignore the legacy of internal colonialism, including its material, cultural and psychological consequences."[97] Mexicans like Josefina's family, who lived on the land that is now New Mexico, were Mexican nationals until the United States invaded Mexican territory and forced the Mexican government to sign the Hidalgo Treaty in 1848. These individuals did not migrate to the United States; the signing of treaty is what made them American citizens.[98] Josefina's story does not account for the ways in which the treaty was violated by large Anglo agribusinesses that, through physical and economic violence, forced small Chicano landowners off of their land.[99] Nor does it address how Mexican Americans were victims of labor policies and practices that forced them to work in lower skilled jobs and for less money than Anglos.[100] The choice to avoid the retelling of this history may serve, as Tripp hopes, to teach readers about the various stories of American heritage, remind readers about the importance of embracing all Americans, and show them that there is common ground to be found among all girls. Still, it may ask girls to participate in the act of noticing/not-noticing in Josefina's story; notice her ethnic difference, do not notice the violent policies and acts against her progeny and community that are yet to come. Notice that Josefina is American but always an "eternal outsider."[101]

The only indication we have of Josefina's future encounters with the United States and its representatives is her interaction with Patrick, the Anglo trader who appears in *Josefina Saves the Day* and who is characterized as a benevolent businessman. This construction of Josefina's US identity as based on an economic transaction is well situated in a contemporary marketing culture that often constructs Latinas as claiming United States citizenship through their relationship to the consumer market rather than to society more broadly.[102] On their first encounter Josefina, playing her flute, and Patrick playing his violin, each think other's instrument sounds like a bird. Usually afraid of strangers, Josefina is warmed by the blue eyes and "friendly smile" on the polite Missouri trader. The positive feelings between the Anglos and the Chicanos continue when Patrick meets Josefina's older sister who looks at him "from under her long, dark eyelashes" and around whom he "seemed to forget how to say thank you—or anything else" because "Francisca was very beautiful."[103] The family and Patrick make music together creating the metaphoric imagery of a harmonious relationship between the United States and Mexican nationals living on the Southwest borderlands. This agreeable relationship is further portrayed by Josefina's account of the increasing influx of American traders. Josefina noticed that some in her community, "were not so enthusiastic" and watched "the wagons with questioning looks, as if they were not convinced that the arrival of the americanos was a good thing."[104] But the BeForever protagonist is filled with excitement; she describes the "delighted shiver" she feels as she awaits the traders' wagons, "the clapping, cheering, and waving as the americanos' wagons lumbered into view," and the way the American flag on the wagons, "looked snappy and clean in the bright sunshine."[105] Though there is skepticism about the opening of the Santa Fe trail from some members of her community, readers are meant to identify with Josefina's enthusiasm.

When a misunderstanding rocks the relationship, it is remedied by Josefina's bravery but also by the discovery that Patrick is as honest and good as first impressions had suggested. We learn that he is not just a fair trader but is also generous and caring. He gives the Montoya sisters the items for which they have fairly bartered as well as special gifts for each sister. Although Josefina's citizenship remains questionable it may be only through this mutually beneficial economic encounter that the protagonist marks her connection to the nation. However, just as the contemporary myth that "buying power" and "political power" are synonymous and can "erase the realities....such as poverty and lack of access to higher education and health care....that many Latina/os continue to face," the story of the easy trading relationship between the Montoya family and the Anglos can erase the racism, economic hardship, and unequal access to power experienced by the Chicanos who lived in New Mexico during the 1820s.[106] This fictitious story of the Montoya's relationship with an American businessman does not simply avoid addressing the exploitation of Mexican American labor yet to come, it suggests the opposite.

Where consumers are led to see Josefina's ethnic Otherness, they are perhaps asked to racialize her as white or ambiguous. Josefina's racial ambiguity is marked by the use of the doll's face mold and skin tone which is used for several other ethnic representations, supporting the claim that "the ethnically ambiguous light-skinned Latina represents the safe and preferred way of representing difference."[107] As the only Latina historical doll she is both historically specific and embodies the generic Latina look employed by marketers who seek to garner the largest share of a diverse Latino/a market and a non-Latino market as well.[108] Given her ambiguous racial identity, as well as a narrative void of economic, social, or physical pain resulting from the oppressive policies and conditions of racial and ethnic injustice, Josefina may fail to assist readers in moving beyond a colorblind or multicultural analytical frame as they work to understand her difference.

CONTRADICTORY LOGICS OF RACE AND ETHNICITY IN THE AMERICAN GIRL BEFOREVER COLLECTION

Whereas the stories about Kit, Melody, Julie, and Rebecca, discussed in Chapter 4, call for communities to organize for change, and Addy and Melody's stories, discussed in Chapter 5, recognize that racism is not the problem of individuals but of laws, institutions, and social hatred, the American Girl stories discussed in this chapter use colorblind narratives, with American status conferred upon those who embrace industriousness rather than those who engage in social change. These tales about Kaya, Kirsten, Rebecca, and Josefina may encourage readers to notice ethnicity and celebrate difference but be blind to the institutionalization of hierarchies around which racial logics are organized.

On a 2017 episode of ABC's sitcom *black-ish*, Diane receives a white historical doll from a neighbor for her birthday. Her mother, Bow, decides she wants to exchange the doll for a black one that would better represent her daughter and serve as a positive role model. Upon arriving at the doll store the mother and daughter learn that there are just two African American historical dolls: Sassy Sadie, an escaped slave, and Sassy Selma, a civil rights activist. Bow is dismayed at the limited selection of black dolls but also at the fact that both of them represent a struggle for justice. Believing that "the images that we see effect who we are and who we aspire to become" and that "our kids seeing themselves reflected in our culture is important," Bow suggests that the company create black dolls that do not focus on their oppression and struggle but focus on African American culture and achievements. Discussed in Chapter 5, Addy and Melody's stories are very much steeped in the struggle for equality and in addressing painful moments in American history. The risk here is that blackness becomes equated with oppression and exploitation. On the other hand, the fictional constructions of the other dolls of color, Kaya and Josefina, do not address a movement for social change at all. There is a brand inconsistency; Addy, Cécile, and Melody's stories explore racism and attend to systemic racism through policy and practice while Kaya and Josefina's stories fail to address racism against the Native and Latino populations in this country. This choice not to depict oppression and injustice in narratives about the dolls of color who are not African American may lead to a focus on their culture outside of their oppression but it also leads to a fictional collection in which the long legacy of Latino and Native American struggles for just treatment in society are neglected.

Notes

1. Valerie Tripp, *The One and Only: A Maryellen Classic Volume 1* (Middleton, WI: American Girl Publishing, 2015), 101, 112–114.
2. Ibid., 110.
3. Stuart Hall, "The Whites of their Eyes: Racist Ideology and the Media," in *The Race and Media Reader*, ed. Gilbert Rodman (New York: Routledge, 2014), 41.
4. Jeanne Brady, "Reading the American Dream: The History of the American Girl Collection," *Teaching and Learning Literature* 4, no. 1 (September/October 1994): 4.
5. Susan Jevens, e-mail message to author, March 10, 2017.
6. Valerie Tripp, e-mail message to author, February 17, 2017.
7. Ibid.
8. Valerie Tripp, in discussion with the author, February 1, 2017.

9. Michelle Healy, "Meet Kaya: The Authentic Nez Perce Doll," *USA Today*, August 11, 2008, D6.
10. Tripp, e-mail.
11. Michelle Wildgen, "The Rise of American Girl Rebecca Rubin," *The Forward*, January 2, 2013.
12. Jessica Harrison, "American Girl Books Honor Readers, Author Valerie Tripp Says," *Cracking the Cover*, September 28, 2015, https://www.crackingthecover.com/11846/american-girl-books-honor-readers-author-valerie-tripp-says/.
13. Samantha Sharf, "Why Mattel's American Girl Needs to Bank on Millennial Moms (And Maybe Dads)," *Forbes*, December 19, 2015, http://www.forbes.com/sites/samanthasharf/2015/12/19/how-mattels-american-girl-is-banking-on-millennial-moms/2/#56775cd07a0d.
14. Laura DeMarco, "American Girl introduces new 1950s doll, Maryellen Larkin, with events around the country," September 22, 2015, http://www.cleveland.com/entertainment/index.ssf/2015/09/american_girl_introduces_new_1.html.
15. Patricia Cohen, "A Line of Dolls Enters the '70s," *New York Times*, August 25, 2007, B7; DeMarco, "American Girl."
16. Claire Kirch, "American Girl Tackles Civil Rights Movement with New Character," *Publishers Weekly*, March 8, 2016, http://www.publishersweekly.com/pw/by-topic/childrens/childrens-book-news/article/69602-american-girl-tackles-civil-rights-movement-with-new-character.html. American Girl says that the doll was three to four years in the making and not a response to the recent call for diverse children's literature. Further information on the renewed focus on the need for diversity in children's literature can be found at http://www.chicagotribune.com/lifestyles/books/ct-prj-daniel-handler-diversity-childrens-books-20141224-story.html.
17. "American Girl Debuts Doll from Civil Rights Era," *CBS News*, February 22, 2016, http://www.cbsnews.com/news/american-girl-30th-anniversary-debuts-third-african-american-historical-doll-melody-ellison/.
18. Ibid.
19. "American Girl: Stories Forever," Vimeo video, 2:48, posted by Weber Shandwick Southwest Studio, June 10, 2014, https://vimeo.com/97829479.
20. American Girl, "American Girl Debuts 1960s Melody Ellison to Its BeForever Lineup," press release, August 25, 2016, http://www.americangirl.com/wcsstore/Tridion/AGStore/Images/melody_press_release924-287641.pdf.

21. Julia Rubin, "All Dolled Up: The Enduring Triumph of American Girl: How Does a Brand Be Everything to Every Girl?" *Racked*, June 29, 2015, http://www.racked.com/2015/6/29/8855683/american-girl-doll-store.
22. Pleasant Company. "Ask the Author: Janet Shaw" retrieved from Children's Literature Independent Information and Reviews, http://archive.is/CIi0J.
23. Ibid.
24. Jevens, e-mail.
25. Susan Guevara, "Authentic Enough: Am I? Are You? Interpreting Culture for Children's Literature," in *Stories Matter: The Complexity of Cultural Authenticity in Children's Literature*, eds. Dana L. Fox and Kathy G. Short (Urbana, IL: National Council of Teachers of English, 2003), 50–51.
26. See Chapter 2 for a greater discussion of neo-historicism.
27. Valerie Tripp, "Anne Scott Macleod Children's Literature Lecture," Unpublished lecture delivered at the Library of Congress, Washington, DC. October 9, 2014.
28. Harrison, "American Girl Books Honor Readers."
29. Ibid.
30. Wildgen, "The Rise of American Girl Rebecca Rubin."
31. Molly Rosner, "The American Girl Company and the Uses of Nostalgia in Children's Consumer Culture," *Jeunesse: Young People, Texts, Cultures* 6, no. 2 (2014): 41; Sonja Zepeda Pérez, "Mis(s)Education: Narrative Construction and Closure in American Girl" (PhD diss., University of Arizona, 2015), 77.
32. Carolina Acosta-Alzuru and Elizabeth P. Lester Roushanzamir, "'Everything We Do is Celebration of You!' Pleasant Company Constructs American Girlhood," *The Communication Review* 6 (2003).
33. Tripp, "Anne Scott Macleod Children's Literature Lecture."
34. Jevens, e-mail.
35. Megan McDonald, *Meet Julie* (Middleton, WI: American Girl Publishing, 2007), 53.
36. Cohen, "A Line of Dolls Enters the '70s."
37. Ibid.
38. Valerie Tripp, *Felicity Saves the Day* (Middleton, WI: American Girl Publishing, 1992; reprint, Middleton, WI: American Girl Publishing, 2000), 7.
39. Valerie Tripp, *Happy Birthday, Felicity* (Middleton, WI: American Girl Publishing, 1992; reprint, Middleton, WI: American Girl Publishing, 2000), 51.
40. Tripp, *Felicity Saves the Day*, 50.

41. Tripp, in discussion with the author.
42. Daniel Hade, "Lies My Children's Books Taught Me: History Meets Popular Culture in 'The American Girls' Books," in *Voices of the Other: Children's Literature and the Postcolonial Context*, ed. Roderick McGillis (New York: Garland, 2000); Veronica Medina, "Theorizing American Girl" (Master's thesis, University of Missouri-Columbia, 2007); Pérez, "Mis(s)Education;" Angharad Valdivia, "Living in a Hybrid Material World: Girls, Ethnicity and Mediated Doll Products," *Girlhood Studies* 2, no. 1 (2009).
43. Veronica Medina, "'And That's What I Think Being an American Girl Is All About!': Girls' Reflections on American Girl and Contemporary American Girlhood" (PhD diss., University of Missouri, 2012), 103.
44. Tripp, "Anne Scott Macleod Children's Literature Lecture."
45. Ibid.
46. Tripp, in discussion with the author.
47. Robin Bernstein, *Racial Innocence: Performing American Childhood and Race from Slavery to Civil Rights* (New York: NYU Press, 2011), 6. Bernstein uses the concept of the performance of not-noticing to explore how white childhood was conferred a false innocence through obliviousness, "not merely an absence of knowledge, but an active state of repelling knowledge."
48. Minnesota was granted statehood in 1858.
49. Janet Shaw, *Kirsten Learns a Lesson* (Middleton, WI: American Girl Publishing, 1986; reprint, Middleton, WI: American Girl Publishing, 2000), 7.
50. Ibid., 16.
51. Ibid., 17.
52. Ibid., 17–18.
53. Ibid., 26.
54. Veronica Medina's analysis of essays by girls about American Girl demonstrates that "diversity—as well as tolerance and acceptance of diversity—is an important component of what makes one an American girl." Medina, "'And That's What I Think Being an American Girl Is All About!' 109.
55. Shaw, *Kirsten Learns a Lesson*, 18.
56. Ibid., 58.
57. Ibid.
58. Ibid., 60; Pérez, "Mis(s)Education," 89.
59. Pérez, "Mis(s)Education," 89.
60. In 2002 American Girl began a three-year experiment with an international collection, Girl of Many Lands. The eight dolls in this collection represented twelve-year-old girls from England in 1592, France in 1711, Turkey in 1720, Ethiopia in 1846, Alaska in 1890, China in 1857, Ireland

in 1937 and India in 1939. As smaller dolls intended for display, the Girls of Many Lands were marketed toward older girls and adults. The line was discontinued in 2005.

61. Felicity lived in Virginia in 1774, fourteen years before statehood, Josefina lived in New Mexico in 1824, twenty-four years before annexation and eighty-eight years before statehood, Kirsten lived in Minnesota in 1854, four years before statehood, and Kaya's Northwest homeland was in parts of the United States that were not officially owned by the United States until the Oregon Treaty of 1846.

62. Kirkpatrick Hill, *Minuk: Ashes in the Pathway* (Middleton, WI: Pleasant Company Publications, 2002), 70–71.

63. Medina, "Theorizing American Girl," 11–13.

64. Healy, "Meet Kaya: The Authentic Nez Perce Doll."

65. Pleasant Company, "Ask the Author: Janet Shaw."

66. Pleasant Company, "Ask the Nez Perce Tribe," retrieved from Children's Literature Independent Information and Reviews, http://archive.is/ CIi0J.

67. Healy, "Meet Kaya: The Authentic Nez Perce Doll."

68. Debbie Reese, "Authenticity & Sensitivity: Goals for Writing and Reviewing Books with Native American Themes," *School Library Journal* 45 (1999): 36.

69. Lucy Ganje, "Native American Stereotypes," in *Images That Injure: Pictorial Stereotypes in the Media*, ed. Paul Martin Lester and Susan Ross (Westport, CT: Praeger, 2003), 113–120.

70. Ann duCille, "Dyes and Dolls: Multicultural Barbie and the Merchandising of American Culture," *differences* 6, no. 1 (1994): 49; Erich Fox Tree, "The Secret Sex Lives of Native American Barbies, from the Mysteries of Motherhood to the Magic of Colonialism," in *Dolls Studies: The Many Meanings of Girls' Toys and Play*, eds. Miriam Forman-Brunell and Jennifer Dawn Whitney (New York: Peter Lang, 2015), 227–256.

71. Fox Tree, "The Secret Sex Lives of Native American Barbies, from the Mysteries of Motherhood to the Magic of Colonialism," 231.

72. Ganje, "Native American Stereotypes."

73. Janet Shaw, *Kaya and the Lone Dog* (Middleton, WI: American Girl Publishing, 2002), 53.

74. Doris Seale and Beverly Slapin, *A Broken Flute: The Native Experience in Books for Children* (Lantham, MD: Altamira, 2006), 386.

75. Carolina Acosta-Alzuru and Peggy J. Kreshel, "'I'm an American Girl… Whatever That Means': Girls Consuming Pleasant Company's American Girl Identity," *Journal of Communication* 52, no. 1 (2002): 147.

76. Ibid.

77. Acosta-Alzuru and Kreshel, "I'm an American Girl."; Valdivia, "Living in a Hybrid Material World."
78. Lisa Marcus, "Dolling Up History: Fictions of Jewish American Girlhood" in *Dolls Studies: The Many Meanings of Girls' Toys and Play,* eds. Miriam Forman-Brunell and Jennifer Dawn Whitney (New York: Peter Lang, 2015), 16–17.
79. Carola Suárez-Orozco and Marcelo M. Suárez-Orozco, *Children of Immigration* (Cambridge, MA: Harvard University Press, 2009).
80. Rebecca Dingo, "Securing the Nation: Neoliberalism's US Family Values in a Transnational Gendered Economy," *Journal of Women's History* 16, no. 3 (2004): 175.
81. Anita Harris, *Future Girl: Young Women in the Twenty-First Century* (New York: Routledge, 2004).
82. Nicole LeConte, "Not One That Looks Like My Daughter: How American Girl Makes History Hegemony" (honors thesis, Connecticut College, 2011).
83. Janet Shaw, *Happy Birthday, Kirsten!* (Middleton, WI: American Girl Publishing 1987; reprint, Middleton, WI: American Girl Publishing, 2000), 21.
84. Janet Shaw, *Happy Birthday, Kirsten!*, 20 as discussed in LeConte, "Not One That Looks Like My Daughter," 27.
85. LeConte, "Not One That Looks Like My Daughter," 27.
86. Jacqueline Dembar Green, *Meet Rebecca* (Middleton, WI: American Girl Publishing, 2009), 1.
87. Jacqueline Dembar Green, *Candlelight for Rebecca* (Middleton, WI: American Girl Publishing, 2009), 32.
88. Jacqueline Dembar Green, *Rebecca and the movies* (Middleton, WI: American Girl Publishing, 2009), 21.
89. Green, *Meet Rebecca,* 68.
90. Green, *Candlelight for Rebecca,* 67.
91. Acosta-Alzuru & Roushanzamir, "Everything We Do is Celebration of You!"; Acosta-Alzuru & Kreshel, "I'm an American Girl."
92. Susan Stiger, "Hispanic Doll Embodies an Era Unique Collection a Hit Among Girls," *The Denver Post,* August 24, 1997, B6.
93. Ibid; "Josefina Mold," http://americangirl.wikia.com/wiki/Josefina_Mold.
94. U.S. Census Bureau, "The Hispanic Population: A Census Bureau Brief," 2001, http://www.census.gov/prod/2001pubs/c2kbr01-3.pdf.
95. Julie Bookman, "Living News for Kids: Meet a New American Girl," *The Atlanta Journal and Constitution,* September 22, 1997, 03B.
96. Medina, "Theorizing American Girl"; Valdivia, "Living in a Hybrid Material World."
97. Medina, "Theorizing American Girl," 11.

98. Rodolfo Acuña, *Occupied America: A History of Chicanos,* 3rd ed. (New York, NY: Addison Wesley Longman, 1987).

99. Ibid.

100. Ibid.

101. Angharad Valdivia, "The Gendered Face of Latinidad: Global Circulation of Hybridity," in *Circuits of Visibility: Gender and Transnational Media Cultures,* ed. Radha Hegde (New York: Peter Lang, 2015), 58.

102. Arlene Dávila, *Latinos Inc.: The Marketing and Making of a People* (Berkeley: University of California Press, 2001).

103. Valerie Tripp, *Josefina Saves the Day* (Middleton, WI: American Girl Publishing, 1998; reprint, Middleton, WI: American Girl Publishing, 2000), 11.

104. Ibid., 18.

105. Ibid., 16–19.

106. Jillian Baez, "Latina/os Audiences as Citizens," in *Contemporary Latina/o Media: Production, Circulation, Politics,* eds. Arlene Dávila and Yeidy M. Rivero (New York: New York University Press, 2014), 275.

107. Valdivia, "The Gendered Face of Latinidad," 64.

108. Davila, *Latinos, Inc.*

CHAPTER 7

Conclusion: Constructing American Girlhood

As I made my final edits to this book, doll news was abundant. In time for the 2017 Toy Fair, the industry's yearly convention in New York City, many companies were making announcements. The Tonner Doll Company would be unveiling its prototype of a doll based on Jazz Jennings, a transgender teen who has written two books and has her own reality show. The UK-based A Girl of All Time, a direct competitor of American Girl, announced that it would be expanding its collection to include more diverse characters including Bex, an English girl with Afro-Caribbean roots. The New York Doll Collection announced its launch of the City Girls, five eighteen-inch dolls each of whom will hail from one of the city's boroughs. And, Mattel revealed that it is creating a hologram Barbie powered with artificial intelligence. American Girl, a subsidiary of Mattel, also made big announcements. Receiving little press coverage, brand executives announced that moving forward the Truly Me collection would provide "girls with the opportunity not just to *pick* a doll that looks like them but design and order dolls that take customization to a new level."[1] What was in the public spotlight, however, was the reveal that over the next year American Girl would bring Felicity Merriman back to the collection, add Nanea Mitchell, a native Hawaiian girl living in Pearl Harbor during World War II, and release three contemporary dolls with stories, including Z. Yang, a Korean-American film maker, country singer Tenney Grant, and Tenney's friend, Logan Everett, the company's first boy doll.

© The Author(s) 2017
E. Zaslow, *Playing with America's Doll*,
DOI 10.1057/978-1-137-56649-2_7

The company's public relations team declared that the impetus for these dolls was a direct result of consumer demand for greater inclusivity in the brand's offerings including a long-standing fan desire for a boy doll. Overwhelmingly fans and news sources considered Nanea and Z. to be "a huge win for diversity."[2] For some, especially those fans who had already been modifying their own girl dolls to be boys, Logan's release was met with delight. However, other fans were less thrilled. For some conservative parents, a boy doll, that would possibly encourage what they consider to be gender non-conforming play, drew ire and concern; one mother wrote in a fan community that when she bought the doll for her toddler son who wanted to play dolls with his American Girl-loving sisters, her husband made her bring it back. Others contended that since cross-sex friendships occur in real life, they should also be available for doll play. Some who feel strongly about the female empowerment message argued that the brand was betraying its original mission.[3] Journalist Rebecca Fishbein wrote, "The thing about American Girl dolls is that they tell stories about brave and strong and occasionally cool things girls have done, like freeing abused horses and fleeing slavery and rescuing their friends from orphanages. It just seems to me like there are millions of stories about brave and strong and occasionally cool boys, and somehow the stuff the boys are doing always looks better than the stuff the girls are doing."[4] Fishbein also worries that American Girl doll play will begin to look more like that of Barbie and Ken with Logan stepping into romantic fantasy plot lines. Some fans suggested that Logan was to blame for the recent announcement that American Girl's underpants were now going to be sewn onto dolls and no longer removable; they speculated that the change was not just a cost-cutting strategy but also to discourage sexual play now that a boy was part of the mix.

American Girl is constantly changing—new collections will emerge and current collections will change—but the core questions at the heart of this book remain the same.

How does a commercial product that is both profit-driven and socially and politically motivated negotiate its offerings to balance mission and revenue? What do feminist-inspired dolls and stories look like when they are for sale and when they are packaged by the Mattel machine, and how do thoughtful consumers understand their consumption of these products? What do American Girl books and dolls communicate to consumers about gender, race, ethnicity, and what it means to be an American? Whose American stories are told and whose are not told, what do they tell us about the gendered and raced relations of power in this country and how is citizenship characterized by this brand that owns the name "American Girl"?

Over the past thirty-plus years, under the watchful eyes of four CEOs, scores of writers, historians, designers, and marketers, representations of gender in American Girl have evolved. The girls within these stories, once struggling to resist the limits prescribed by the period-determined femininity of their mothers, now more often demonstrate a vocal opposition to the constraints of the private sphere and also serve their communities by fighting for social change. Kit writes and takes photographs to raise awareness of impoverished children; Rebecca gives a speech in support of worker's safety and rights; Melody sings, protests, and organizes to fight for racial equality; and Maryellen highlights the struggles of girls who want to participate in science. In all of these stories, social hierarchies of gender and social class are portrayed as supported not only by individuals but also by institutions—laws, governments, and corporations—that can be resisted. Girl consumers who participated in this study consistently identified the theme of the brand's narratives not only as "no one can get in my way" but also as "fighting for what is right" and "making a difference in your community."

Conversely, as the narratives of the BeForever historical dolls challenge social norms, the American Girl clothing, accessories, and experiences have become increasingly more gender normative. Whereas the historical collection previously had accessories that were laden with cultural and historical significance and the books continue to offer narratives in which varied scripts of girlhood are possible, the current accessories collection is limited to hair related trimmings, fashion and purses, beds, and food objects. Similarly, while there had been, in an earlier era, American Girl experiences at Colonial Williamsburg and other living history museum environments, current experiences are limited to retail which in addition to consumption, revolve around beauty and fashion design. This limited product line and experiential interaction offers girls no tools to support the narrative scripts in which their public sphere lives and resistive voices are encouraged; instead the BeForever characters are given objects that situate them within the normative feminine arenas of beauty culture, bedroom culture and food culture.

Further, exploring the debate that concerns portraying communities of color exclusively as living in oppression and struggle, I identify a lack of constancy in the brand's construction of racial logic. African American characters in the BeForever collection are depicted as living within a nation that has institutionalized racism, against which there must be constant struggle, while depictions of Native American and Latina girls have been focused on highlighting the integrity of the community before Anglo influences. African American Addy and Melody, and to a lesser extent Cécile, challenge the racist society in which they live, while Kaya and Josefina's stories are both about their ethnic culture with almost no hint of racism, ethnic discrimination, or structural oppression in their communities. While this difference can be understood, in part, because for African Americans in this country there is no story to tell before Anglo intervention, there is also the risk that oppression becomes a stand-in for culture in African American stories. So, too, does this dichotomy create the risk that Native American and Latino culture becomes romanticized and the oppressive conditions in which they live are minimized or erased. Further, it leads to an inconsistent racial logic and inconsistent portrayal of the lived experiences of people of color in the United States.

In stories about protagonists who are neither African American nor Anglo Saxon Protestant, cultural specificity is explored but often depicted as relatively insignificant, with Americanness taking on the role as the more important identifier. For this group of protagonists, it is not investment in social change that characterizes their American experience but their industriousness and entrepreneurial spirit. This thematic construction positions readers in an act of noticing/not-noticing difference, a position that supports the myth of social mobility and the neoliberal fantasy that institutional oppression is a thing of the past and that individual hard work is the antidote for uneven wealth, access to social institutions, and political power.

Drawing on my interviews with American Girl executives, authors who write for American girl, and mothers and their daughters who play with American Girl, as well as my close reading of the American Girl BeForever series, dolls, and accessories, this book argues that American Girl can be understood within the realm of commodity activism. Considering the production and consumption of these dolls and books as an act of (feminist) commodity activism allows for the exploration of "cultural resistance …that emerges from *within* the neoliberal hegemonies of entrepreneurial individualism and materialist pleasure."[5] Even as the middle- to upper-class mothers who participated in this study sometimes question what they call the "ridiculous" level of consumption involved in the American Girl universe and bemoan, as several mothers did, that the "company as a whole is not representing the full diversity of what America is and what America is becoming," they understand their consumption of American Girl as an intentional act to support their personal ideological positions regarding gender, racial, and/or social class equality and justice. These mothers recognize that children's toys and dolls do not just sit upon their shelves or offer them a distraction to idle away their time but serve as powerful ideological tools of socialization. Within a world that they perceive as becoming increasingly sexual for younger girls, and in which excessive consumption feels like it is a *fait accompli*, they see American Girl as a company that they can generally trust to share their values. American Girl not only provides their daughters' pleasure but allows the mothers in my study to provide their daughters easily digestible representations of "smart, independent, powerful, and wholesome" girls who teach them to advocate for themselves but also to stand up for essential social change in the United States. Even as these mothers, to varying degrees, recognize the contradictory imperatives at the core of this capitalist brand owned by a toy conglomerate, they generally believe that they are contributing to the public good by raising daughters who can be self-determined but also learn to fight for social justice and equality, and that American Girl can help them to reach this goal. Similarly, the authors with whom I spoke genuinely understand their craft as political. Although individual authors have differing motivations and approaches to their writing, the three I spoke with all understand their American Girl BeForever narratives as making a contribution to educating children about the positive ways they can interact in society and participate in an effective social change built on optimism and hope.

This parental and authorial intention of commodity activism is under ongoing revenue-driven threat from corporate forces within Mattel. Having lost the contract for Disney princesses to Hasbro in 2014, a three to five hundred-million-dollar business it controlled for twenty years, the company is scrambling to regain its share of the doll market in all categories including Barbie and American Girl.[6] As it explores new avenues for profit, one technique the company has used is to capitalize on social change movements by adding diversity to its collections. For the first time since its inception, it has responded to the movement for more realistic body images in Barbie. A few years after nearly 90,000 signatures compelled *Seventeen* magazine to commit to stop digitally altering girl models to make them look thinner and to represent the "real beauty" of girls of "all sizes, shapes, and skin tones," and the 2014 outcry against Victoria's

Secret "The Perfect Body" ad campaign that led the lingerie company to change its slogan to "A Body for Every Body," Mattel announced that it would begin to sell Barbie dolls in different body formats including curvy, with thicker thighs and a rounder belly.[7] In 2015, two years after the launch of the Black Lives Matter movement began its online campaign and street protests, Mattel announced that its Barbie collection would be expanded to feature a more racially and ethnically diverse collection including African American, Asian, and mixed-race dolls.[8] One year later Melody Ellison was released as the most recent BeForever historical doll and in 2017 Gabriela McBride became American Girl's first African American Girl of the Year doll.[9] Diversity throughout the corporation may very well be a response to consumer demand in a changing era but it may also simply be a marketing strategy. Only time will tell how long commodity activism will continue to serve the financial interests of the company and how the current conservative political regime in the country will impact this approach to product development.

NOTES

1. Juliana Chugg, "Mattel's Toy Fair Presentation/Gallery Tour," (speech), February 17, 2017, http://files.shareholder.com.
2. Carla Herreria, "American Girl to Make Korean and Hawaiian Dolls, A Huge Win For Diversity," *Huffington Post*, February 16, 2017, http://www.huffingtonpost.com/entry/american-girl-hawaiian-korean-dolls_us_58a62b2be4b037d17d263e47.
3. Caity Weaver, "Leave American Girls Alone," *The New York Times*, February 19, 2017, https://www.nytimes.com/2017/02/18/opinion/sunday/leave-american-girls-alone.html; Rebecca Fishbein, "I Hate This Boy American Girl Doll," *Gothamist*, http://gothamist.com/2017/02/14/doll_eviscerated.php.
4. Fishbein, "I Hate This Boy American Girl Doll."
5. Roopali Mukherjee, "Diamond (Are from Sierra Leone)," in *Commodity Activism: Cultural Resistance in Neoliberal Times*, eds. by Roopali Mukherjee and Sarah Banet-Weiser (New York: NYU Press, 2012), 125.
6. Claire Suddath, "The $500 Million Battle Over Disney's Princesses," *Bloomberg*, December 17, 2015, https://www.bloomberg.com/features/2015-disney-princess-hasbro/. The transition went into effect on January 1, 2016 but the brand knew of its pending loss since September 2014.
7. Eliana Dockterman, "Barbie's Got a New Body," February 8, 2016, *Time*, 46–51.

8. John Kell, "Barbie's Comeback: Include More Diversity, and a Voice," *Fortune,* http://fortune.com/2015/02/17/barbies-comeback-plan/.
9. Melissa Henriquez, "How American Girl Dolls Are Rocking Inclusion Lately," *kveller*, January 4, 2017, http://www.kveller.com/how-american-girl-dolls-are-rocking-inclusion-lately/.

Bibliography

General Bibliography

Acuña, Rodolfo. *Occupied America: A History of Chicanos.* 3rd ed. New York, NY: Addison Wesley Longman, 1987.

Acosta-Alzuru, Carolina and Elizabeth P. Lester Roushanzamir. "'Everything We Do Is Celebration of You!' Pleasant Company Constructs American Girlhood." *The Communication Review* 6 (2003): 45–69.

Acosta-Alzuru, Carolina and Peggy J. Kreshel. "'I'm an American Girl… Whatever That Means'": Girls Consuming Pleasant Company's American Girl Identity." *Journal of Communication* 52, no. 1 (2002): 139–161.

Alexander, Suzanne. "Doll Line Is History – A Pleasant Hit." *Wall Street Journal,* August 22, 1991.

American Girl. "American Girl Debuts 1960s Melody Ellison to Its BeForever Lineup." Press release, August 25, 2016. http://www.americangirl.com/wcsstore/Tridion/AGStore/Images/melody_press_release924-287641.pdf

"American Girl." *Fast Company,* September 1, 2006. https://www.fastcompany.com/57754/american-girl

American Girl. "Fast Facts." http://www.americangirl.com/corporate/fast-facts

"American Girl: Stories Forever." Vimeo video, 2:48, posted by Weber Shandwick Southwest Studio, Uploaded June 10, 2014. https://vimeo.com/97829479

"American Girl Debuts Doll from Civil Rights Era." *CBS News,* February 22, 2016. http://www.cbsnews.com/news/american-girl-30th-anniversary-debuts-third-african-american-historical-doll-melody-ellison/

American Psychological Association, Task Force on the Sexualization of Girls. *Report of the APA Task Force on the Sexualization of Girls.* Washington, DC: American Psychological Association, 2007.

© The Author(s) 2017
E. Zaslow, *Playing with America's Doll,*
DOI 10.1057/978-1-137-56649-2

Ang, Ien. *Watching Dallas: Soap Opera and the Melodramatic Imagination.* New York: Methuen & Co. Ltd., 1985.

Anton, Carrie, Laurie Calkhoven, and Erin Falligant. *American Girl Ultimate Visual Guide.* New York: DK Publishing, 2016.

Arnold, Annette. "Samantha's Ice Cream Social." *The Northwest Indiana Times,* September 30, 1998. http://www.nwitimes.com/uncategorized/samantha-s-ice-cream-social/article_87ac3ace-fdf9-5249-9763-2de0a6147a24.html

Austin, Whitney Thornberry. "We Are The 'Felicity Generation' Making History: Inspiration for the Modern Revolutionary." January 12, 2016. http://makinghistorynow.com/2016/01/we-are-the-felicity-generation/

Baez, Jillian. "Latina/os Audiences as Citizens." In *Contemporary Latina/o Media: Production, Circulation, Politics,* edited by Arlene Dávila and Yeidy M. Rivero, 267–284. New York: New York University Press, 2014.

Banet-Weiser, Sarah. "Free Self-Esteem Tools?: Brand Culture, Gender, and the Dove Real Beauty Campaign." In *Commodity Activism: Cultural Resistance in Neoliberal Times,* edited by Roopali Mukherjee and Sarah Banet-Weiser, 39–56. New York: NYU Press, 2012.

Banet-Weiser, Sarah and Roopali Mukherjee. "Introduction: Commodity Activism in Neoliberal Times." In *Commodity Activism: Cultural Resistance in Neoliberal Times,* edited by Roopali Mukherjee and Sarah Banet-Weiser, 1–21. New York: NYU Press, 2012.

"Barbie, Meet American Girl of Today Doll." *The Arizona Republic,* December 25, 1995, B7.

Bennet, Brit. "Addy Walker: American Girl." *The Paris Review,* May 28, 2015. http://www.theparisreview.org/blog/2015/05/28/addy-walker-american-girl

Bernstein, Robin. *Racial Innocence: Performing American Childhood and Race From Slavery to Civil Rights.* New York: NYU Press, 2011.

Bishop, Rudine Sims. "Evaluating Books by and About African-Americans." In *The Multicolored Mirror: Cultural Substance in Literature for Children and Young Adults,* edited by Merri Lindgren, 31–44. Fort Atkinson, WI: Highsmith, 1991.

Boltanski, Luc and Eve Chiapello. *The New Spirit of Capitalism.* New York: Verso, 2005.

Bonilla-Silva, Eduardo. *Racism Without Racists: Color-Blind Racism and The Persistence of Racial Inequality in the United States.* Lanham, MD: Rowman & Littlefield, 2003.

Bookman, Julie. "Living News for Kids: Meet a New American Girl." *The Atlanta Journal and Constitution* (September 22, 1997), B3.

Borghini, Stefania, Nina Diamond, Robert V. Kozinets, Mary Ann McGrath, Albert M. Muñiz, and John F. Sherry. "Why are Themed Brand Stores so Powerful? Retail Brand Ideology at American Girl Place." *Journal of Retailing* 85, no. 3 (2009): 363–375.

Brady, Jeanne. "Reading the American Dream: The History of the American Girl Collection." *Teaching and Learning Literature* 4, no. 1 (September/October 1994): 2–6.

Brookfield, Molly. "From American Girls into American Women: A Discussion of American Girl Doll Nostalgia." *Girlhood Studies* 5, no. 1 (2012): 57–75.

Brotman, Barbara. "The Multicultural Playroom: Today's Dolls Have Ethnicity That's More Than Skin Deep." *Chicago Tribune*, October 31, 1993. http://articles.chicagotribune.com/1993-10-31/features/9310310429_1_black-dolls-white-dolls-ethnic-groups

Brown, Lyn Mikel and Carol Gilligan. *Meeting at the Crossroads*. New York: Ballantine Books, 1992.

Buckingham, David. *Children Talking Television*. London: The Falmer Press, 1993.

Canedy, Dana. "Takeovers Are Part of the Game; Any Hot Toy Can Grow Up to Be a Unit of Mattel or Hasbro." *New York Times*, February 9, 1999. http://www.nytimes.com/1999/02/09/business/takeovers-are-part-game-any-hot-toy-can-grow-up-be-unit-mattel-hasbro.html

"Changes for Pleasant." *Wisconsin State Journal*, December 1, 1996, A7.

Chen, Eva. "Neoliberalism and Popular Women's Culture: Rethinking Choice, Freedom and Agency." *European Journal of Cultural Studies* 16, no. 4 (2013): 440–452.

Cherland, Meredith Rogers. *Private Practices: Girls Reading Fiction and Constructing Identity*. London and Bristol, PA: Taylor and Francis, 1994.

Chuppa-Cornell, Kim. "When Fact Is Stranger than Fiction: Hair in American Girl Stories and Dolls." *The Lion and the Unicorn* 37, no. 2 (2013): 107–125.

Clark, Roger, Heidi Kulkin, and Liam Clancy. "The Liberal Bias in Feminist Social Science Research on Children's Books." In *Girls, Boys, Books, Toys: Gender in Children's Literature and Culture*, edited by Beverly Lyon Clark and Margaret Higonnet, 71–82. Baltimore: Johns Hopkins University Press, 1999.

Clehane, Diane. "Why Is American Girl Rebranding Their Historical Line Without An Asian Doll?" *Forbes*, July 8, 2014. http://www.forbes.com/sites/dianeclehane/2014/07/08/why-is-american-girl-rebranding-their-historical-line-without-an-asian-doll/#3c9ae58b2fa2

Cohen, Patricia. "A Line of Dolls Enters the '70s." *New York Times*, August 25, 2007. https://mobile.nytimes.com/2007/08/25/books/25girl.html

Council on Interracial Books for Children. *Guidelines for the Future: Human and Anti-Human Values in Children's Books: A Content Rating Instrument for Educators and Concerned Parents*. New York: Council on Interracial Books for Children Racism and Sexism Resource Center for Educators, 1976.

Cross, Gary. *Kids' Stuff: Toys and The Changing World of American Childhood*. Cambridge, MA: Harvard University Press, 2009.

Daiken, Leslie H. *Children's Toys Throughout the Ages*. New York: Praeger, 1953.

Damour, Lisa. "For Teenage Girls, Swimsuit Season Never Ends." *New York Times*, August 10, 2016. https://well.blogs.nytimes.com/2016/08/10/for-teenage-girls-swimsuit-season-never-ends/

Dávila, Arlene. *Latinos Inc.: The Marketing and Making of a People*. Berkeley: University of California Press, 2001.

De Lauretis, Teresa. *Technologies of Gender: Essays on Theory, Film, and Fiction.* Bloomington, IN: Indiana University Press, 1987.

Deane, Paul. *Mirrors of American Culture: Children's Fiction Series in the Twentieth Century.* Metuchen, NJ: Scarecrow Press, Inc., 1991.

DeMarco, Laura. "American Girl Introduces New 1950s Doll, Maryellen Larkin." *The Plain Dealer,* September 22, 2015. http://www.cleveland.com/entertainment/index.ssf/2015/09/american_girl_introduces_new_1.html

Diamond, Nina, John F. Sherry Jr., Albert M. Muniz Jr., Mary Ann McGrath, Robert V. Kozinets, and Stefania Borghini. "American Girl and the Brand Gestalt: Closing the Loop on Sociocultural Branding Research." *Journal of Marketing* 73, no. 3 (2009): 118–134.

Dingo, Rebecca. "Securing the Nation: Neoliberalism's US Family Values in a Transnational Gendered Economy." *Journal of Women's History* 16, no. 3 (2004): 173–186.

Doane, Ashley. "The Changing Politics of Color-Blind Racism." *Research in Race and Ethnic Relations* 14 (2007): 159–174.

Dockterman, Eliana. "Barbie's Got a New Body." *Time,* February 8, 2016, 46–51.

Douglas, Susan and Meredith Michaels. *The Mommy Myth: The Idealization of Motherhood and How It Has Undermined Women.* New York: Free Press, 2004.

Dow, Bonnie. *Prime-Time Feminism: Television, Media Culture and the Women's Movement Since 1970.* Philadelphia: University of Pennsylvania Press, 1996.

Dr. Mama Esq. "Black Girls and the American Girl Doll Dillemma [Sic]." *CocoaMamas,* January 23, 2014. https://cocoamamas.com/2014/01/23/black-girls-and-the-american-girl-doll-dillemma/

Drill, Christina. "2012: The End of the American (Girl Doll) History." *Verbicide,* January 24, 2012. http://www.verbicidemagazine.com/2012/01/24/end-of-the-american-girl-doll-history/

duCille, Ann. "Dyes and Dolls: Multicultural Barbie and the Merchandising of American Culture." *differences* 6, no. 1 (1994): 48–68.

duCille, Ann. *Skin Trade.* Cambridge, MA: Harvard University Press, 1996.

Dumaine, Brian. "Pleasant Co.: How to Compete With a Champ." *Fortune,* January 10, 1994, 106.

Edmondson, Brad. "The Demographics of Guilt." *American Demographics* 8 (1986): 33–35, 56.

Edwards, Sally. *Beyond Child's Play: Sustainable Product Design in the Global Doll-Making Industry.* Amityville, NY: Baywood Publishing Company, 2010.

Egoff, Shelia. *Thursday's Child Trends and Patterns in Contemporary Children's Literature.* Chicago, IL: American Library Association, 1981.

Eisenstein Stumbar, Sarah and Zillah Eisenstein. "Girlhood Pastimes: American Girls and The Rest of Us." In *Growing Up Girls: Popular Culture and the Construction of Identity,* edited by Sharon R. Mazzarella and Norma Odom Pecora, 87–96. New York: Peter Lang, 1999.

Elium, Jeanne and Don Elium. *Raising a Daughter: Parents and the Awakening of Healthy Woman*. Berkeley, CA: Celestial Arts, 1994.

Faludi, Susan. *Backlash: The Undeclared War Against American Women*. New York: Crown Publishers, 1991.

Feminist Asian Dad. "American Girl Power." September 10, 2016. https://feministasiandad.com/2016/09/10/american-girl-power/

Fishbein, Rebecca. "I Hate This Boy American Girl Doll." *Gothamist*, February 14, 2017. http://gothamist.com/2017/02/14/doll_eviscerated.php

Fisherkeller, JoEllen. *Growing Up with Television: Everyday Learning Among Young Adolescents*. Philadelphia: Temple University Press, 2002.

Forman-Brunell, Miriam and Jennifer Dawn Whitney. *Dolls Studies: The Many Meanings of Girls' Toys and Play*. New York: Peter Lang, 2015.

Formanek-Brunell, Miriam. *Made to Play House: Dolls and the Commercialization of American Girlhood, 1830–1930*. New Haven: Yale University Press, 1993.

Fox Tree, Erich. "The Secret Sex Lives of Native American Barbies, from the Mysteries of Motherhood to the Magic of Colonialism." In *Dolls Studies: The Many Meanings of Girls' Toys and Play*, edited by Miriam Forman-Brunell and Jennifer Dawn Whitney, 227–256. New York: Peter Lang, 2015.

Francis, Beth. "Popular American Girl Dolls Give Children a Chance to Play and Learn." *Gannett News Service*, August 1, 1996.

Frank, Thomas. *The Conquest of Cool: Business Culture, Counterculture, and the Rise of Hip Consumerism*. Chicago: University of Chicago Press, 1997.

Fraser, Antonia. *Dolls: Pleasures and Treasures*. New York: G. P. Putnam's Sons, 1963/1967.

Freeman, Sara. "Jerry Frautschi and Pleasant Rowland: Who Is Jerry Frautschi?" *Isthmus*, April 7, 2011. http://isthmus.com/archive/from-the-archives/jerry-frautschi-and-pleasant-rowland-who-is-jerry-frautschi/

Ganje, Lucy. "Native American Stereotypes." In *Images That Injure: Pictorial Stereotypes in the Media*, edited by Paul Martin Lester and Susan Ross 113–120. Westport, CT: Praeger, 2003.

Gatewood, Willard B. *Aristocrats of Color: The Black Elite, 1880–1920*. Fayetteville, AR: University of Arkansas Press, 2000.

Giddens, Anthony. *Modernity and Self-Identity: Self and Society in the Late Modern Age*. Cambridge: Polity, 1991.

Goldman, Robert, Deborah Heath and Sharon L. Smith. "Commodity Feminism." *Critical Studies in Mass Communication* 8, no. 3 (1991): 333–351.

Gonick, Marnina. "Between 'Girl Power' and 'Reviving Ophelia': Constituting the Neoliberal Girl Subject." *NWSA Journal* 18, no. 2 (2006): 1–23.

Gordon, Avery and Christopher Newfield. "Introduction." In *Mapping Multiculturalism*, edited by Avery Gordon and Christopher Newfield, 1–16. Minneapolis: University of Minnesota Press, 1996.

Guevara, Susan "Authentic Enough: Am I? Are You? Interpreting Culture for Children's Literature." In *Stories Matter: The Complexity of Cultural Authenticity in Children's Literature*, edited by Dana L. Fox and Kathy G. Short, 50–51. Urbana, IL: National Council of Teachers of English, 2003.

Hade, Daniel. "Lies My Children's Books Taught Me: History Meets Popular Culture in 'The American Girls' Books." In *Voices of the Other: Children's Literature and the Postcolonial Context*, edited by Roderick McGillis, 153–164. New York: Garland, 2000.

Hains, Rebecca. *The Princess Problem: Guiding our Girls Through the Princess-Obsessed Years*. Naperville, IL: Sourcebooks, 2014.

Hall, G. Stanley and Alexander Caswell Ellis. *A Study of Dolls*. New York: EL Kellogg & Company, 1897.

Hall, Stuart. 2014. "The Whites of their Eyes: Racist Ideology and the Media." In *The Race and Media Reader*, edited by Gilbert Rodman, 37–51. Routledge: New York, 2013.

Halzack, Sarah. "American Girl's Pint-Size Antidote for Its Multi-Million Dollar Problem." *The Washington Post*, July 21, 2016. https://www.washingtonpost.com/news/business/wp/2016/07/21/american-girls-pint-sized-antidote-for-its-multi-million-dollar-problem/?utm_term=.a6f5a0bc92dd

Harris, Aisha. "The Making of an American Girl." *Slate*, September 21, 2016. http://www.slate.com/articles/arts/culturebox/2016/09/the_making_of_addy_walker_american_girl_s_first_black_doll.html

Harris, Anita. *Future Girl: Young Women in the Twenty-First Century*. New York: Routledge, 2004.

Harrison, Jessica. "American Girl Books Honor Readers, author Valerie Tripp Says." *Cracking the Cover*, September 28, 2015. https://www.crackingthecover.com/11846/american-girl-books-honor-readers-author-valerie-tripp-says/

Harvey, David. *A Brief History of Neoliberalism*. New York: Oxford University Press, 2005.

Healy, Michelle. "Meet Kaya: The Authentic Nez Perce Doll." *USA Today*, August 11, 2008, D6.

Hebdige, Dick. *Subculture: The Meaning of Style*. New York: Routledge, 1979.

Herreria, Carla. "American Girl to Make Korean and Hawaiian Dolls, A Huge Win For Diversity." *Huffington Post*, February 16, 2017. http://www.huffingtonpost.com/entry/american-girl-hawaiian-korean-dolls_us_58a62b2be4b037d17d263e47

Henriquez, Melissa. "How American Girl Dolls Are Rocking Inclusion Lately." *Kveller*, January 4, 2017. http://www.kveller.com/how-american-girl-dolls-are-rocking-inclusion-lately/

Hochschild, Arlie. *The Second Shift: Working Parents and the Revolution at Home*. New York: Avon, 1989.

Holcomb, Betty. *Not Guilty!: The Good News About Working Mothers*. New York: Scribner, 1998.

hooks, bell. "Representing Whiteness in the Black Imagination." In *The Race and Media Reader*, edited by Gilbert B. Rodman, 85–93. New York: Routledge, 2013.

"How Women Have Changed America." *Working Woman* 11 (1986): 129.

Inness, Sherrie. "'Anti-Barbies:' The American Girls Collection and Political Ideologies." In *Delinquents and Debutantes: Twentieth-Century American Girls' Cultures*, edited by Sherrie A. Inness, 164–183. New York: New York University Press, 1998.

"Interview with Ruth Handler." *Barbie Nation*, directed by Susan Stern. DVD. San Francisco, CA: Bernal Beach Films, 1998.

Jackson, Sue and Tiina Vares. "Media 'Sluts':'Tween' Girls' Negotiations of Postfeminist Sexual Subjectivities in Popular Culture." In *New Femininities*, edited by Rosalind Gill and Christina Scharff, 134–146. New York: Palgrave Macmillan, 2011.

Jackson, Sue, Tiina Vares, and Rosalind Gill. "'The Whole Playboy Mansion Image': Girls' Fashioning and Fashioned Selves Within a Postfeminist Culture." *Feminism & Psychology* 23, no. 2 (2013): 143–162.

Jenkins, Henry. *Textual Poachers: Television Fans and Participatory Culture.* New York: Routledge, 2012.

Kell, John. "Barbie's Comeback: Include More Diversity, and a Voice." *Fortune*, February 17, 2015. http://fortune.com/2015/02/17/barbies-comeback-plan/

Kelly, R. Gordon. *Mother Was a Lady: Self and Society in Selected American Children's Periodicals, 1865–1890.* Westport, CT: Greenwood Press, 1974.

Kirch, Claire. "American Girl at 25." *Publishers Weekly*, May 2, 2011. http://www.publishersweekly.com/pw/by-topic/childrens/childrens-industry-news/article/47124-american-girl-at-25.html

Kirch, Claire. "American Girl Tackles Civil Rights Movement with New Character." *Publishers Weekly*, March 8, 2016. http://www.publishersweekly.com/pw/by-topic/childrens/childrens-book-news/article/69602-american-girl-tackles-civil-rights-movement-with-new-character.html

Koss, Melanie D. "Diversity in Contemporary Picture Books: A Content Analysis." *Journal of Children's Literature* 41, no. 1 (2015): 32–42.

Lamb, Sharon and Zoë D. Peterson. "Adolescent Girls' Sexual Empowerment: Two Feminists Explore the Concept." *Sex Roles* 66, no. 11–12 (2012): 703–712.

Lamb, Sharon. *The Secret Lives of Girls: What Good Girls Really Do – Sex Play, Aggression, and Their Guilt.* New York: The Free Press, 2001.

Landsman, Leanna. "Induction Speech for Pleasant Rowland to Association of American Publishers Hall of Fame." 2009. http://publishers.org/2009-pleasant-t-rowland#leanna

Larrick, Nancy. "The All-White World of Children's Books." *Saturday Review* 48, no. 11 (1965): 63–65.

Lavitt, Wendy. *Dolls.* New York: Knopf, 1983.

LeConte, Nicole. "Not One That Looks Like My Daughter: How American Girl Makes History Hegemony." Honors Thesis, Connecticut College, 2011.

Lehnert, Gertrud. "The Training of the Shrew: The Socialization and Education of Young Women in Children's Literature." *Poetics Today* 13, no. 1 (1992): 109–122.

Levy, Ariel. *Female Chauvinist Pigs: Women and the Rise of Raunch Culture.* New York: Free Press, 2006.

Lindsey, Robert. "A Million Dollar Business." *New York Times,* June 19, 1977, 91.

Mackoff, Barbara. *Growing a Girl: Seven Strategies for Raising a Strong, Spirited Daughter.* New York: Dell Publishing, 1996.

Marcus, Lisa. "Dolling Up History: Fictions of Jewish American Girlhood." In *Dolls Studies: The Many Meanings of Girls' Toys and Play,* edited by Miriam Forman-Brunell and Jennifer Dawn Whitney, 15–35. New York: Peter Lang, 2015.

Marshall, Elizabeth. "Consuming Girlhood: Young Women, Femininities, and American Girl." *Girlhood Studies* 2, no. 1 (2009): 94–111.

Marshall, Elizabeth. "Marketing American Girlhood." In *Rethinking Popular Culture and Media,* edited by Elizabeth Marshall and Özlem Sensoy, 129–135. Milwaukee: Rethinking Schools, 2011.

McCabe, Janice, Emily Fairchild, Liz Grauerholz, Bernice A. Pescosolido, and Daniel Tope. "Gender in Twentieth-Century Children's Books Patterns of Disparity in Titles and Central Characters." *Gender & Society* 25, no. 2 (2011): 197–226.

McRobbie, Anegla with Jenny Garber. "Girls and Subcultures." In *Feminism and Youth Culture: From 'Jackie' to 'Just Seventeen,'* edited by Angela McRobbie, 1–15. Boston: Unwin Hyman, 1978.

Medina, Veronica. "'And That's What I Think Being an American Girl Is All About!': Girls' Reflections on American Girl and Contemporary American Girlhood." PhD diss., University of Missouri, 2012.

Medina, Veronica. "Celebrating Whiteness American Girl-Style: Representing Race at American Girl's Twentieth Anniversary." Paper presented at Department of Women's and Gender Studies Colloquium, University of Missouri, Columbia, MO, March 2009.

Medina, Veronica. "Theorizing American Girl." Master's Thesis. University of Missouri-Columbia, 2007.

"Meet Pleasant." *Wisconsin State Journal,* December 1, 1996, A6.

Mehren, Elizabeth. "Playing With History." *Los Angeles Times,* November 28, 1994, E1.

Mickenberg, Julia. *Learning from the Left: Children's Literature, the Cold War, and Radical Politics in the United States.* New York: Oxford University Press, 2005.

Mickenberg, Julia and Philip Nel. "Radical Children's Literature Now!" *Children's Literature Association Quarterly* 36, no. 4 (2011): 445–473.

Miller, Kay. "Dolls Are a Pleasant Surprise." *Star Tribune,* November 19, 1991, E1.

Miskec, Jennifer. "Meet Ivy and Bean, Queerly the Anti-American Girls." *Children's Literature Association Quarterly* 34 (2009): 157–171.

Moore, Anne Elizabeth. "Operation Pocket Full of Wishes." *In These Times,* March 2005. http://inthesetimes.com/article/2006

Moore, Todd. "Unpleasantries at Pleasant Company." *Capital Times*, September 16, 1993, A1.

Morrissey, Tracie Egan. "Growing Up, Everyone Did Dirty Things With Their Barbies." *Jezebel*, September 12, 2007. http://jezebel.com/299195/growing-up-everyone-did-dirty-things-with-their-barbies

Morrison, Kara. "American Girl Dolls Are no Fad Toy: Popularity Continues to Grow After 30 Years." *The Republic*, August 21, 2015. http://www.azcentral.com/story/entertainment/kids/2015/08/21/american-girl-dolls-popularity-continues-grow-scottsdale-store/32119301/

Mukherjee, Roopali. "Diamonds (Are from Sierra Leone): Bling and the Promise of Consumer Citizenship." In *Commodity Activism: Cultural Resistance in Neoliberal Times*, edited by Roopali Mukherjee and Sarah Banet-Weiser, 114–133. New York: NYU Press, 2012.

Mukherjee, Roopali and Sarah Banet-Weiser, eds. *Commodity Activism: Cultural Resistance in Neoliberal Times*. New York: NYU Press, 2012.

Neal, Molly. "Cataloger Gets Pleasant Results." *Direct Marketing Magazine* 55, no. 1 (May 1992): 33.

Neuman, Susan B. *Literacy in the Television Age: The Myth of the TV Effect*. Norwood, NJ: Ablex, 1995.

Nielsen, Fred. "American History Through the Eyes of the American Girls." *The Journal of American and Comparative Cultures* 25, no. 1/2 (2002): 85–93.

Omi, Michael and Howard Winant. "Racial Formation." In *Race Critical Theories: Text and Context*, edited by Philomena Essed and David Theo Goldberg, 123–145. Malden, MA: Blackwell, 2002.

Orenstein, Peggy. *Girls & Sex: Navigating the Complicated New Landscape*. New York: Harper Collins, 2016.

Page, Christine. "A History of Conspicuous Consumption." In *SV – Meaning, Measure, and Morality of Materialism*, edited by Floyd W. Rudmin and Marsha Richins, 82–87. Provo, UT : Association for Consumer Research, 1992.

Pang, Kevin. "Doll Tale Sets Off Student Protest: American Girl Book Lies, Pilsen Teens Say." *Chicago Tribune*, March 30, 2005. http://articles.chicagotribune.com/2005-03-30/news/0503300334_1_american-girl-place-marisol-luna-student-protest

Peek, Philip M., and Kwesi Yankah, eds. *African Folklore: An Encyclopedia*. New York: Routledge, 2004.

Peers, Juliette. "Adelaide Huret and the Nineteenth Century French Fashion Doll: Constructing Dolls/Constructing the Modern." In *Dolls Studies: The Many Meanings of Girls' Toys and Play*, edited by Miriam Forman-Brunell and Jennifer Dawn Whitney, 157–184. New York: Peter Lang, 2015.

Pérez, Sonja Zepeda. "Mis(s)Education: Narrative Construction and Closure in American Girl." PhD diss., University of Arizona, 2015.

Petersen, Jennae. "American Girl, Your Slave Doll is a Big, Fat, Offensive FAIL." *Green & Gorgeous*, October 26, 2015. http://www.greenandgorgeous.net/2012/10/26/american-girl-your-slave-doll-is-a-big-fat-offensive-fail/

Peterson, Sharyl Bender and Mary Alyce Lach. "Gender Stereotypes in Children's Books: Their Prevalence and Influence on Cognitive and Affective Development." *Gender and Education* 2, no. 2 (1990): 185–197.

Philpott, Sarah Lewis. "'Those Events Really Happened!' How Elementary Students Transact with History and Historical Fiction While Reading the American Girl Series." PhD diss., University of Tennessee, 2013.

Pipher, Mary. *Reviving Ophelia: Saving the Selves of Adolescent Girls.* New York: Ballantine, 1994.

"Pleasant: A Christmas Story." *Wisconsin State Journal*, December 1, 1996, A7.

Pleasant Company. "Ask the Author: Janet Shaw." Accessed from Children's Literature Independent Information and Reviews on February 1, 2017. http://archive.is/CIi0J

Pleasant Company. "Background Information: American Girl." Press release. Received by mail December 1996.

Pleasant Company. "Background Information: Pleasant T. Rowland." Press release. Received by mail December 1996.

Pleasant Company. "Pleasant Company." Accessed December 1996. www.pleasantco.com

Pleasant Company. "Pleasant Company. *At a Glance!* 1995." Press release. Received by mail December 1996.

"Pleasant Learns a Lesson." *Wisconsin State Journal*, December 1, 1996, A7.

Projansky, Sarah. "Mass Magazine Cover Girls: Some Reflections on Postfeminist Girls and Postfeminism's Daughters." In *Interrogating Postfeminism: Gender and the Politics of Popular Culture*, edited by Yvonne Tasker and Diane Negra, 41–72. Durham, NC: Duke University Press, 2007.

Pugh, Allison J. "Selling Compromise Toys, Motherhood, and the Cultural Deal." *Gender & Society* 19, no. 6 (2005): 729–749.

Raphel, Adrienne. "Our Dolls, Our Selves." *The New Yorker*, October 9, 2013. http://www.newyorker.com/business/currency/our-dolls-ourselves

Reese, Debbie. "Authenticity and Sensitivity: Goals for Writing and Reviewing Books with Native American Themes." *School Library Journal*, 45 (1999): 36–37.

"Rejecting Barbie, Doll Maker Gains." *New York Times*, September 1, 1993, D1.

Romalov, Nancy Tillman. "Children's Series Books and the Rhetoric of Guidance: A Historical Overview." In *Rediscovering Nancy Drew*, edited by Carolyn Stewart Dyer and Nancy Tillman Romalov, 113–120. Iowa City, IA: University of Iowa Press, 1995.

Rosch, Leah. "Sugar Daddies." *Folio: The Magazine for Magazine Management* 23 (1994): 52–56.

Rosenfeld, Megan. "Wholesome Babes in Toyland." *The Washington Post*, May 24, 1993. https://www.washingtonpost.com/archive/lifestyle/1993/05/24/wholesome-babes-in-toyland/b4ed92ca-1571-4ec9-9290-4dfb4ded0b7b/?utm_term=.02e371d091bb

Rosner, Molly. "The American Girl Company and the Uses of Nostalgia in Children's Consumer Culture." *Jeunesse: Young People, Texts, Cultures* 6, no. 2 (2014): 35–53.

Rousselot, Elodie. "Introduction: Exoticising the Past in Contemporary Neo-Historical Fiction." In *Exoticizing the Past in Contemporary Neo-Historical Fiction*, edited by Elodie Rousselot, 1–16. New York: Palgrave Macmillan, 2014.

Rowland, Pleasant. "AG 25th Birthday Tribute Speech." Uploaded on November 29, 2011. https://www.youtube.com/watch?v=_ltX5W6eZYw

Rubin, Julia. "All Dolled Up: The Enduring Triumph of American Girl." *Racked*, June 29, 2015. http://www.racked.com/2015/6/29/8855683/american-girl-doll-store

Rudolph, Jennifer. "Identity Theft: Gentrification, Latinidad, and American Girl Marisol Luna." *Aztlán: A Journal of Chicano Studies* 34, no. 1 (2009): 65–91.

Rush, Emma and Andrea La Nauze. *Corporate Paedophilia: Sexualisation of Children in Australia*. Australia Institute, 2006.

Rutter, Virginia Beane. *Celebrating Girls: Nurturing and Empowering our Daughters*. Berkeley, CA: Conari Press, 1996.

Sadker, Myra and David Sadker. *Failing at Fairness: How Schools Cheat Girls*. New York: Touchstone. 1994.

Schachter, Abby W. "Could Today's 'American Girl' Be Any Blander?" *Acculturated*, February 27, 2013. http://acculturated.com/could-todays-american-girls-be-any-blander

Sharf, Samantha. "Why Mattel's American Girl Needs to Bank on Millennial Moms (And Maybe Dads)." *Forbes*, December 19, 2015. http://www.forbes.com/sites/samanthasharf/2015/12/19/how-mattels-american-girl-is-banking-on-millennial-moms/2/#56775cd07a0d

Schiller, Amy. "American Girls Aren't Radical Anymore." *The Atlantic*, April 23, 2013. http://www.theatlantic.com/sexes/archive/2013/04/american-girls-arent-radical-anymore/275199

Schlosser, Lisa Mae. "'Second Only to Barbie': Identity, Fiction, and Non-Fiction in the American Girl Collection." *MP: An Online Feminist Journal* 1, no. 4 (May 20, 2006). http://academinist.org/wp-content/uploads/2010/06/Schlosser.pdf

Schor, Juliet. *The Overspent American: Why We Want What We Don't Need*. New York: Harper Perennial, 1998.

Seale, Doris and Beverly Slapin. *A Broken Flute: The Native Experience in Books for Children*. Lantham, MD: Altamira, 2006.

Seiter, Ellen. *Sold Separately: Children and Parents in Consumer Culture*. New Brunswick, NJ: Rutgers University Press, 1993.

Sekeres, Diane Carver. "The Market Child and Branded Fiction: A Synergism of Children's Literature, Consumer Culture, and New Literacies." *Reading Research Quarterly* 44, no. 4 (2009): 399–414.

Sequeria, Jillian. "A Tale of Two Barbies: Did Mattel's Labor Law Violations Fly Under the Radar?" *Lawstreet*, December 1, 2015. http://www.chinalaborwatch.org/newscast/501

Silverstein, Michael J., Neil Fiske, and John Butman. *Trading Up: Why Consumers Want New Luxury Goods – And How Companies Create Them*. New York: Penguin, 2008.

Sloane, Julie with Pleasant Rowland. "A New Twist on Timeless Toys." *Fortune Small Business*, October 1, 2002. http://money.cnn.com/magazines/fsb/fsb_archive/2002/10/01/330574/index.htm

Sodenbergh, Peter. "The Stratemeyer Strain: Educators and the Juvenile Series Books, 1900–1980." In *Only Connect: Reading on Children's Literature*, edited by Shelia Egoff, G. T. Stubbs, and L.F. Ashley, 63–73. New York: Oxford University Press, 1980.

Soto, Gary. "Why I've Stopped Writing Children's Literature." *Huffington Post*, September 25, 2013. http://www.huffingtonpost.com/gary-soto/childrens-literature-writing_b_3989751.html

Squires, Catherine R. *The Post-Racial Mystique: Media and Race in the Twenty-First Century*. New York: NYU Press, 2014.

Stangenes, Sharon. "Barbie Backlash." *Chicago Tribune*, January 4, 1990, C1.

Steinberg, Shirley R. "The Bitch Who Has Everything." In *Kinderculture: The Corporate Construction of Childhood*, edited by Shirley R. Steinberg and Joe L. Kincheloe, 207–218. Boulder: Westview, 1997.

Stephens, John. *Language and Ideology in Children's Fiction*. New York: Longman, 1992.

Stiger, Susan. "Hispanic Doll Embodies an Era Unique Collection a Hit Among Girls." *The Denver Post*, August 24, 1997, B6.

Story, Nancy Duffey. "Pleasant Company's American Girl Collection: The Corporate Construction of Girlhood." PhD diss., University of Georgia, 2002.

Suárez-Orozco, Carola and Marcelo M. Suárez-Orozco. *Children of Immigration*. Cambridge, MA: Harvard University Press, 2009.

Suddath, Claire. "The $500 Million Battle Over Disney's Princesses." *Bloomberg*, December 17, 2015. https://www.bloomberg.com/features/2015-disney-princess-hasbro/

Susina, Jan. "American Girls Collection: Barbies With a Sense of History." *Children's Literature Association Quarterly* 24, no. 3 (1999): 130–135.

Taxel, Joel. "Multicultural Literature and the Politics of Reaction." In *Stories Matter: The Complexity of Cultural Authenticity in Children's Literature*, edited by Dana L. Fox and Kathy G. Short, 143–164. Urbana, IL: National Council of Teachers of English, 2003.

Taylor, Judith, Josée Johnston, and Krista Whitehead. "A Corporation in Feminist Clothing? Young Women Discuss the Dove 'Real Beauty' Campaign." *Critical Sociology* 42, no. 1 (2016): 123–144.

Tomchak, Anne-Marie. "#BBCtrending: The Secret World of Animated Doll Videos." *BBC News*, March 31, 2015. http://www.bbc.com/news/magazine-32042509

Toth, Sara. "Trend Setters." *South Bend Tribune*, July 15, 2005.

Tripp, Valerie. "Anne Scott Macleod Children's Literature Lecture." Unpublished lecture delivered at the Library of Congress, Washington, DC. October 9, 2014.

Urla, Jacqueline and Alan C. Swedlund. "The Anthropometry of Barbie: Unsettling Ideals of the Feminine Body in Popular Culture." In *Deviant Bodies: Critical Perspectives on Difference in Science and Popular Culture*, edited by Jennifer Terry and Jacqueline Urla, 277–313. Bloomington, IN: Indiana University Press, 1995.

U.S. Census Bureau. "The Hispanic Population: A Census Bureau Brief." 2001. http://www.census.gov/prod/2001pubs/c2kbr01-3.pdf

Valdivia, Angharad. "Living in a Hybrid Material World: Girls, Ethnicity and Mediated Doll Products." *Girlhood Studies* 2, no. 1 (2009): 73–93.

Valdivia, Angharad. "The Gendered Face of Latinidad: Global Circulation of Hybridity." In *Circuits of Visibility: Gender and Transnational Media Cultures*, edited Radha Hegde, 53–67. New York: Peter Lang, 2015.

Van Gelder, Lindsy. "The Importance of Being Eleven." *Ms* (July/August 1990): 77.

Ward, Janie Victoria and Beth Cooper Benjamin. "Women, Girls, and the Unfinished Work of Connection: A Critical Review of American Girls' Studies." In *All About the Girl: Culture, Power, and Identity*, edited by Anita Harris, 15–28. New York: Routledge, 2004.

Weaver, Caity. "Leave American Girls Alone." *The New York Times*, February 19, 2017. Accessed February 19, 2017. https://www.nytimes.com/2017/02/18/opinion/sunday/leave-american-girls-alone.html

Weitzman, Lenore J., Deborah Eifler, Elizabeth Hokada, and Catherine Ross. "Sex-Role Socialization in Picture Books for Preschool Children." *American Journal of Sociology* 77, no. 6 (1972): 1125–1150.

West, Rebecca Joan. "Some of My Best Dolls Are Black: Colorblind Rhetoric in Online Collecting Communities." PhD diss., University of Loyola Chicago, 2014.

Wildgen, Michelle. "The Rise of American Girl Rebecca Rubin." *The Forward*, January 2, 2013. http://forward.com/culture/168334/the-rise-of-american-girl-rebecca-rubin/

Williams, Joan. *Unbending Gender: Why Family and Work Conflict and What to Do About It*. New York: Oxford University Press, 2000.

Wright, Felicity. "American Girls to Treasure." *The Washington Post*, August 27, 1991, C5.

Zaslavsky, Claudia. "'Africa Counts' and Ethnomathematics." *For the Learning of Mathematics* 14, no. 2 (1994): 3–8.

Zaslow, Emilie. *Feminism, Inc.: Coming of Age in Girl Power Media Culture*. New York: Palgrave Macmillan, 2009.

Zaslow, Emilie. "GFCFSF: Mothers Challenge Evidence-Based Medicine & the Privitization of Motherhood." In *Mothers and Food: Negotiating Foodways from Maternal Perspectives*, edited by Tanya Cassidy and Florence Pasche Guignard, 245–258. Branford, ON: Demeter Press, 2016.

Zipes, Jack. "Taking Political Stock: New Theoretical and Critical Approaches to Anglo-American Children's Literature in the 1980s." *The Lion and the Unicorn* 14, no. 1 (1990): 7–22.

AMERICAN GIRL BOOKS

Shaw, Janet. *Meet Kirsten*. 1986. Reprint, Middleton, WI: American Girl Publishing, 2000.

———. *Kirsten Learns a Lesson*. 1986. Reprint, Middleton, WI: American Girl Publishing, 2000.

———. *Kirsten's Surprise*. 1986. Reprint, Middleton, WI: American Girl Publishing, 2000.

———. *Happy Birthday, Kirsten!* 1987. Reprint, Middleton, WI: American Girl Publishing, 2000.

———. *Kirsten Saves the Day*. 1988. Reprint, Middleton, WI: American Girl Publishing, 2000.

———. *Changes for Kirsten*. 1988. Reprint, Middleton, WI: American Girl Publishing, 2000.

Tripp, Valerie. *Meet Molly*. 1986. Reprint, Middleton, WI: American Girl Publishing, 2000.

———. *Molly Learns a Lesson*. 1986. Reprint, Middleton, WI: American Girl Publishing, 2000.

———. *Molly's Surprise*. 1986. Reprint, Middleton, WI: American Girl Publishing, 2000.

———. *Happy Birthday, Molly!* 1987. Reprint, Middleton, WI: American Girl Publishing, 2000.

———. *Molly Saves the Day*. 1988. Reprint, Middleton, WI: American Girl Publishing, 2000.

———. *Changes for Molly*. 1988. Reprint, Middleton, WI: American Girl Publishing, 2000.

Adler, Susan. *Meet Samantha*. 1986. Reprint, Middleton, WI: American Girl Publishing, 1998.

———. *Samantha Learns a Lesson*. 1986. Reprint, Middleton, WI: American Girl Publishing, 1998.

Schur, Maxine Rose. *Samantha's Surprise*. 1986. Reprint, Middleton, WI: American Girl Publishing, 1998.

Tripp, Valerie. *Happy Birthday, Samamtha!*. 1987. Reprint, Middleton, WI: American Girl Publishing, 1998.

———. *Samantha Saves the Day*. 1988. Reprint, Middleton, WI: American Girl Publishing, 1998.

———. *Changes for Samantha*. 1988. Reprint, Middleton, WI: American Girl Publishing, 1998.

Tripp, Valerie. *Meet Felicity*. 1991. Reprint, Middleton, WI: American Girl Publishing, 2000.

———. *Felicity Learns a Lesson*. 1991. Reprint, Middleton, WI: American Girl Publishing, 2000.

———. *Felicity's Surprise.* 1991. Reprint, Middleton, WI: American Girl Publishing, 2000.

———. *Happy Birthday, Felicity!* 1992. Reprint, Middleton, WI: American Girl Publishing, 2000.

———. *Felicity Saves the Day.* 1992. Reprint, Middleton, WI: American Girl Publishing, 2000.

———. *Changes for Felicity.* 1992. Reprint, Middleton, WI: American Girl Publishing, 2000.

Porter, Connie. *Meet Addy.* 1993. Reprint, Middleton, WI: American Girl Publishing, 1998.

———. *Addy Learns a Lesson.* 1993. Reprint, Middleton, WI: American Girl Publishing, 1998.

———. *Addy's Surprise.* 1993. Reprint, Middleton, WI: American Girl Publishing, 1998.

———. *Happy Birthday, Addy!* 1994. Reprint, Middleton, WI: American Girl Publishing, 1998.

———. *Addy Saves the Day.* 1994. Reprint, Middleton, WI: American Girl Publishing, 1998.

———. *Changes for Addy.* 1994. Reprint, Middleton, WI: American Girl Publishing, 1998.

Tripp, Valerie. *Meet Josefina.* 1997. Reprint, Middleton, WI: American Girl Publishing, 2000.

———. *Josefina Learns a Lesson.* 1997. Reprint, Middleton, WI: American Girl Publishing, 2000.

———. *Josefina's Surprise.* 1997. Reprint, Middleton, WI: American Girl Publishing, 2000.

———. *Happy Birthday, Josefina!* 1998. Reprint, Middleton, WI: American Girl Publishing, 2000.

———. *Josefina Saves the Day.* 1998. Reprint, Middleton, WI: American Girl Publishing, 2000.

———. *Changes for Josefina.* 1998. Reprint, Middleton, WI: American Girl Publishing, 2000.

Tripp, Valerie. *Meet Kit.* Middleton, WI: American Girl Publishing, 2000.

———. *Kit Learns a Lesson.* Middleton, WI: American Girl Publishing, 2000.

———. *Kit Surprise.* Middleton, WI: American Girl Publishing, 2000.

———. *Happy Birthday, Kit!* Middleton, WI: American Girl Publishing, 2001.

———. *Kit Saves the Day.* Middleton, WI: American Girl Publishing, 2001.

———. *Changes for Kit.* Middleton, WI: American Girl Publishing, 2001.

Hill, Kirpatrick. *Minuk: Ashes in the Pathway.* Pleasant Company Publications. 2002.

Shaw, Janet. *Meet Kaya.* Middleton, WI: American Girl Publishing, 2002.

———. *Kaya's Escape.* Middleton, WI: American Girl Publishing, 2002.

————. *Kaya's Hero*. Middleton, WI: American Girl Publishing, 2002.

————. *Kaya and the Lone Dog*. Middleton, WI: American Girl Publishing, 2002.

————. *Kaya Shows the Way*. Middleton, WI: American Girl Publishing, 2002.

————. *Changes for Kaya*. Middleton, WI: American Girl Publishing, 2002.

McDonald, Megan. *Meet Julie*. Middleton, WI: American Girl Publishing, 2007.

————. *Julie Tells Her Story*. Middleton, WI: American Girl Publishing, 2007.

————. *Happy New Year, Julie!* Middleton, WI: American Girl Publishing, 2007.

————. *Julie and the Eagles*. Middleton, WI: American Girl Publishing, 2007.

————. *Julie's Journey*. Middleton, WI: American Girl Publishing, 2007.

————. *Changes for Julie*. Middleton, WI: American Girl Publishing, 2007.

Yee, Lisa. *Good Luck, Ivy*. Middleton, WI: American Girl, 2008.

Green, Jacqueline Dembar. *Meet Rebecca*. Middleton, WI: American Girl Publishing, 2009.

————. *Rebecca and Ana*. Middleton, WI: American Girl Publishing, 2009.

————. *Candlelight for Rebecca*. Middleton, WI: American Girl Publishing, 2009.

————. *Rebecca and The Movies*. Middleton, WI: American Girl Publishing, 2009.

————. *Rebecca to the Rescue*. Middleton, WI: American Girl Publishing, 2009.

————. *Changes for Rebecca*. Middleton, WI: American Girl Publishing, 2009.

Buckey, Sarah. *Meet Marie-Grace*. Middleton, WI: American Girl Publishing, 2011.

Patrick, Denise Lewis. *Meet Cécile*. Middleton, WI: American Girl Publishing, 2011.

Buckey, Sarah. *Marie-Grace and the Orphans*. Middleton, WI: American Girl Publishing, 2011.

Patrick, Denise Lewis. *Troubles for Cécile*. Middleton, WI: American Girl Publishing, 2011.

Buckey, Sarah. *Marie-Grace Makes a Difference*. Middleton, WI: American Girl Publishing, 2011.

Patrick, Denise Lewis. *Cécile's Gift*. Middleton, WI: American Girl Publishing, 2011.

Ernst, Kathleen. *Captain of the Ship: A Caroline Classic, Vol. 1*. Middleton, WI: American Girl Publishing, 2014.

————. *Facing the Enemy: A Caroline Classic, Vol. 2*. Middleton, WI: American Girl Publishing, 2014.

Tripp, Valerie. *The One and Only: A Maryellen Classic Volume 1*. Middleton, WI: American Girl Publishing, 2015.

————. *Taking Off: A Maryellen Classic 2*. Middleton, WI: American Girl Publishing, 2015.

Patrick, Denise Lewis. *No Ordinary Sound: A Melody Classic Volume 1*. Middleton, WI: American Girl Publishing, 2016.

————. *Never Stop Singing: A Melody Classic 2*. Middleton, WI: American Girl Publishing, 2016.

American Girl Curricular Guides

Scales, Pat. *A Teacher's Guide to Captain of the Ship: A Caroline Classic.* 2014.
Scales, Pat. *A Teacher's Guide to Finding Freedom: An Addy Classic.* 2014.
Scales, Pat. *A Teacher's Guide to Manners and Mischief: A Samantha Classic.* 2014.
Scales, Pat. *A Teacher's Guide to Read All About It: A Kit Classic.* 2014.
Scales, Pat. *A Teacher's Guide to Sunlight and Shadows: A Josefina Classic.* 2014.
Scales, Pat. *A Teacher's Guide to The Big Break: A Julie Classic.* 2014.
Scales, Pat. *A Teacher's Guide to The Journey Begins: A Kaya Classic.* 2014.
Scales, Pat. *A Teacher's Guide to The Sound of Applause: A Rebecca Classic.* 2014.
Scales, Pat. *A Teacher's Guide to The One and Only: A Maryellen Classic.* 2015.
Scales, Pat. *A Teacher's Guide to No Ordinary Sound: A Melody Classic.* 2016.

INDEX[1]

---

[1] Page numbers followed by 'n' refers to notes.

© The Author(s) 2017
E. Zaslow, *Playing with America's Doll*,
DOI 10.1057/978-1-137-56649-2

K
Kanani Akina doll, 116
Kaya doll. *See also* Native American experiences
  character's story, 25, 139–42, 146–8, 167n61, 174
  as ethnic Other, 151–4, 159–60, 174
  family work and, 77
  mold, 115
  normative femininity and, 92
  photo, 151
  race and, 115–16, 138–9, 148, 150–1, 162–3
Kelly, R. Gordon, 37
King, Billie Jean, 86
King, Martin Luther Jr., 84
King, William, 106
Kirsten Larson doll
  accessories, 21
  character's story, 19–20, 23, 41, 139, 146, 167n61
  as ethnic Other, 154, 156–7
  historical collection and, 12n7
  inclusion in living history exhibit, 29
  mold, 114
  Native American experience and, 148–50
  race/ethnicity and, 107, 139–40, 148, 162
  release, 15, 19–21
  voice and, 77
Kit Kittredge doll
  accessories, 97
  character's story, 25, 74–5, 82, 86, 142
  community building and, 82–4
  family work and, 74–5
  gender representation and, 95

material culture and, 88–9
normative femininity and, 91
photo, 83
race and, 119
release, 29
social change and, 100, 162, 173

L
Lamb, Sharon, 11, 53
Larrick, Nancy, 39
Lehnert, Gertrude, 38
Logan Everett doll, 28, 115, 171–2

M
Mackoff, Barbara, 46, 51
Made to Play Dolls and the Commercialization of American Girlhood (Forman-Brunell), 42
Marcus, Lisa, 155
Marie-Grace Gardiner doll
  Cécile Rey and, 127
  character's story, 26
  family work and, 77, 101n14
  historical collection and, 12n7
  mold, 115
  normative femininity and, 92. 94
Marisol Luna doll, 20, 35–6, 116
Marshall, Elizabeth, 73
Marshall Field's department store, 16
Maryellen Larkin doll
  accessories, 91
  character's story, 26, 137, 139–40, 173
  community building and, 81
  family work and, 75
  heterosexual coupling and, 92
  normative femininity and, 91

CPSIA information can be obtained
at www.ICGtesting.com
Printed in the USA
BVHW040158070819
555291BV00015B/152/P